WORE NEGARI

WORE NEGARI

A Memoir of an Ethiopian Youth
in the Turbulent '70s

Mohamed Yimam

Library of Congress Control Number:		2013916806
ISBN:	Hardcover	978-1-4836-9897-7
	Softcover	978-1-4836-9896-0
	Ebook	978-1-4836-9898-4

This book was printed in the United States of America.

Rev. date: 10/01/2013

To order additional copies of this book, contact:
Xlibris LLC
1-888-795-4274
www.Xlibris.com
Orders@Xlibris.com
135874

CONTENTS

PART II

PART III

For my father Sheikh Yimam Mohamed who taught me
by his own example to value modern education, respect other religions,
and accept the equality of women.

ACKNOWLEDGMENTS

I would like to thank Nancy Bringhurst and Tilahun Afessa for reading the very first draft some twenty years ago when the book was in its rawest form and offering critical review.

My most sincere appreciation to Omar Mohamed, Professor Adeno Addis, and Bill Cannon, who read the manuscript and provided much needed feedback. I am grateful to Yared Tibebu for his insightful suggestions. I am also indebted to Dr. Efrem Yemane-Brehan for his edits. Thank you, Efrem, for your infectious enthusiasm (you don't know how much I needed that) and attention to detail from which the book benefited immensely.

Special thanks to Sahle Ibrahim who is intimately linked with the story and many of the individuals in the book. *Wore Negari* is a story of our shared experience.

My biggest thanks goes to my beloved wife, Lubaba Yimam, for her persistent encouragement so *Wore Negari* could see the light of day.

PREFACE

That the atmosphere was different—pregnant with something momentous—we could neither tell nor recognize. In Addis, people went on with their daily lives like any other time. Students, whose restlessness was often a barometer for measuring the general state of the country's wellbeing, were intent on attending classes. Buses ran as usual. Taxis hassled. For all that can be surmised, nothing appeared different than usual. Life slugged on its miserable way for most people. The year was 1974.

As the fall semester ended, Ethiopians celebrated Christmas, followed by Epiphany. The Western New Year came around that time, and with it started the spring semester for Haile Selassie University, which uses the Gregorian calendar to mark the academic year.

And then, suddenly and unexpectedly, what was to climax into a protracted period of social convulsions began to happen, albeit without much fanfare. It started with a demonstration here, a strike there, a mutiny in an army barrack. The spark that ignited the revolution started with a teachers' union boycott of a planned education reform dubbed "Sector Review." These micro events occurring in some random fashion were cumulatively heading toward a calamitous event. Only we didn't know it. Only we had no inkling as to what these events—unconnected and unorganized as they were—were setting in motion. In that sense, we were like the proverbial frog in the slowly simmering pot. As the heat increased, the frog got even more comfortable until the water slowly reached the simmering point. By the time it figured it out, it was too late to escape, and the frog had boiled.

Near Haile Selassie University, in a smoke-filled tea room where students from the provinces congregate to watch a variety music show and American sci-fi movies, we gathered for musical entertainment as we often did on weekends.

I happened to remember this evening for some reason, and out of the blue came an improvisation of a song by a trendy popular singer from Gondar, Tamerat Mola. It was an ancient melody that no one particularly cared for, let alone drew some deep meaning out of. But the lyrics were prophetic.

According to Ethiopian folklore, *azmari* (singer) can foresee events that were going to happen. It is said that *azmari* predicted the rise of Emperor Tewodros or upcoming battles that would be fought and won in nineteenth century Ethiopia. Kings paid attention or ignored them at their own peril. The public got its information from the musings of *azmari*. The song was *Denyew Deneba*:

ደንየው ደነባ

ደነየዉ ደነባ

የባላአባቱ ልጅ

ተው ም'ን'ሽር ግዛ

ተው ዲ'ም'ትፈ.ር ግዛ

No one actually paid much attention to these prophetic words. It was a call for the landlord class to arm and prepare for an event brewing in the atmosphere that would forever transform the life of the gentry—whom we derisively called *balabat or neftegna* (armed settler) in Ethiopia.

Author's Note

I first drafted most parts of this book in the summer of 1992 over a two-month period without worrying about the quality, style, or format. I just wrote what came to my mind, and the stories flowed without much effort. I was unemployed at the time and looking for a job. It was a crisis period for me, and crisis forces a person to focus one's mind in understanding oneself, past and present. Ever since I came to the US, I have promised to write my story by way of telling the story of my friends who were lost in the event we sometimes call the Ethiopian Revolution. Call it survivor's guilt, I felt I had to tell my friends' stories so that they are not forgotten altogether and erased from the country's consciousness.

I went ahead and shared the rough draft with two friends, an American and an Ethiopian, and sat on it for a long time, leaving it on floppy disk.

In my midfifties some twenty years later, I faced a serious health, life, and professional crisis and started thinking about rewriting and editing this story. I felt that I had to finalize this story and attempt to get it published, or at least just give the finished manuscript to Addis Abeba University. I figured it should be somewhat useful to understanding the period of 1970s in Ethiopia and may add to the growing body of literature and discourse on that period. Although we see many biographies and journals and even novels based on that period, I know Ethiopians, culturally, are loath to telling their own stories to others. It is not like us to share our feelings, our innermost conflicts, and bring it out to an unforgiving public. But it seems that is changing, and more and more people who have participated in significant events in the past are contributing to the growth of this genre of writing.

We who are in this book, except perhaps for Birhanu Ejigu, Wolde Ab Haile, and Mezgebnesh (Mezy) Abayu, Yohanese Berhane, and other party leaders that I cursorily mention, were not Ethiopian People's Revolutionary Party (EPRP) leaders who shaped the party's development in any meaningful way. Although we had high-sounding titles, we were, in many ways, like the average EPRP member. We followed orders, completed our assignments, participated in committees, and were passive actors. We did not originate policy or shaped strategy or lead people in peaceful demonstrations or violent actions. That does not mean, however, that what we did had no impact. It certainly did, and I don't want to minimize our role for the sake of absolving ourselves of guilt or culpability, but what I rather mean is what we did was not of our initiative or self-directed. This was certainly true of me. What started in February (*Yekatit*) of '74 was a great historical event that swept most of us willy-nilly into a powerful revolutionary current; I was one of those who were definitively moved by this major historical plate tectonics. But I never really felt that I understood the movement and made an effort to play any role in attempting to shape it. I did not. In many ways that was true of many EPRP members too. So our story is not any different from others, and understanding our narrative means having some insight into the phenomenon that we call EPRP.

My story is not one of heroism or a vivid description of survival after being subjected to horrific tortures and other human-interest stories that mesmerize a reader. Mine is simply a story of a group of young people, average and ordinary, who found themselves thrown into extraordinary times and had to struggle first within themselves and later with their peers in order to join the movement for a much bigger cause than they had prepared themselves for.

This book is not like Kiflu Tadesse's *The Generation*, Part I and II. *The Generation* was an attempt to recount EPRP's story as the author saw it from a leadership position. I don't know how to categorize that book, but it can't be called a memoir or a journal, although it is not written as a history book either. I am sure there are historians who one day will write about the history of this period using the tools of the craft.

The other book that I read about this period—and this was more recently—is the history of the All Ethiopian Socialist Movement, popularly known as Meison, by Andargachew Asseged, which is an attempt to reconstitute the movement's history using internal documents the author had access to. This was written earlier, right after the collapse of Meison, and has both the advantage of temporal proximity and sufficiency of documentation that Kiflu Tadesse's work lacked. That book is also written in an Amharic style that is not easy to appreciate, although the book by itself offers a wealth of information that both historians and students who want to learn about this period can find to be exhaustive.

There are other writings about this period that were not published but used to circulate among the different leftist groups. Some were written to score points and continue the now worn debate among the different leftists groups that was effectively settled by the triumph of the Derg. Even the Derg now seems a footnote in Ethiopia's history.

My book is different; it is only meant to be a human-interest story about a group of young individuals, who in a generic sense, represent all the typical leftist youth of Ethiopia in that period. It's intended to depict their struggle within themselves and in their organization for an ideal that represents the aspirations of millions of Ethiopians for economic and political justice. My effort is not ideological. Thank goodness the ideology that convulsed the Ethiopian youth is dead. Rather, it is to show our strength and weakness, and above all, our inherent humanity in an inhuman situation.

Surely the type of character that you find in this book can also be found in Meison, TPLF, EPLF, OLF, and other organizations. Aside from the ideology, there was something profound, a genuine commitment to an ideal, that connected us all together. That connection may have also made our fighting all the more ferocious and cruel. That is the nature of civil wars. They are feted to be brutal, barbaric, depraved, and insane. So were the fight between Meison and EPRP, and between TPLF and EPRP. What makes the fate of EPRP so singularly more tragic was that it was an organization embattled on all fronts, from within and without. In the big cities it battled with the Derg and its supporter organization; in the rural north, its guerrilla units fought with TPLF, which dealt its final and mortal blow. EPRP was a tragic organization that from its inception was doomed to fail and to bring down with it the most public-minded generation in Ethiopia's history.

After I came to the United States, I had a conversation with Mezy; I don't remember what the subject was, but I am sure it was a mundane issue unrelated to the revolution or the Derg or the Red Terror. In the middle of the conversation, she spoke of something that happened before "Birhanu was martyred (*Birhanu sayesewa*)." Since I had never heard her use this hallowed word before, it struck me as odd. The truth of the matter is I don't remember her using this solemn word when referring to the sacrifices of others. But none of their deaths, one can fairly conclude, had as much personal poignancy as the death of her husband. As for me, I have never used that term to describe the sacrifices that were paid by so many young people at such a delicate age. Had their cause won, their sacrifice would likely have been ennobled. Alas, that was not the case, and one would always wonder, albeit with a heavy heart and a grave silence, if their sacrifice had all been in vain.

In the past thirty years my life has undergone so many changes. Like all immigrants, it is wrapped up in the many daily struggles that one has to go through in the West to settle, start a new life, and raise a family. In all these daily struggles, I often remember my friends. Not a day goes by without one or the other coming to my mind.

I often imagine Birhanu walking near Ras Makonnen Bridge always carrying an attaché case. I see as he walks he swirls around at every occasion, ever so conscious of the Derg security that could nab him any minute. He often walked the streets of Addis carrying incriminating documents. The daily risk he faced never fazed him though. He had been in and out of prison a couple of times before he finally met his death somewhere in Sidamo.

I remember the gentle, kind, and handsome face of Wolde Ab—full of smiles, drinking his macchiato while engaged in conspiratorial discussions.

I remember the unruly afro of Kassaye, a lanky youth who strikes one as a carefree individual, far removed from such lofty ideals as brining about a revolution.

I always remember Mohamed Arabi huffing and puffing his cigarettes. Mohamed had a way of looking at you not with his eyes, but with his forehead like he was going to charge at any moment. I remember our last minutes as he urged me to fall as one (*Abren Enwudeke*) before he was struck in a hail of machine-gun fire.

I remember Aya, who never seemed to have enough cigarettes and was always craving for more.

I often remember Abraham, a jolly jack who seemed more concerned with his looks and outfit like any normal young man. Who would have suspected that he had any revolutionary zeal in his persona?

I remember Bezabeh, a small-built boy who looked much younger than his age. One would mistake him for a twelve-year old. Bezabeh struck me as a walking dead who entertained a death wish and sought trouble at the risk of his life. I never cared to know what he did, but judging by his utterances, it was deadly serious. Bezabeh was caught and died a horrific death at the notorious security prison. None of us who knew him was affected.

I remember the poet Jale Bia struggling to give voice to a cause that was being lost and to the individuals who were players.

I remember Mesfin, Yohannes, Ahimed Abetew, Mohamed Ali, Hassen Abegaz, Hassen Hussein, Sirak Teferra, Abdureheman Haji, Abdurehman, Tekalegne, Kadri, Dilnessa, Teodros, and many others whose names I don't recall and who were lost during the revolution.

I hope this book beams some light into these and many other individuals not mentioned. I want this book to be a glimpse into their humanity. I do admit, in many ways the tone of this book is critical of the organization but not of these individuals who fought for it. It is not my intention to criticize people who are deceased and are in no position to contradict this story and tell their own version of it.

This book should be seen as window to understanding the Ethiopian left and the psychology of the revolution. It is not a story of EPRP, but it is a story of a small group of individuals who in many ways represent the Ethiopian left, and more precisely, EPRP.

Talking to many former members of EPRP, I have come to realize that it would be a herculean task to write a definitive story of EPRP. EPRP's story can only be a collection of individual stories that can't yet be woven together to provide a complete picture of the organization. But these pieces that represent the recollection of individuals who took part in the phenomenon may be connected to form a more coherent narrative of the organization.

I hope this book will form but one small part of a larger story that has to be told to enable people to understand the period of the 1970s, one of the most consequential periods in Ethiopian history.

The title, *Wore Negari* comes from a powerful propaganda piece in one of the issues of *Democracia*, EPRP's main newsletter. After the so-called urban armed struggle started, *Democracia* claimed the party's aim was not just to kill for the sake of killing (I am paraphrasing) "*Bandas* (those who collaborated with the Derg)." If that was the goal, boasted *Democracia*, we would not have left any "*banda*" alive for posterity. *Le Wore Negari inquan anetwem neber*. I always thought this sentence was a fitting epitaph on the gravestone of EPRP. A few of us who are lucky enough to be left behind should take our obligation to serve as Wore Negari seriously. I know my friends would appreciate the effort.

PART I

Genesis of Radicalization: Ideological Seduction

DESSIE

Woizero Siheen Comprehensive High School, the only high school of its kind in Wollo in the 1960s for a population of roughly five million, was a venerable, exciting, and vibrant institution. The high school band—considered the best in the nation—produced accomplished musicians who were touted as celebrities in Dessie. Before I was admitted to the school, I would often come to the campus to observe with awe as some of the students practiced music on the piano, saxophone, or another instrument. Tadesse Mengiste was my favorite; I would wait for hours just to hear him practice. Another student, whose name escapes me, was also reported to have received a music scholarship to a university in the United States, where we boasted although we had no proof of it, no other black student from Africa was ever accepted. The school educated aspiring poets, writers, and dancers, and was an exciting place of learning. Its annual parents' day was probably the most festive public parade in the city, and we all looked forward to it every year. Selected poems were recited; the band dazzled the public with colorful display; students vigorously debated issues in front of parents and admirers. Students like the late Amare Techan, an actor and orator who died while working on the Amharic film Guna; Tesfaye Eshete, a writer, poet, and playwright who later became a journalist; and Ali Zegeye, an orator of his time who ran for the Ethiopian parliament quoting John F. Kennedy. Each assumed almost celebrity status in our lives. Tekola Hagos, the artist, was a bigger-than-life figure in the school.

There were also academic luminaries, many of whom had gone on to become successful in and out of the county.

Woizero Siheen is also to be remembered for having produced two of the best known revolutionaries in the Ethiopian Student Movement in their time—Wallelegn Mekonen and Birhanu Ejigu. Some may add to the list Birhane Meskel, a student at the high school at one time, but these two were the most authentic Wollo-born revolutionaries, whose tragic life is emblematic of the Ethiopian left. Here I am making a broad generalization and leaving out many prominent leftists like Asefa Endeshaw and the hundreds of Dessie youth like Hassen Hussein who died for EPRP. Wallelegn, a university student and probably the most ardent proponent of the so-called National Question in Ethiopia, was shot dead while trying to hijack a domestic Ethiopian Airlines flight to Khartoum. Another group of university students, which included Berhane Meskel, had successfully hijacked a plane before and Wallelegn, Martha Mebrahtu, and their associates were trying to repeat that success in a spectacular way. Wallelegn's militancy and revolutionary activity had a tremendous influence on Birhanu Ejigu, then a high school student and later one of EPRP's foremost leaders and organizers. For Birhanu and other aspiring revolutionaries, Wallelegn's adventurous (by today's definition, terrorist acts) constituted revolutionary commitment whose spirit was to be emulated. Their life was to be lived in the service of the Ethiopian people, ready to face whatever risks they had to encounter in the process.

Both Birhanu and Wallelegn exemplified this spirit of the Ethiopian students. Although Wollo was one of the poorest of the provinces, they did not see that as cause of their lives. They might have even come to look at *Wolloye* as a culturally privileged group by virtue of the fact that they were mostly Amharic speaking. No, they had to look outside of their immediate surrounding and liberate the "ethnically oppressed." They looked at themselves as part of a larger human movement toward freedom under socialism. In that sense, they were exceedingly idealistic and almost detached from reality.

Birhanu lived and died by this ethos of struggling for Ethiopian people, whose most serious problem, as he saw it included "national" subjugation. After the second *assessa (*the search-and-destroy operations launched by the Derg), Birhanu died while trying to organize the Guji Oromo near Kibre Mingist into an incipient guerrilla army. EPRP was making a last-ditch effort near the home of the Guji Oromo, close to Kibre Mengist, where Birhanu lost his life. Tragically, he died incognito—neither understood nor appreciated. Nobody had a full accounting of where and how he died. Some say he committed suicide while in custody by swallowing a cyanide capsule; others claim he was shot dead while trying to resist arrest. Nobody really knows what happened to this day. Why would an intelligent young man who knew no other Ethiopian language besides Amharic decide to engage in such a risky, not to say reckless, venture (not to say adventure) in a faraway land among a people he didn't know but deeply cared for in a very idealist way? To ask this question is to get a glimpse into EPRP, its youthful idealism and its foibles, and to appreciate the tragedy that befell the Ethiopian youth of our generation.

*   *   *

CHILDHOOD

I am the oldest child in a family of nine children. Four died before the age of two and five of us survived to grow up into adulthood. I am not sure how my father who was born in Gragn Meda (twenty-five kilometers from Dessie) and my mother who was born in Boru (ten kilometers from Dessie) met and married. My father, a product of Islamic education in rural Wollo, taught himself basic arithmetic using Arabic numbers and used his skill to make a living in the grain retail trade

I was born in a house with a thatched roof in in Silk Amba, Dessie. We used locally-made lamps that burned naphtha for light since there was no electricity. The slightly better off used a kerosene lamp. Water was scarce in Silk Amba as in many places in Dessie. My mother had to carry water every other day from Bokesesa, a stream at the bottom of a gorge close to Borkena River, roughly four kilometers from where we lived. Coming back from the gorge carrying the water on her back in a jar (*insra*) made of pottery was daunting. I remember women in a single file carrying their water on their back, head leaning forward as they navigated the treacherous trail. The stronger ones would even sing while gasping for air in an effort to lighten the burden. The water was used for drinking and cooking. We washed our clothes at the Borkena River once or twice a month.

We also did not have pit latrine. We used the wooded backyard for a bathroom. At sunset every day, it was not unusual to see our mothers and sisters go with a can of water, get relief, wash, and come back to the house to serve our food.

I started my education at a *madrassa* in one of the two mosques in Dessie. Our teacher, Haji Yasin, the grandfather of Sheih Alamoudin, one of the richest men in the world today, was the *imam* at the mosque. He was a giant man with a massive turban who was feared by all the little kids and respected by parents.

I had memorized the first eight to nine chapters of the Koran when our *madrassa* evolved into an elementary school that taught reading, writing, and other subjects in Arabic. Most of the teachers spoke basic colloquial Arabic of the Yemen dialect. Sometime in the middle of my elementary school years the Ethiopian government provided our school with a teacher for English and mathematics.

After some four years of schooling, I finally managed to read and write in Amharic and perform basic arithmetic. I had enormous difficulty learning to read and write in Arabic. I was particularly poor at dictation (*imla*). It was a testimony to how poorly classes were taught that most students, except for a few who had Arabic-speaking fathers (the mothers were invariably Ethiopians), never learned to speak or write in Arabic. In sixth grade, the government provided our school with another teacher. He wasted the year talking about trivial stuff instead of teaching. At the end of the year, when we took the national sixth-grade leaving exam, we all failed. Had we not been allowed to combine our classroom results with the exam scores, none of us would have made it to junior high school. That was the year the national exam was introduced to Ethiopian sixth graders.

Seventh grade was the most difficult year for me academically. I was completely lost as all subjects were taught in English. At night I would sit on a chair by our bed in front of the naphtha-burning lamp and try to study by memorization. All five of us—my brother, sister, and my parents—slept in one bedroom and two beds. My mother would often wake up and urge me to sleep. Toward the end of the year, I sought the help of a friend who was a grade above me for an English homework. His explanation opened my eyes. After this timely assistance, my understanding improved and I made it to eighth grade through hard work and memorization. That summer I was determined to start reading in English. I borrowed a dictionary from a friend and wrote down every new word I encountered and searched for its meaning. This was a tiresome task but it paid off. I became a good student and passed the national eighth grade exam with 94 percentile—a proud moment in my life.

I came to ninth grade much more confident and optimistic. I was deeply shy and insecure about many other things, but my academic future looked promising.

There were other problems in my family that preoccupied me. My father became seriously ill with asthma when I was in sixth grade, and stayed home for an extended period. This alarmed me so much I broke down and wept in front of my father's oldest brother, the titular head of our extended family. The fear of death of my father was a shock to my hitherto carefree life. My father left bed and went back to work but was never the same man. He often spent the whole night coughing and spitting. The whizzing in his lung scared me the most and kept me awake at night.

FRIENDS

I grew up with Mohamed Ahimed, who lived in a house adjacent to ours until he moved to another neighborhood at the end of elementary school. Mohamed's father built a new house and moved the family away from Silk Amba, which was not considered a desirable place to live because of the lack of availability of water. In eighth grade Mohamed's mother offered to let me sleep in their house. Mohamed and I shared a bedroom. For the first time in my life I was able to study under electric light. This contributed to my improved academic performance in eighth grade. Most importantly, though, I did not have to hear my father's incessant coughing, which affected my sleep and concentration.

The new living arrangement was wonderful to my psyche, confidence, and comfort. Mohamed's family was gracious; they never made me feel unwelcome, and allowed me to share dinner as often as I had to. I felt like I was part of the family. And when Mohamed went to Massawa (where his father worked) in the summer, I had the room to myself and enjoyed my privacy. I also borrowed Mohamed's watch and clothes and attended school.

My other close friend, who also happened to be my second cousin, was Omar Mohammed. Ever since he enrolled in the *madrassa* we were pretty much inseparable, even in high school. In ninth grade, Mezgebnesh (Mezy) Abay, another second cousin, and I became good friends. We were in the same class in eighth grade but did not know we were related. She grew up in her grandfather's home and was named after him. Her father, my mother's cousin, was a Christian convert.

Perhaps one of the most influential people I knew in high school and he was still in middle school was an older man we called Shieh Indreas. He taught himself English and flew through elementary school. For a man who studied Islam in rural Ethiopia, he was amazingly well-read and progressive. He was called Shieh Indreas *mutazilite* (a Muslim philosophical school founded in the eighth century AD emphasizing reason in religious interpretation, free will in opposition to predestination, and the unity and justice of Allah). We grilled Sheih Indreas about Islam, science, and modernity. I helped him with his English and he taught me not to be afraid to ask and try to understand Islam through questions and answers. Sheih Indreas also infected me with what is often called the "Middle East bug"—a lifelong passion mostly informed by Jewish liberal and progressive writing.

Birhanu Ejigu and I were introduced when I started tenth grade and he was in eleventh grade by a mutual friend who later became deeply religious and moved to Saudi Arabia. Our friendship, which took time to mature, became the most consequential in my life.

Birhanu, Omar, Mohamed Ahimed, Aziz, another friend from high school, and a number of other students from Woizero Siheen taught classes in the summer and evenings in the elementary school (*madrassa*) that Omar and I attended. We taught elementary and middle school students and charged a nominal fee. Since many of us were poor, the money was used to buy shoes and clothes and provided us with extra spending money. We often bought bread from one of the local bakeries and walked by the crown prince's palace, arguing over a slew of topics that never seemed to end.

When I was in tenth grade, we rebelled against a principal who deployed harsh disciplinary tactics ostensibly for commendable academic reasons, but enraged the student body into a spontaneous revolt. Rumor had it that he boasted he would whip these unruly Wolloye into an orderly society. A major riot—the first of its kind resulting in damages to school property and injuries to teachers—erupted. In the ensuing lawlessness, I remember a beautiful Indian teacher being fondled by a bunch of students while her husband watched in horror. That was unheard of before, but we were soon to become acclimatized to such vulgarity. The riots cost the principal his job, but we also wasted a significant amount of academic time; this was to continue off and on until the revolution broke out and wrecked the public education system altogether. The principal Ato Asrat was transferred to Bahir Dar Polytechnic Institute and later became one of the most trusted advisors of Mengistu Haile Mariam. In fact, he is credited with having negotiated Mengistu's departure and asylum in Zimbabwe following the victory of the Ethiopian people's Revolutionary Democratic Front (EPRDF).

Toward the end of tenth grade, after a great deal of reflection I decided to leave high school and attend a teacher training institute. My family's deteriorating financial condition and my father's poor health was the main reason. I had started eleventh grade and was thinking of seriously preparing for the Ethiopian school-leaving certificate exam when I was informed that I had been accepted to Jima Teacher Training Institute (TTI), the newest institute in the country. I was terribly conflicted, but I decided to accept the offer. Days before I left, I introduced Mezy to Birhanu.

Mohammed's father gave me the money for the bus ticket and clothing and I left for Jimma with other candidates. I cried halfway to Addis Abeba after I said goodbye to my friends.

It was the year I was in Jima that Marxism-Leninism was introduced to a few students in Woizero Siheen in 1969 by a third-year university student who was doing his national service. Birhanu, who was a senior at this time and president of the debate club, became immersed in this study. It seemed like Birhanu had found his calling in life. The same year, the emperor's security assassinated Tilahum Gizaw. Birhanu wrote to me a ten-page letter passionately describing the event and the struggle that followed in Addis. When the senior class in Woizero Siheen graduated, Birhanu refused to wear a suit and a tie. He wanted to make a statement. Radicalization was taking hold.

I returned from Jimma TTI a year later for the summer. I had become a bit withdrawn and more introspective. There were also noticeable changes in Birhanu, who in a matter of one year had been transformed into a budding revolutionary. He talked about class struggle, dialectical and historical materialism, revolution, armed struggle, and other lofty ideas that were not exactly the topic of discussion of a typical teenager. A year before we would have normally discussed the Apollo mission, Amharic novels, or some other topic that a person of our age would be interested in. We would just pick a random topic and argue against one another for the sake of argument. This exercise was usually very productive and trained us on how to make points and debate issues. We would never admit it, but we learned from each other and strengthened our friendship. On weekends and after school, we had plenty of time to fill in such mundane activity, which turned out to be a productive social and intellectual engagement.

The very first night after I came back to Dessie, I engaged Birhanu in similar vein on some issue that I don't now remember. The argument quickly digressed into issues of a political nature. Birhanu managed to segue into the Ethiopian situation and spoke passionately about national oppression and class struggle. In just one night, he gave me a short introduction into social development, from primitive communism to modern socialism. I immediately noticed that Birhanu had become so well versed in the revolutionary lexicon that I had no clue what he was talking about. I felt like I was left many years behind and could not catch up. Before this I was a good debater and rarely lost an argument among my friends. But at that time, I felt stupid, ill-informed, and reactionary.

I was deeply pro-American in my political orientation. A frequent user of an excellent high school library built and staffed by the United States

Information Agency (now defunct agency devoted to "public diplomacy"), I already knew relatively more about America. The first English book I ever read was about JFK. I had read books on Abraham Lincoln, Thomas Jefferson, and Martin Luther King Jr., so it was obvious I was pro-American. I listened to Voice of America, read *Newsweek*, *Time*, and *Ebony*, and followed events in America with enthusiasm. I had even wanted to come to America on an American field service program for a year, although that changed when I went to Jimma TTI. I was unabashedly pro-American in my feelings, which became the butt of jokes for Birhanu.

On the other hand, Birhanu had become so intensely anti-American that he referred to the Peace Corps volunteers as CIA spies. This was news to me. I always had good relationships with the Peace Corps volunteers and had an excellent relationship with Gerry Jones, who taught me history, one of my favorite subjects in high school. Naturally I started to defend my teachers and argued against the spy insinuation. In the heat of these exchanges I said, "Give me some proof that Gerry, my teacher, is a spy and I will twist his neck." It was a hyperbole, stated more for its dramatic effect than an expression of intent. Birhanu quickly shot back, "I am not sure you are capable of doing that since Mr. Jones has already twisted your heart." Unaccustomed to the vicious leftist rhetorical style, I was confused and felt defeated. I felt I lost the argument both at the moral and intellectual level.

After the initial shock was over, Birhanu suggested that I open up my eyes and start reading. He gave me materials for beginners. I was convinced that I had to catch up on this Marxism stuff and be conversant enough or I thought I would be left behind forever.

What probably added to my insecurity was my earlier decision to go to Jima TTI. In those days, a teacher training institute was not the place for people who wanted to get a college education or have higher aspirations. While the quality of the students that were now attending TTIs had considerably improved—as students found out that it was easier way to find a job once one has finished high school—many bright students still avoided going to TTIs. The academic program was considered to be inferior to other senior high schools since students had to focus more on learning the pedagogical skills at the expense of a rigorous high school curriculum that prepared students for college. Academic skills were deemphasized in favor of teaching skills. We were only taught enough subject matters as was needed to teach in elementary schools, or at most, in junior high schools. To make matters worse, Jimma TTI was new and offered very few courses that prepared the trainees to take the Ethiopian School Leaving Certification Exam (ESLCE). So I was beginning to feel that I was lagging behind my friends academically and might not be as successful in college. I interpreted my lack of preparation in this discussion and my friend's grasp of Marxism as proof of my predicament.

That summer I read as much Marxism-Leninism and Mao Tse Tung materials as I could put my hands on. I followed the suggestion of Aziz and Birhanu. By the end of the summer, I was beginning to feel conversant and converted.

JIMMA

I went back to the TTI for my last year after a summer well spent with my buddies reading, teaching, debating, and playing soccer on the streets. I felt very confident that I was now equipped with an activist philosophy, which was unknown by the vast majority of the trainees in the institute. In the second year, I was selected to be president of the debating club, editor of the student magazine, and secretary of the drama club. My position was not directly related to my leftist philosophy, but my confidence was lifted by what I felt I knew and others did not. By then I had read materials from selected works of Mao Tse Tung including on protracted war and on dialectical and historical materialism from Novosty Press publications. I was feeling knowledgeable about the ideology and its lessons for Ethiopia's future.

As the president of the debate club, I organized a secret program to celebrate the one-year anniversary of assassination of Tilahu Gizzaw. We convened students by telling them there would be a program that would feature some speakers from the institute and invited them to attend. I discussed this with a few who were also known in the campus for one reason or another: Sahle, Endale (Abera), and Zenebe; we agreed that all four of us would make the presentation. Abera was a radical student from Sidamo who later became a member of the Pentecostal Church. Zenebe, at the time, was a first-year student from Addis who had made a name for himself as a real rabble-rouser in high school before he came to TTI. He always struck me as a demagogue, but seemed to have some following in the freshman class. Sahle, also from Sidamo, was considered the coolest and smartest student in the institute. We wanted to keep things secret regarding the purpose of the program for security reasons. Nothing like it was ever attempted at the new TTI and so no one would have suspected what was going to happen other than the four of us. I knew this was a risky venture, but I had to do it to prove my worth as a militant student.

We chose different topics to speak about. My speech, which was delivered from my notes, focused on what I called the Ethiopian condition. I spoke about the country's rich history and its current appalling backwardness, and attributed that to the feudal system. Zenebe went even further and attacked the royal family. Sahle spoke on the relative contribution to Ethiopia's economic underdevelopment by emperors Menilik and Haile Selassie. He attributed to Emperor Menilik's reign whatever little national infrastructure and services the country had at the time, including the Addis-Djibouti railway, telegraph and postal services, and the beginning of modern education. By comparison, Emperor Haile Selassie's regime did little despite the relative peace the world enjoyed at the time (compared to Menilik's time) and the friendship the emperor had with the rich Western world, which he could have utilized to leverage aid to fund the expansion and improvement of the infrastructure and services that Emperor Menilik had begun. At the end of the program, we sang "*Fano Tesemara* (ፋኖ ተሰማራ)"—the battle cry of the Ethiopian student movement, a call to arms to follow in the footsteps of Ho Chi Minh and Che Guevara. This was unheard of before at the institute. The next day the institute was closed for the Christmas break, so we had no way of gauging how the student body reacted. When I came to Dessie for a visit during the Christmas break, I bragged to my friends how well I spoke at the gathering and how impressed the audience was. Deep down, however, I was worried that I might be arrested or expelled for organizing the secret gathering. Luckily for me, nothing happened when I returned.

Continuing on my newfound activism, I assumed a leadership role when Jimma TTI joined other teacher training institutions in a protest against a new Ministry of Education policy of awarding certificates for students when they complete their studies. The policy stipulated students would take an assessment at the end of the program to test their pedagogical readiness to become teachers. This was going to be a national exam, and students, for the most part, were alarmed, read more into it (as was typical in those days), and reacted negatively. Additionally, the ministry stated that students would receive a certificate for completion of the program rather than a diploma, as was customary prior to the change of policy. This was seen by the trainees as a major issue that was intended to lower the TTI graduate's profile. More importantly, there was an unsubstantiated rumor that after graduation our salaries would be cut to 175 birr a month instead of the 250 birr we were expecting. Many TTIs, including the one in Addis, boycotted classes, demanding a change in this policy. We followed Kotebe TTI and boycotted classes as well. School officials talked to us and explained the issue, but we did not budge. Finally, we said we would leave Jimma and go to our respective cities unless the ministry rescinded this policy and met our demands. Our meetings took place at night. When this was known by *Dejamatch* Tsehai Enku Selassie, the famous governor of Kaffa, he asked to speak to the student body. At our meetings at night, when we were debating whether or not to wait and listen to the governor, Zenebe argued against it. I said that there is nobody under the sun that was more powerful than the governor in Kaffa Province, and that it would be wise for us to give him a chance to talk to us. This seemed to sway students to remain in campus. The next day, the governor spoke. The governor's speech was forcefully delivered. He compared us to a farmer who would scare people who offer to help him weed his crop with a snake. "በገዛ አረሟ አበብ ይዞ ታስፈራራ," he yelled with a threatening gesture. He might have even said that he would hang the ring leaders of the boycott on campus if we were to continue with the boycott, pointing to the oak tree at the main gate of the TTI. I don't think anybody doubted that he could do what he was saying. That was a guy who saw no boundary to his duties and powers in his jurisdiction. Sahle recalls hearing about the governor's encounter with the Gulte Night Club dancers who were walking on the road dressed in miniskirts. He got out of the car and beat the hell out of the hapless girls for wearing miniskirts. He was clearly a forceful speaker and was recognized as a powerful governor at that time.

We decided to stay awhile and see what his intervention would bring. After some time, for reasons that I don't remember now, the trainees decided to board buses and leave the campus altogether. Our convoy of buses heading for Addis, and subsequently to other places, left Jimma but was stopped in Wolliso, close to Addis Abeba by security forces. We stayed overnight, sleeping in the buses and local motels in the town. The next day, the commander of the Addis Abeba police told us to send our representatives and talk to the Ministry of Education. Four individuals, including Zenebe, Abera, and I, were selected to go to Addis. We went to the Addis Abeba police headquarters, where we were met by the commander. The commander was a soft-spoken grandfatherlike figure who gently advised us, without making any threats, to return to our campus. He then told us that he would take us to the prime minister's office and allow us to present our case. After sometime in his office, we were escorted to the infamous *makelawi* security prison by a police car. Here we were met by a senior officer, the second-in-command in the Ethiopian security apparatus. He had us wait for a while in the reception area of his office while he and the police commander talked inside. While waiting in the reception area, I remember reading English weekly magazines. The police commander had earlier warned us the security officer was a "highly educated" man with a master's degree from a university in America. From this office, we were driven to Amest Kilo and ushered to an intimidating conference room in the prime minister's office. For me, this was the first time to be at the corridors of power. Sitting at the imposing conference room where the Ethiopian cabinet met was an unnerving and intimidating experience. We finally sat down by the massive table across from the police commander, the security officer, and the deputy minister of education. The atmosphere in the conference room was so intimidating we were in no position to assert our claims forcefully as we had thought we would. We were given a chance to speak, and we took turns expressing our positions. The minister dismissed the whole issue of certificate vs. diploma as a semantic difference and massive confusion on our part. He explained to us the difference between a degree, a diploma, and a certificate. He said that in a way even a degree is a certificate of achievement at some level and that we had nothing to worry about it regardless. He also assured us the test was going to be used as a national assessment tool, but not for the purpose of failing trainees at a time when the country's need for elementary school teachers was growing by leaps and bounds. If we passed our classes, we were sure to be able to graduate, regardless of our score on the national assessment. I don't remember if any concession was made by the government, but we accepted the explanation and returned to the student body.

We brought this news back and informed the students. After describing what happened that day, we told them that we had no reason to worry and we should return back to our school and finish our studies. The students generally expressed a collective sigh of relief, and were happy to return. A few weeks after this, the Kotebe TTI students were suspended for one year. When students heard this, they were really happy that this did not happen to them. I also felt extremely happy about this outcome. All along I was concerned about the prospect of not finishing my studies that year. I wrote an exaggerated version of this story to Birhanu, who was now teaching in Addis, to impress him about my leadership skills.

Also in Jimma, I did something that was very educational for me but did not really digest it at that time. Sahle, Abera, and I decided to stage Tsegaye Gebre Medhin's one-act play (which requires only three actors), called *Yekermo Sew*. Although none of us had any experience acting or directing, we decided to do it on the spur of the moment. Memorizing *Yekermo Sew* proved to be a daunting task for Abera, but Sahle and I did not have an easy time either. When finally the play was staged, the audience found it wanting. Abera often forgot his lines. Students were not too impressed by our effort. A few weeks later, Goitom Bihon's play was staged and it was a phenomenal success. Many members of the audience watched in rapt attention; many visibly cried at what we thought was a rather run-of-the mill love story typical of Ethiopian novels at the time. The three of us thought that his play really was a simple story that lacked literary merits, but little did we know what the audience wanted. That summer, I saw a production of *Yekermo Sew* in Dessie by the national theater with Wogayehu Negatu as Abeye Zerfu, one of the three characters in the play. I played Abeye Zerfu. It was at the time that I realized how our heroic yet naive attempt to stage Tesegaye Gebre Medhin's great literary work fell flat at the artistic level.

HARAWECHA

I graduated from Jimma TTI and was assigned to teach in Harawecha, Hararghe, through a lottery system. We dreaded the lottery drawing for fear of picking up places that were too far from big cities. Harawecha, a small town about 100 kilometers from Harar and Dire Dewa, was a couple hours' drive from the main road that connects Addis Abeba to Harar.

My reading of Marxism continued after I became a teacher in Harawecha. I was able to get some more shipments of books from China for free. I received a shipment of the *Collected Works of Mao Tse Tung* and felt knowledgeable as to why the Chinese revolution succeeded. Mao was easy to read, and his writing made a lot of sense. I always had a strong distaste for Stalin, probably as a result of the many American books that I had read on Communism. Lenin posed a different set of problems. His writing style was generally difficult, his sentences long, and his prose rushed; reading him required a big intellectual effort. I read *Imperialism: the Last Stage of Capitalism*, a book that was considered a must-read at that time, with a lot of effort but little enthusiasm. I also read Nkrumah's take on this theory, *Neo Colonialism, the Last Stage of Imperialism*. Marx was unapproachable, but I managed to read his book on the French revolution and some others, although how much I understood was debatable. Friedrich Engels was impressive to me even when he was difficult. Later, I became fascinated with Trotsky. Trotsky's biography was compelling, and seemed in his tragic failings to have won my sympathy. I did most of this reading in my second year of teaching. The first year I spent most of the time preparing to take ESLCE. After I got a passing grade in the first year, I devoted my spare time to reading Marxism, philosophy, and Russian novels.

The most memorable book I read at this time, which was sort of a counterweight to my leftist indoctrination, was Will Durant's *The Story of Philosophy*. Rarely had a book engaged me so thoroughly as this book. I recommended this to Birhanu, but he dismissed it outright as bourgeoisie philosophical trash. My second year of my short-lived teaching career was intellectually the most stimulating. With the ESLC worry behind me, I delved myself into books, and not just Marxist books, and began to consider both the philosophical and political questions posed in Will Durant's books and the Marxist writers. I was especially fascinated by the discussion on religion. Never a person of strong faith to begin with, I started questioning the very existence of God. However, I never intellectually really resolved the question to any degree of satisfaction. While by this time my attitude toward the two major organized religions, Islam and Christianity, was deeply skeptical, I still could not resolve intellectually whether God existed or not. I was more inclined to believe that concepts of a creation without a creator or a creation with a creator, according to Kant's framing, was intellectually confounding. Believing in a creation by a creator was intellectually impossible to fathom and required a leap of faith for which I was not ready yet. In a small town called Harawecha, situated on a plateau overlooking the vast Ogaden desert, I pondered these issues by myself and never really got a convincing answer. By contrast, Birhanu had no problem seeing the world that evolved to be without any divine intervention. He was an atheist to his skin and never wavered. As in many other things, he had certainty, whereas I was full of questions, unresolved and unresolvable.

I also read Leo Tolstoy's novels. *War and Peace* was especially most gratifying. I was profoundly affected by the characters, dazzled by the panorama of the vast Russian heartland, the wisdom of its peasants, and greatness of its military leaders. Once again, I recommended the book to Birhanu, but he was never able to get into it. The Russian novelist that had the most influence on him was Dostoevsky, whose books, especially *The Brother's Karamazov*, he loved. I had difficulty reading and never really understood Dostoevsky. Even after I came to the United States, *The Brothers Karamazov* was not intelligible to me.

As a teacher in Harawacha, I earned about 250 birr (twenty-four dollars a month at the then exchange rate) per month but limited my expenses to about fifty birr. In those days, you could get a lot of mileage out of that kind of money in rural Ethiopia. A teacher in rural Ethiopia garnered enormous respect and was paid handsomely by today's standards. Teaching was also prestigious. Teaching rural children who were always impeccably polite, enormously respectful, and uniformly hungry for learning was a satisfying experience. I would never forget travelers who dismounted from their horses every time they saw me going to and from school, often surrounded by adoring students, some of whom were as old as I was.

I shared a house with another teacher who grew up in Adowa; we had an elderly lady who cooked, washed, and took care of our rented place. It was a comfortable living, but I was determined to give it up to pursue higher education.

Harawcha was a small town with only an elementary school to its name. There was a telephone station that I used to dial Dessie and occasionally talk to my parents. But my parents have to come to Dessie telecommunication center for us to make the connection. The mail worked very well. There was a town center with a few shops and local bars. In Harawecha, I came face to face with the national question for the first time. My students often asked me why I did not speak Afan Oromo since I was named Mohamed. The Ormo in the area actually called themselves Muslims or Kotu alternatively. Given my name, my students thought I was a Kotu who was too embarrassed to admit his ethnicity. I also used the term *gala* so liberally that it took me awhile to realize the derogatory connotation of the term in the mind of students.

One of the teachers also happened to have an uncle in Arsi who was an absentee landlord in the surrounding area. When he came to Harawcha to visit his tenants and collect his dues, he would often invite us to a lavish lunch where roasted and raw goat meat was served by some of his tenants. I enjoyed the dinner, but I also noticed the fear of the tenants and the unfairness of the arrangement. That was my real-life exposure to the explosive mixture of the national question and feudalism at that time.

From the start, my plan was to teach for only two years and save enough money to support my family while I went to college. It worked out very well up to that point; I had close to 3,000 birr saved in the bank. I had both the motivation and discipline to realize that I needed the education.

As I said above, the reason that I did not go directly to the university after high school was because I realized my family needed my support as their financial situation was getting desperate. With four other children to feed, my father's health deteriorating and his small retail activity dwindling by the day, it was becoming increasingly apparent that my family would not make it without my support. Coming from a close-knit family, it was unspoken but understood that I would help my family out. I was the oldest child, with the next sibling still struggling through primary grades; I saw this responsibility, like many youth of my generation, as a natural obligation of the oldest son or daughter of the family.

The second year I was in Harawecha, I came for a Christmas break to Dessie. On the way back to Harar, I dropped by Birhanu's apartment for a couple of days. One night, we went out to drink and we argued about something very seriously. It was a heated exchange that got out of hand. Although I was a patient listener, whatever Birhanu said got under my skin. Fuming with anger, I left Birhanu at the bar and took a taxi to another friend's house. The next day or the day after, I took the bus back to Harawecha, vowing never to see Birhanu again.

Months later, I received a long letter from Mezy, who was at the university, telling me that she had fallen in love with Birhanu and had started dating him. She mentioned she was now pregnant and staying with him. She pleaded that I reconcile with Birhanu and reestablish our friendship for her sake. After reading her letter and finding out about her pregnancy, it did not seem right to me to put her in the middle of our fight. I let bygones be bygones and visited them at their apartment near Ras Makonnen Bridge after I finally left Harawecha.

TOURING FAMINE STRICKEN AREAS: RADICALIZATION TAKES ROOT

In the summer of 1973, while preparing to enroll in the university, Birhanu, who was then working as a high school teacher in Addis Abeba, told me that he was visiting the drought-affected areas of Wollo to gather information for a report he was preparing. Right at this time, the northern part of Ethiopia, especially Wollo and Tigray, were faced with a drought of biblical proportions—a calamity the likes of which we had never seen before. The famine, hidden from the rest of the world, caused the death and destruction of a quarter million and the dislocation of millions others.

I did not ask who this report was for or any other details, but decided to accompany Birhanu to Bati and Asaita on the road to Assab, and to Woldia and Kobo on the road to Mekelle.

This was a very educational but depressing trip for me. On the way to Bati, we saw a landscape filled with thousands of animal carcasses scattered near the highway. We visited relief camps and saw children and old people die right in front of our eyes in Bati. We saw children who were minutes away from dying painfully drifting to death—a haunting spectacle that one can never ever forget. In Kobo, we saw people eating leaves and grasses. We saw abandoned neighborhoods and ghost villages. We saw the skeletons of thousands of cattle at every frequent interval on the road to Assaita. I had never been exposed to a tragedy of this magnitude, and was overwhelmed.

We talked to peasants and asked them if they thought this was a manmade disaster or was God's punishment for the sins of the people. Birhanu, an avowed atheist, and I, an agnostic at heart, had other agendas in asking these questions. A peasant in Haike expressed his opinion: "There was no reason for God to do the horrible things visited upon us poor folks; most of us are God-fearing religious people." Another one near Kobo, on the other hand, claimed that this was God's punishment. He illustrated his point by saying that some of the more prosperous peasants in Raya Ena Azebo used to shoot through their harvest to see whose harvest was bigger and thick enough to dodge a bullet, and whose harvest was thin enough to let a bullet pass through. None blamed the government, probably because such expression of dissent was unheard of; it was obviously a risky thing to say to a bunch of city strangers. Again in a place near Kobo, a traveling elderly peasant told us the story of a peasant who had to sell his gun to survive. The peasant in the story had a blood feud with another person, and selling his gun would have been unthinkable under normal circumstances.

As I traveled, I thought how strange these stories sounded, and how little I knew of my country. We could not talk to the Afars because of the language barrier, and because the Afar, with their guns on their shoulders and their swords ominously tucked by their side, never seemed approachable. A proud people with unquestioned supremacy over the north-eastern desert land in Ethiopia, they evoked terror on town folk like us. I never forget how the minibus drivers, who normally treated the other peasant passengers with disdain, treated the Afars with a grudging respect. They were never hassled, pushed around, or ill-spoken of.

At night, Birhanu and I discussed the famine; we were convinced that a serious agrarian revolution that would transform the land-holding system was needed in the country. For us, there was no doubt what we witnessed was a manmade disaster that could have been averted by a socialist government. Neither aware of the local culture nor the economics involved, we blamed the land-holding system in Wollo for causing this disaster. We concluded that irrespective of the technology or land-management techniques employed by the peasants, this natural catastrophe was caused by the regime of Emperor Haile Selassie and the archaic land-holding system.

In Bati Junior High School, we asked a geography teacher and a graduate of Woizero Siheen whom we both knew, what he thought was the reason for the famine. He told us that he was teaching his students that the irregularity of the monsoon rain was the reason for missing the planting season. We suppressed our laughter at his naiveté, smugly displaying our political sophistication and "superior" understanding of the problem. We saw the solution to the problem within the context of an agrarian revolution and the imposition of a socialist regime.

Against the backdrop of the famine that seemed a tragedy caused by the willful neglect of the feudal regime, Birhanu and I talked about revolution.

It seemed to me that he was determined to pursue the life of a revolutionary with all the pursuant hardships and problems. He spoke of sacrifice and in glowing terms about the revolutions in China and Vietnam and how they have been able to do away with recurrent famines. We agreed the feudal system had become archaic in Ethiopia and had to be removed. It seemed so easy to see the connection between the famine and the feudal system although our conclusion by no measure was supported by deep knowledge of the system or how it had brought this horrendous tragedy.

I was awed by my friend's youthful determination to dedicate his life to the cause of the Ethiopian people. He appeared to be like a heroic figure with a historic mission compared to me, who exhibited what seemed be spinelessness and fear of death. I was brutally honest with myself. I surely feared for my life and felt guilty about it. Not only did I feel guilty, but I also became inherently insecure about it. I attributed my fear to my concern for my family, who now seemed to have placed all their hopes of a better future on me. So I meekly argued that revolution would be a dangerous thing to pursue and tragic to my family. I sort of wanted some understanding and sympathy about my predicament, although deep inside I also felt my reason was sheer cowardice. For a long time, this dilemma would haunt me even as I slowly began to be sucked into the radical political movement that was forever to change my life and that of my country.

In Woldia, Birhanu and I visited Mezy and her parents while still touring the affected areas. She was pregnant and had come to visit her parents. Birhanu was meeting the family for the first time and was apprehensive about it. He had suspicions that her parents were not fond of their daughter's choice for a husband. A feisty young man who was used to doing things his way, Birhanu was determined to fight them if it came to that. To him, it did not matter what they thought and how they would take it; it was her choice that mattered. For Mezy, it was more complicated. She felt it was important that her parents accepted the relationship. She wanted their blessing even though she knew they could not do much about it. Her parents were not too happy about the situation either, but felt that they had to accept the choice of their daughter. Mezy was bright, stood in the top three or 5 percent of her class and her parents were aware of her independence. They became reluctantly resigned to living with Mezy's choice of a son-in-law.

Haile Selassie University

In August 1973, against the advice of my father and the reluctant acquiescence of my mother, I quit my teaching job in Harawecha and enrolled at Haile Selassie University. I took the train to Harawecha and took Birhanu with me to collect my last payments for July, August, and September. On the train back from Dire Dawa, Birhanu ran into Yonas Admassu, a member of the Haile Selassie University faculty and Yohannes a.k.a. Johnny or Arabu who was a graduate of the university and later a politburo member of EPRP. We chewed *khat* (the mildly narcotic green leaf) all the way and discussed literature, philosophy, and Marxism. I was quiet for the most part, listening to these individuals who impressed me as intelligent and articulate revolutionaries. I also had a nasty cough that lasted for the duration of the long train ride.

Even as I finally left my teaching position, I had serious doubts and second thoughts about my decision to join the university. I was worried about money and whether my savings, into which I was now liberally dipping, would last and support my family. It was also not lost on me that the university may not remain open to finish my education and find a job. But I decided to go ahead and become a student.

I registered for English, Amharic, Ethiopian geography, Ethiopian history, and introduction to science, and became a freshman in the 1973-1974 academic year, the eve of the most fateful year in Ethiopia. I felt I should take it easy and acclimatize to the rigor of higher education before I signed up for more demanding subjects like economics and mathematics. With me, starting as a freshman, was Sahle Ibrahim, a graduate of Jimma TTI who I was somehow able to nudge into joining the university earlier than he had planned. Academically gifted, I know Sahle would have joined the university sooner or later. He had not meant to spend his life teaching elementary students.

The university that I came to was a hotbed of revolutionary activity, filled with firebrands and aspiring revolutionaries who saw it more and more as a breeding ground for revolutionaries than as an academic institution. Two years before, students had withdrawn from the university when their often impossible political demands that could never be met under the existing political structure were refused by the administration. The majority, except for some who refused to withdraw and were labeled saboteurs, wasted a year without education. For many students who came from the provinces in Ethiopia, leaving the university compound required a tremendous sacrifice. Although I had a strong suspicion this might happen again, I was resolved to get education and enrolled in the university according to my plan.

Life in the university was not that challenging. The crowding of the dormitory, which in retrospect seemed intolerable, did not bother me that much since I was used to sleeping with forty students in the TTI dormitories. I rarely complained about the food. I was bothered by the long line and by the irresponsibility of students who come late and cut, or in the jargon of the students, "hijacked" the line.

The first semester was uneventful. I was assigned to one of what were then called *prefabs* or prefabricated rooms, with each dorm accommodating twenty or more students. I was studious, nervous, and extremely eager to learn. I tried to concentrate and do as well as I could in my studies. I became so anxious that I started to have problems with my sleep, a problem I had never had before. I was also beginning to have doubts about my capacity to learn and do well in school. Socially, I was easily adjusted.

The first semester of the first year was typically a difficult period in the university. By the end of the semester, hundreds of freshmen were forced out as "Christmas graduates" for failing to maintain a C average. This was mostly true in the sciences, where students face enormous difficulty for lack of adequate high school preparation. I did not think the program in the arts stream was that difficult, but here also quite a number of students faced expulsion.

Given the level of stress that first-year students face, I do not remember if there was counseling or stress reduction sessions to alleviate student's tension at the university. Many students used *khat* to study, concentrate, and work longer hours. I remember very few who were not using *khat* in this manner. It was also the favorite entertainment drug. I started using it although I was not sure whether it was helping me to remember things or not. It was good to get you focused until the effect wears off in eight to ten hours. Whether it helps in the retention of what was learned was dubious even then. But students liked to study in groups and *khat* facilitated group study.

The *khat* culture is an important aspect of the university life but little is written about it. *Khat* was also very important later among the revolutionary individuals. Almost everyone I knew ate *khat*. People I thought were very senior in EPRP ate *khat* and discussed ideology and strategy under the influence. Most of what we read, theoretical or propaganda pieces, were written under the influence of *khat*. Despite that, *khat*, as I could remember, played such a crucial role in the university and the student movement, it is amazing that nothing is written about it.

Khat is a depressant drug. Depending on the type, the peak and the valley vary. But it always has a peak followed by a fall into a low, a typical mood swing that is noticeable in every *khat* abuser. The more regular users probably suffer from less violent mood swings, but the beginners swing between high and low extremes. To kill the depressant effect, people drink alcohol once the effect of the *khat* begins to wear off. This helps but also has the effect of making one dependent on two drugs, *khat* and alcohol. Once you learn to combat the depressant effect with alcohol, you become hooked on alcohol. You crave it after the *khat* effect wears off, and if you do not get it you sort of hit the abyss. It becomes a vicious cycle. After the alcohol wears off, you have a hangover for which the *khat* becomes a very good medicine. So you go on like that every week.

This, in retrospect, seems a big anomaly, but then it was part of the life of many university students that I knew. I do not want to give the impression that *khat* was universally used, but it was so widespread I would be surprised if there was any student that had not tried it.

I got into the *khat* and alcohol culture faster than I thought. Before I joined the university, two beers was my limit, and even that was intoxicating. Now I would probably drink every weekend later during the revolution almost every day or whenever I could get it. I moved up to hard liquors like *katikalla*, which was cheaper and more potent. So with university life, I began to acquire bad habits, risky behavior, and everything else that came with them. It seemed these bad habits were the norm, so it was hard to think of them as abnormal at that time.

My midterm result was good enough that I realized I would not be dismissed from the university. Actually I got one of the highest grades in the entire arts department in the introductory science course. This was a hooch-pooch science course for liberal arts students, and included astronomy, geology, biology, and other basic sciences. Because I was weak in science, I studied it harder than any of my other subjects. I was trying to understand the hardcore dialectical materialism, and thought basic grasp of science would help with my understanding of Marxism. I studied this every day and discussed it with friends.

At the university, I did not make that many friends. I socialized with Sahle. In my dorm, I shared a bunk bed with an Oromo student, Taddesse Gena, who was from Arsi and with whom I became good friends. Taddesses' ancestors were Muslims. His father or his grandfather may have converted to Christianity, probably to maintain their economic and social status. Taddesse and I studied and hung out together and were good friends until the revolution and *Zemecha*, when he was sent to the rural south, through which he escaped to Kenya. Later he returned to Ethiopia and reconstituted his life. Beide Melaku, a graduate of Woizero Siheen also spent time with us. With Sahle often working with us, we formed a circle of friends that studied and socialized together. We would often go to Birhanu and Mezy's apartment to eat and socialize.

SIGNS OF UNREST

In spring of 1974, the *Yekatit* (February) crisis erupted; classes started on time but began to be disrupted by the rapid agitation in the city. Soon this spilled into the university as the mostly leftists activists in the university felt they had to provide leadership. It was becoming increasingly clear this was not going to be a normal academic year.

The election in the university to form the student government, USUAA, coincided with the general deterioration of events outside campus. The campus politics was often conducted in a divisive atmosphere with factions fighting and posturing against one another for leadership positions. Even the invitation of a scholar like Ali Mazuri to speak to the student body was preceded by live conflict that involved nebulous factions. For freshmen like me, it was difficult to gauge what was going on. I seriously contemplated becoming a member of the congress representing the freshman class but copped out. I was not in the campus the night of the election. I boycotted the debate for no apparent reason.

The issue of withdrawal from the university became the most hotly debated topic in the campus. Students had withdrawn from the university about two years before and many students were questioning the wisdom of such action the second time around. Partly for personal reasons (I dreaded the interruption of my education) and partly because it did not seem that sensible to me, I argued against withdrawal and begrudged the individuals who seemed to instigate it. To me, the student movement was only effective in so far as students remained on campus and waged their struggle as students. Leaving campus denied the students the organizational wherewithal to be effective. Birhanu and I argued on the opposite side of this issue. Although he would not be personally affected by a withdrawal, he insinuated those who wanted to stay were not revolutionary enough and were doing it for selfish reasons. He read opportunism in my position and bluntly said it.

At that time, expression of self-interest was considered a bourgeois mentality that was not worthy of the Ethiopian people.

The leader of the group that was actively opposed to withdrawal was Melesse Tekle, a veteran of the student movement who had already been in and out of the university for more than seven years. He articulated the opposition's argument very well and fought hard to dissuade students from what he thought was a fruitless exercise in withdrawal.

The election was held and the leaders were selected. The elected officers except for Aboma seemed uniformly unimpressive and rather mediocre. That was because my high expectation did not seem to square with the crop of available leaders at that time. It may also be due to my unrealistic expectations. Some of the candidates that I thought looked strong, including Dawit Yohannes, lost. Of course, being new, my judgment was based on how well one spoke English and how smart he/she sounded.

One of the most memorable events to me at this time was the inauguration of the USUAA office holders. At the inauguration, Girmachew Lemma, a former president of USUAA delivered the keynote address. Members of the faculty, including Eshetu Chole and Fikre Merid, also spoke, but Girmachew was in a class by himself. He was an electrifying speaker who mesmerized the audience. Charismatic and towering, he had a commanding presence that eclipsed anyone who stood near him. The audience interrupted his speech with a tumultuous applause so frequently that it was difficult to hear him finish but a few complete sentences. This was an incredible phenomenon to me. Many other people I know remember this as vividly as I do. To this day, when I hear a good speech it reminds me of this famous speech by Girmachew.

In Girmachew I saw a leader that I was instantly attracted to and seemed capable of leading people to do anything that he wanted them to do. Girmachew worked as a legal counsel in the Ethiopian Trade Union and became one of the leaders of EPRP. He participated and led during the major demonstration that engulfed Addis Abeba at that time. He was in Addis Abeba right up to the height of the Red Terror. I was told by a person who knew him closely that he died trying to escape arrest.

I never knew how high Girmachew was in the leadership structure of EPRP. I have also heard others express doubt about his ability to lead. He was a gifted orator (there seems to be a universal agreement about that), and so far as I could tell, extremely intelligent. On top of that, he was down-to-earth and unassuming. It was incredible to me that he would stay in Addis during those fateful years. He was undoubtedly the easiest person to recognize at a time when the only way you could survive was by moving from place to place. To make matters worse, Girmachew suffered from a bad foot, which was attributed to torture, and had difficulty moving or running. To be constrained from regular movement inside or outside Addis was to be a sitting duck for the notorious *kebele* revolutionary squads.

The night of the inauguration, Girmachew's big gun was added to the group who argued for withdrawal. Girmachew called for action to support high school students whose blood was "flooding the streets" of Addis and who were now out of school. If that meant withdrawal from the university, he was all for it. That speech by Girmachew sealed the debate in favor of a vociferous and tenacious group who probably were a small minority. Added to Girmachew's force of personality was the rapidly deteriorating political situation in the country.

In one of the last debates before the decision to withdraw from the university was made, I remember a group of young students, mostly from Tigray, forcefully arguing for withdrawal. These youthful-looking, intense, and passionate students were determined to get students out of the university. I could not exactly determine who was who, but this group was later to form the core of TPLF leadership and "transform" Ethiopia for better or worse. I specially remember one who spoke so forcefully for withdrawal, and in a prophetic statement that I always remember, declared, "We shall withdraw, we shall go to rural Ethiopia, organize the people, and struggle to liberate the peasants." Few in history have lived up to their words to the fullest. I am not sure if this speaker was Meles, the late prime minister or Abaye Tsehai, but these individuals knew what they wanted and was going after it. The irony of this was Meles Tekle, whose name was assumed as a *nom de guerre* by Legesse after the former was executed by the Derg, fought harder than anyone else against withdrawal. The individuals who later formed the TPLF, on the other hand, fought for withdrawal with equal determination and succeeded.

The day we returned textbooks to the university, Mezy and I ran into Meles Tekle, who seemed dispirited by the decision to withdraw. He told her that he would never come back to the university again and finish his studies. That also proved prophetic since Melese Tekle was one of the four individuals that Derg executed for allegedly trying to blow up the municipality building.

I saw Melese Tekle many times in Addis Abeba. He seemed somewhat reckless for a university student leader of his notoriety. I remember speaking to a Tigray student who went to school in Dessie with me. In his opinion, Melese Tekle acted foolishly by remaining so visible in Addis at a time when many of his cohorts, with less notoriety, were going underground. Melese Tekle asked pointed questions and argued with Derg members when they came to campus. He spoke against the officers so openly that he made a very easy target of himself.

At this time events in the country began to move with dizzying speed. The Haile Selassie regime looked helpless as sectors of society began to agitate and join the rebellion. The small demonstrations that usually involved high school and university students in the past were now joined by teachers and taxi drivers. Soon the Muslim society, claiming historical grievances, joined the demonstrations with a massive show of force the likes of which Addis Abeba had never seen before. The demonstrations were joined by Addis Abeba students who supported the Muslim community's search for equality with their Christian brothers.

At this time many of the revolutionary individuals who lived outside in Europe and the United States started coming back to the country and forming organizations that would shape and guide the hitherto spontaneous massive rebellion and articulate it in political terms.

It is in these early years we became giddy with the possibilities of change and our lives became intertwined with the massive events taking place in the country, which got its clues from the restive Addis Abebans. Like my friends, I took part in many of these demonstrations and distributed leaflets.

While this was going on, members of the armed forces selected a group of individuals consisting of over a hundred officers and noncommissioned officers to direct the military's demands to the emperor. The committee that became known as the Derg gathered at the fourth division army headquarters in Addis and finally began to assert itself and assume power. It started by bringing certain elements of the old regime under control, all in the name of the emperor. The Derg got its cues from the radical individuals who formed the nascent revolutionary organizations that became known as Meison and EPRP. Through trial and error it coopted the left's ideas, and at times it came with its own slogans as it tried to find its footing. The left pushed and the Derg mainly moved in its direction. As the Derg began to fill more confident and acquired more legitimacy by responding to the revolutionary demands, it became the de facto political power. As the regime tried to cope up with the crisis, Haile Selassie's cabinet was forced to resign. Lij Endalkachew Mekonen became the prime minster and pleaded with the country for patience to make the necessary changes. The rebellious society now being led by even more radicalized revolutionaries ridiculed the new prime minister, making it impossible to govern. He was then replaced by Michael Emeru, the son of Ras Emeru, perhaps the most beloved and respected of the Ethiopian nobility, but the country's track was irrevocably set on a change and removal of the monarchy and the old order forever. The cisis continued unabated.

MEMBERSHIP IN A CELL: A RELUCTANT REVOLUTIONARY

Sahle introduced Birhanu and I to his primary and junior secondary school friend from Awassa named Mesfin, an air force cadet in Debre Zeit. At that time, Mesfin had received a scholarship to study medicine in Yugoslavia and would have left Ethiopia if it was not for Yekatit and the Ethiopian Air Force noncommissioned officers' mutiny, in which Mesfin played an active role. Major Sissay, who was later killed by Mengistu Haile Mariam in the earliest power struggle within Derg, was one of his instructors. Mesfin respected Major Sissay as a professor but had precious little to say about his other qualities.

Mesfin and Birhanu bonded immediately and were kindred spirits. Birhanu believed that Mesfin had the same stuff that revolutionaries are made of. Birhanu sought these acquaintances with a strategic view. Friendships were not made for just friendship's sake for him. Relationships needed to be cultivated for the purpose of swelling the ranks of revolutionaries. For Birhanu, Sahle was mostly fun-loving. Mesfin was serious and had the making of a revolutionary. While Sahle was kind of a free-thinker who had not yet determined what he wanted to be, Mesfin was purposeful and intense. Sahle gave the impression that he was not the kind of person who would abide by party principles; Mesfin looked like he could fit in a party hierarchy.

Mesfin looked up to Birhanu and seemed to be taken in by the latter's revolutionary fervor. He started coming to Addis from Debre Zeit, the Ethiopian Air Force base, and spend the weekend with us. We talked of revolution and Marxism-Leninism, to which Mesfin was just being introduced but instantly took a liking to. One night, Mesfin brought an Uzi submachine gun that the Ethiopian soldiers carry, and showed Birhanu how to handle it. Sahle recalls the morning Mesfin brought the weapon. He took it first to Sahle's dormitory, the newly built accommodation near Afncho Ber. None of the other three students who shared the dorm with Sahle were in the dorm at the time. Mesfin opened the sports bag he was carrying with him and pulled out the Uzi to show to Sahle. They left the bag under his bed and went to the cafeteria to have lunch. They discussed the Uzi over lunch and agreed it would be better if he discussed it with Birhanu.

One night I remember Birhanu's childlike enthusiasm playing with such a dangerous toy. It was obvious Birhanu understood where the movement was heading and was preparing himself for it. He was also interested in individuals who shared his commitment and bringing them to the movement.

Mesfin participated in a leadership role in the 1974 mutiny of the air force when cadets arrested their senior officers and briefly took charge of Debre Zeit City. The mutiny was quickly put down by the nearby airborne unit, which was led by a flamboyant airborne officer named Alem Zewde. Alem Zewed was considered pro-Endalkachew, and the underground people thought that he would be used to suppress the burgeoning rebellion that was breaking everywhere. But Alem Zewede's ascendency was quickly brought under control when the fourth division stationed in Addis joined the rebellion.

We were all impressed by Mesfin's role. He manned a checkpoint, carried a machine gun, and spoke of the rebellion with enthusiasm. Birhanu dubbed this rebellion the "Debre Zeit Commune," much like the short-lived Paris Commune that Marx enthusiastically wrote about. When the rebellion was suppressed, Mesfin brought his weapon and left the Ethiopian Air Force for good. With Mesfin also came another young air force cadet who later played an active role that I knew very little about and was transferred to Assimba, EPRP's rural base of armed operation.

After Mesfin left the Ethiopian Air force, he rented a house across from Yared Music School. I don't remember where the money for the rent came from, but Birhanu's underground associates must have been the source for it. Mesfin and Sahle knew another student from Awassa, Mohamed Arabi, who was a student at Ecole Normal, a French college in Addis. Mohamed became a regular at the house. With Mohamed came Abraham Kebede, his classmate. Soon Kassaye, a graduate of Addis Technical College and a close of friend of Abraham, joined the group. Kassaye, was looking for a job at that time and appeared frustrated by his failure despite his technical skills. Kassaye used to tell jokes about another graduate of the technical college who laid his diploma outside the school and started begging for money. The ideas was to solicit sympathy from the public on the plight of graduates with much needed technical skills in the country but who were unable to find gainful employment. Tough times were coming ahead, a harbinger of a much worse situation for which the Haile Selassie regime was ill prepared. With Kassaye came another student from Wollega named Bezabeh. Bezabeh was a high school graduate whose father was an officer in the Ethiopian army or police stationed in Eritrea. Then came Aya, another high school dropout. Aya knew the others, but I never knew how. Aya lived with his mother. He earned some money from rent and often bought *khat* for us. Aya was often chided for being very stingy, although we still managed to get him to part with his money and cigarettes.

Dil Nessa (nicknamed Dulla), another person from Wollega, also visited the house and helped financially. He often bought us *khat*, alcohol, and food. He was like a rich uncle who provided for the group. Dulla later played a serious role as owner of a furniture store that became a front for EPRP's underground activities. He supported many people that were affiliated with EPRP financially and by other means. In fact, Bezabih was like a young bother to Dula; he was sheltered at Dula's sister's house for a long time. The furniture shop in Piassa was a safe haven for many EPRP people to meet and even spend the night. He also employed some EPRP people with full knowledge of the danger associated with it. Weapons were stored in the shop. The weapons were seized when the shop was raided by the *kebele* forces and Dula was arrested.

Now, when I look back, I don't know how this group actually came into being other than what I am writing here. The people in the group knew each other far better than I knew them. In a way, I was new to them all and was the odd man out. We were like any other group of young men. None of us had planned to become an underground cell of a political organization. That came in time and was more the outcome of what was happening outside in the society than what was going on within us. Certainly Birhanu was the hidden hand behind our transformations. He was the only one who saw a purpose for our being and nudged us in the direction of underground activities. Mesfin provided the link.

From my side, Beide, a student from Dessie, frequented the house. Also, my dorm mate, Tadesse, occasionally dropped by just to socialize. Tadesse was apolitical, and was there to chew *khat* and stay off campus, as classes were completely disputed by then. For a while we had access to the dormitory and cafeteria. We would take our friends to campus and share our meal until the university was completely closed.

Our activity consisted of a scheduled reading and discussion of Marxism-Leninism. We discussed political lessons always with *khat*. If we could not buy *khat*, we would not read or discuss. We usually spent nights discussing the material. We were not as such following any particular outline. We read at random; some started from the beginning and others could be considered advanced. I helped answer many of the questions. Since I had been exposed to it longer than they had, I gave them what I thought was the right interpretation.

I enjoyed reading and was happy to be able to fill the long, idle day with books. This kind of life was new to me. My friends were good friends before I met them, and like good friends, shared everything. They wore each other's clothes, slept on the same bed or mattress, shared their food, and lived a communal life. Unlike me, they did not seem to have any family responsibility. Mesfin came from a poor family, but he never spoke of his family or was ever preoccupied with it. I began to adapt to their lifestyle and shared my money. My savings, which was intended for my family, was now being withdrawn at regular intervals and liberally spent for *khat* and drinks; my life was now irreversibly set on a different course than I had intended when I joined the university.

This was the first half of 1974. The emperor was still nominally the country's leader, but Derg was making all kinds of changes in the name of a hapless emperor who was now like a caged lion. While events were rapidly deteriorating, there was no danger to our safety. We mostly read and discussed books that were shipped from Russia and China. Ideologically, we preferred the books from China. We thought the Chinese revolution was purer and more profound, and held relevant lessons for our situations. All of us in general, Kassaye, Mesfin, Mohammed, and Bezabeh in particular, were fascinated by how a small group of guerrilla fighters who started from a small base of operation in a remote area could finally defeat a powerful government and establish the People's Republic of China. Conceptually, it was easy to understand, and for people like us, prone to accept such simple proposition without having to worry about implementation yet, the idea had a powerful hold on our thinking. We read *Fanshen: A documentary of Revolution in a Chinese Village* by William Hinton and Red Star over China by Edgar Snow. We found these two books extremely influential. The first one is a detailed sociological panorama of the revolutionary transformation of a Chinese peasantry in one village. Fanshen was extremely readable and easy to understand. *Red Stat over China* was also a fascinating account of the Red Army's "Great March" from its base of operations to save the revolution from the Kuomintang regime and liberate China. These books painted a poignant picture of revolution that captured our imagination and hence we often read them more than once. They were like our Bible. We also read books on the American socialist movement by Paul Sweezy and Paul Baran. We read these books seriously, but not critically. We were happy to fill our abundant free time with books.

During this time, I noticed that we were getting news of what was going on in the Derg through Mesfin. For example, we saw a draft copy of what was to become the Land Proclamation Act that had Mengistu's signature.

I remember being impressed by what looked like the assertive, confident penmanship of Mengistu. Sometimes the information would be given directly to Mesfin from Birhanu and passed on to us. I began to realize that Mesfin was our liaison (our link, as we then said) with an underground organization that we suspected existed but did not actually know.

I was still good friends with Mezy and Birhanu. They also treated me as a close friend. I was regularly at their house often on special occasions. They all knew that I had a profound distrust of what they were doing and was not ready to commit myself to the revolution, which they were living and breathing. My constant excuse was my family. I always found myself in tough spot, eager to be like my friends, unburdened by my family ties. In this, my situation was not any different from many others, but weighed on me so much that I was often torn by inner conflicts.

By this time Sahle lived in Awassa with his family but came to Addis often. Whenever he came to Addis, he would drop by the house and socialize with us. One day, while Sahle was in the house, Mesfin told us that Abraham, Aya, Kassaye, Bezabeh, and I were invited to Birhanu's house to attend some business. I don't remember us including Beide also, who later found himself in the organization. We left Sahle out. Sahle deftly and with humor brushed off the lack of explanation for us leaving him. If his feeling was hurt, he did not show it that night. He joked that we had important business to attend. Those days also I was conscious that some discussion was going on between Birhanu and Mesfin from which I was excluded. I felt sensitive about that. I had suspicions for why I was being left out, but still, my ego was hurt.

We went to Birhanu's house, got much needed food—*injera* with spiced and butter-treated *shero wat* that Mezy and Birhanu's sister, Tsedale, cooked. After dinner, Birhanu mentioned to us the existence of a clandestine political organization, and speaking uncharacteristically with some hesitation, told us that we all have demonstrated our revolutionary spirit and have been recommended to be members. He was referring to our participation in demonstrations and distributing leaflets. EPRP was an underground movement whose political program was still unknown even among the intelligentsia in Ethiopia. Our reaction ranged from enthusiasm to muted indifference. He asked us what we thought about it. I felt the question was directed at me but waited until the others spoke. Mohammed said that he was pleased to be a member and others nodded. I probably mumbled "*teru new*" (it's okay) with visibly less conviction, adding that it is good we have become members.

We were told of our responsibilities as party members. Birhanu made a small speech exhorting us to be disciplined and steadfast in our struggle as true revolutionaries.

I had a bad feeling about it all, although I did not express it. I know this was not done openly and fairly but I had no argument against it. More importantly, I felt that somehow from now on I have sort of lost some control of my life. Deep down I resented what Birhanu had done to me and to the others.

In my case, I was sure that I did not want to be a part of this but did not raise any objection. This is how those of us who were invited became party members; no serious discussion of what it entailed or it meant for our lives. This was our official initiation into the brotherhood of revolutionaries for which Mohamed, Kassaye, Abraham, Aya, and Bezabeh paid the ultimate price, and Mesfin languished in prison for an extended period of time. After Mesfin was released from prison, he died in a car accident. I am not sure how it happened, but I suspect alcohol was involved—a legacy of life and association with an underground movement.

We came back from the house having confirmed what some of us might have all along suspected; we were a cell that was a part of an organization that hitherto was really unknown by the general public. For me we were just a study group of like-minded individuals that enjoyed books, alcohol, and *khat*. I had not anticipated this sudden turn into something so serious. As if to give me time to get acclimatized to my new role, the situation in Addis at this time never gave me reason for concern about my safety. That came later.

A Visit to Arsi

Sometime in the summer of 1974, I went to visit Arsi with my friend Tadesse Gena. We first went to Assella, where his father owned a business. We visited Chilalo Agricultural Development Unit (CADU), a Swedish-funded agricultural training center in Asela. Arsi seemed to my untrained eyes a very rich and prosperous province. Modern farming was slowly being introduced in the area, often at the expense of the small farmers, but Arsi, it was said, could grow enough food to feed the rest of Ethiopia. This was the most memorable trip I had made in Ethiopia. We drove in his father's Toyota to a very rural area where his mother and relatives lived. His father managed the business from Asela.

Before I left for Arsi, I had written a short piece about the pace of change that the Derg was implementing at that time. I don't remember the details, but I argued that every movement in history faced a decision on how fast or how slow to develop before its enemies organize and defend their interest. I must have read that somewhere. I used the phrase "snail's pace" (*ende aeli mazgem*) implying that the Derg had to make up its mind on how fast to dismantle the old order or something to that effect. I gave it to Birhanu, who in turn had it published in Addis Zemen. While listening to the radio in Arsi, I heard a commentator quote from this article I had written under the name Adefresse. I chose the pen name from the title of an impressive Amharic novel by Dagnachew Worku that I read in TTI. The book was recommended to me by Derebew Adjugna, my Amharic teacher at TTI, who gave me a tremendous confidence in my writing skills. Adefresse was later used by Birhanu and Yohannes and kind of became a famous EPRP pen name. Birhanu and another teacher used this pen name in a polemic against Abe Gobegna, the most-read Amharic writer at the time.

Anyway, while sitting somewhere in a village in Arsi eating and drinking, I remember being thrilled and feeling important at being quoted on the radio.

Tadesse and I also went to visit his sister who lived by the Koka hydroelectric dam. We rode on horseback to his sister's house, where we were generously entertained. After food and drink, his brother-in-law rented us a boat to paddle on the lake. Later that night, when it was almost dark, Tadesse insisted that we return to his father's house, and I reluctantly agreed to end the festivity. When we were alone and heading back, Tadesse told me that they would have slaughtered a calf had we stayed overnight. I was touched and impressed both by the wealth and tradition of his people.

I left Arsi, where I had so much fun, including hunting and walking and riding on horseback through a beautiful forest, to the nearby town of Shashmene, from where I took the minibus to Addis. I felt like I had spent a magical moment in that place that I could never replicate now when I visit other places. Something of my soul has remained in Arsi.

HAILE SELASSIE IS OVERTHROWN

After I returned from Arsi, just before the emperor was deposed I went to Dessie wearing an air force jacket that I borrowed from Mesfin. That was my new look, and some of the younger people that knew me noticed. A relative of mine told me that his friends commented that I looked like a fighter. That was their image of a guerilla fighter, but not what fighters looked like. I was told that people thought I was a "revo" like Birhanu and showed some respect for me.

Going to Desssie often brought me down to reality. I could see the grinding poverty that my family lived under. I could see my brothers and sisters, what they wore, what they had to eat, which always raised a profound moral dilemma about my commitment to my family. My father was at that time in an "I told you so" frame of mind although he did not openly say it. He had realized giving up my teaching career to go to the university was a mistake. He did not like the fact that I left a nice job that paid very well only to find myself unemployed. But he was quiet and deferential as usual. My mother meekly raised the issue of finding another job but that did not look like an option that I could entertain.

Toward the end of the summer, the Derg became rather bold in its attacks on the emperor. It was systematically stripping the emperor of his legitimacy through a well-orchestrated propaganda against his lifestyle, his neglect of his people, and other alleged transgressions. In interview after interview designed to undermine the emperor's legitimacy to the Ethiopian people, former dissidents spoke how politically they were persecuted by the emperor. These stories shocked the public and offered it a glimpse into a life beneath the veneer of a decent, God-fearing emperor who loved his people. The Derg was especially skillful in using the 1972 famine, which was hidden from the world because the emperor was celebrating his eightieth birthday, to demonstrate that the emperor did not care for his people. It played up the image of a detached emperor surrounded by corrupt officials so effectively that the public, especially Addis Abebans, seemed ready for the overthrow of the emperor. However, I remember my mother was shocked to hear all of this propaganda. When I told her that the emperor could be deposed, she could not believe my words. Incredulous, she asked me who the next king of the country would be. I told her we may never have a king again. She thought that was an incredible statement. A country that could exist without a king was not intelligible to her. She feared that may be the beginning of something dreadful coming to the country. It never occurred to me what I was talking about was a new order of society unlike any other that my mother knew or heard about. Although we talked as if we knew what the people wanted, we really did not appreciate what all these impending changes meant to them.

It was obvious that the Derg was going to depose the emperor. I felt they would do it in the Ethiopian New Year. In the spring before the emperor was deposed, our cell talked to a young NCO who happened to be member of the Derg and was a classmate of Kassaye. Kassaye brought him over one night for one of our *khat* sessions and we discussed politics, especially the Derg's systematic effort to bring under control the powerful individuals of the regime. This was a time when the Derg members were available and talked things openly with anyone they knew. Of course, the members were not officially known. It was also not known who the inner circle of the Derg was. At this early stage, Derg's decisions were reached through a collective process. The young NCO told us of Mengistu, who at that time was emerging as one of the powerful leaders. He was respectful of Mengistu. He was evasive about our question whether or not the Derg will depose the emperor. We were obviously all for that and argued that the people would not resist if the emperor was removed. They were very cautious, but we could not wait.

Their strategy to slowly remove the locus of power from under the emperor's control and isolate the royal family members, senior military officers, and other individuals who could organize resistance to the Derg worked flawlessly. The Derg was cunning, skillful, systematic, and efficient. They had practically all the members of the former regime with power under control, and they did so without heavy bloodshed. Their mantra was "Ethiopia Forward, but without Bloodshed." A few resisted; the most notable of which was the governor of Keffa, who refused to give his hands up and was later killed while trying to organize some resistance from rural Ethiopia. But the Derg was so methodical in the way it organized the deposition of the emperor, even Birhanu admitted it was brilliantly executed.

I returned to Addis when the Derg announced the overthrow of the emperor. There may have been some shock with the more traditional elements of society, but most took it in stride. The Derg had prepared the people for this. Addis Abebans were specially prepared for the overthrow with a TV documentary that showed the emperor wining and dining in royal extravaganza juxtaposed with the image of starved peasants that were dying by thousands every day. People were especially indignant that the emperor's dog was treated with so much dignity while other Ethiopians were dying en masse from famine. The propaganda reached a responsive chord and Addis Abebans quietly and later with some jubilation accepted the deposing of the emperor.

My friends and I walked around the city that morning and saw tanks stationed near the municipality building. One tank was surrounded by jubilant young people who were also fraternizing with the crew. A young girl gave flowers to a crew member and kissed him on his cheeks. The youth were obviously delighted to see the era of the kings ended in Ethiopian history. Later that day, people demolished the statue of the emperor near Cinema Empire.

THE ORGANIZATIONS
BEHIND THE CHANGES

At this time there were at least four underground papers that were being disseminated: *Democracia*, *Ye Sefiw Hizb Dimts* (The Voice of the Masses), *Abeyot* (Revolution), and *Key Bandira* (Red Flag). The two underground organizations that published *Democracia* and *Abeyot* later merged to form EPRP after a protracted discussion. Democracia became the main organ of EPRP, and Abeyot was renamed *Lab Ader* (Proletaria) and became the organ of labor under EPRP. There were also serious efforts to bring EPRP and Meison to work together, which yielded no result.

Democracia and *Ye Sefiw Hizb Dimts* were considered to have bigger circulations, although it appeared to us at that time *Democracia* had wider circulation. The underground political oppositions to the old regime and later to the Derg coalesced around these newspapers.

I remember our cell was consulted about the title of *Democracia* before it became the main organ of EPRP. Birhanu asked us what we thought of *Democracia* as a title of a newspaper. We all liked it and I commented it was a neat idea. It also made ideological if not political sense. In Marxist theory, as interpreted by Mao Tse Tung, the first phase of a socialist revolution for a country just coming out of feudal economic order, is what Mao called "the New Democratic Revolution." This was said to be different from the "bourgeoisie democratic revolution" because it occurs only in a world environment where there is a block of socialist countries. This thinking was widely accepted around revolutionary circles and hence the name *Democracia* to signify the revolutionary democracy phase of this struggle. That was my rationale for applauding the decision and probably why EPRP, which had not declared itself a party yet, called its propaganda organ *Democracia*. I simply liked the sound of it and what the name represented and was for it.

Our cell was considered one of the most dedicated and hardworking. We printed *Democracia* in our crude printing presses. In fact, Kassaye redesigned the letterhead for printing *Democracia* with relatively better-looking (very primitive technology by today's standards) fonts. The stamp was made from discarded rubber of a sandal shoe from which each letter of *Democracia* was carved out. We also distributed the papers to as many people as we knew. I remember Mohamed and I spending a day in Akaki, the industrial zone of Addis, distributing *Democracia*. We often discussed *Democracia* and used it to guide our thinking and help us understand the changes that were taking place.

Initially the Derg seemed ideologically clueless, often vacillating between developing what it called an Ethiopian solution to the problem and adopting more conventional leftist policies. There was a great deal of discussion in the papers about the direction the country was supposed to take. Famous academics like Prof. Mesfin Wolde Mariam and Dr. Negussie Ayele and the novelist Haddis Alemayehu advocated for a more evolutionary change, taking into consideration the rich tradition of the country. But their voices were no match to the emerging radical and leftist ideology that was now adopted by activists and the organized intelligentsia. The activists' push was more effective as the Derg seemed to be easily swayed by the leftist groups that were slowly making themselves felt in and outside the Derg through organized activities. Consequently, the Derg began to rapidly move to the left and utilize all the available leftist jargon at the time. We, of course, did not think highly of this and believed that the Derg can neither be socialist nor communist. This lurch to the left by Derg was very disorienting for many leftists. First the Derg came up with what was called Ethiopian Socialism. *Democracia* ridiculed it. What Democracia said made theoretical sense for us. But we never discussed political tactics or strategy, but mainly ideology and it was very easy to see that what the Derg was doing did not square with what Lenin, Mao or Marx have written. EPRP skillfully exposed this contradiction for us that we were easily convinced that EPRP was the true Marxist and the Derg was at best a pseudosocialist, or at worst a fascist organization. Its mission in history was to foil a genuine proletarian revolution that only the EPRP leading the "proletariat" was capable of bringing.

Ye Sefiw Hizb Dimts (VOM), however, traded a more nuanced route and began to tilt toward the Derg's new position. Meison was buoyant about the declaration of socialism and began to push the Derg toward agrarian reform and other declarations. Meison adopted what was then called a strategy of constructive criticism and began to show greater support for the Derg, while at the same time rejecting what it referred to as the left adventurism of

EPRP. Meison was also critical of some polices of the Derg, but its strategic tilt was toward working with elements within the Derg that were pushing for radical changes.

I read the *Ye Tsefew Hizb Dimts* (VOM) frequently. It was always printed on a better quality paper and was cleaner to carry. However, I thought *Democracia* was better written; the style was elegant, although I was very impressed with the depth and quality of some issues of *Ye Tesefe Hizb Dimts*. The *Proletariat* traded a more leftist route. The paper looked shabby and the style was very dry. I saw very few issues of *Red Flag*. All these could be due to my bias, but that is what it seemed like at that time.

This was an exciting time. Derg still stated that it wanted to bring change without bloodshed for which the left mocked it. Abe Gubegna, who was the most radical author in his own time and perhaps the most-read novelist in Ethiopia, wrote an article supporting Derg's thrust and applauding the bloodlessness of the changes up to that point. The author, in trying to make his point as forcefully as he could, also stated that individuals thirsty for blood should satisfy themselves with their wives' menstrual cycle. This unfortunate phrase, which may have been a slip-up, was seen as intentional and in poor taste. Abe Gubegna, who had written more political novels than any other author and was closely watched by the emperor's security, was very much out of the loop in his political thinking at that time. On top of that, what he said about blood lacked both good taste and tactic.

Birhanu, who in high school was a great admirer of the author and another member of the teachers' union, responded under the pen name Adefresse in Addis Zemen. Abe Gobena made an easy target and the two were out to get him. The famous Ethiopian author was mocked and ridiculed in a vicious leftist polemics. Part of the criticism was as witty as it was devastating. Abe Gobegna never recovered from it. I do not remember reading anything political he wrote after that debacle.

In the early part of 1975, a sweeping and radical Land Proclamation Act was declared. *Democracia* supported it with condition, and declared these changes would be meaningless without the organs of self-rule in rural Ethiopia. We participated in a huge demonstration that started in Arat Kilo and went downtown through the back of Emperor Menlik's palace to what became known as the Revolutionary Square. At the back of Emperor Menlik's palace facing the OAU were some members of the Derg, including Col. Mengistu Haile Mariam. They stood watching the crowd pass by and waved. It was rumored at that time that Mengistu was behind the land proclamation. It was also rumored that he pushed for this change, while the others, most notably Colonel Atnafu, wavered and even opposed the law. The demonstrators expressed their support to Mengistu. Some, including a few young people, broke through the guards and hugged him. It was a spontaneous and genuine applause, and he seemed to enjoy it. Interspersed with the placards that supported the Land Proclamation Act, which ended feudalism as we knew it, were others that were asking for a provisional civilian government, then EPRP's most famous slogan. A group of young people surrounding Girmachew carried these placards. Kassaye and Mesfin were in this group.

The sweeping Land Proclamation Act was as radical as EPRP wanted it. In fact, some of its members had a hand in its formulation. In just one stroke of the pen, it destroyed the hated feudalism. The proclamation was especially significant in the south, east, and west of the country where the feudal land tenure system was based on ethnic hegemony. It was profound and revolutionary, which made it very difficult for the Derg's opposition to say anything against it.

Meison now completely parted ways with EPRP and began to attack EPRP fiercely. Meison saw this as a splendid opportunity to work with the government in organizing the peasantry so the proclamation could be fully implemented. Organizing the peasantry at this time was considered very crucial and whoever could control the peasant's association could probably control the revolution. EPRP, in what seems in retrospect a strategic error, failed to see what this proclamation could do to its ambition to come to power as the head of an organized revolutionary movement.

The declaration made EPRP's stand complicated. Its position was such that without political power in the hands of the people, the agrarian reform could only be used to legitimize the Derg and bring the peasants under its influence. The peasant association, it suspected correctly, was going to be used to strengthen the Derg's control over the population. Hence, EPRP would continue to oppose the Derg and fight for the formation of a provisional democratic government. In essence, EPRP was going to either force the Derg to give up its political power or the latter was going to say that its situation was untenable and willingly bring others into the government and share power with them.

I don't think EPRP had a realistic appreciation of the political realignment that the Land Proclamation Act was going to force on the Ethiopian political landscape. With this one act, the Derg took from EPRP the potential support of the Ethiopian peasantry. How was EPRP ever going to win the support of the rural masses when the very issue that has animated the left for so long and was encapsulated in the elegant "Land to the Tiller" slogan was now made superfluous, if not redundant? Only one issue remained that was potent enough to mobilize the rural poor, and that was the so-called national question. But this was the issue that EPRP did not know how to translate into a meaningful movement. In any case, whoever was to use this issue as a multinational movement had to first deal with the well-entrenched and powerful movements in Eritrea. Here again EPRP did not seem to find a way to deal with the card it was dealt with.

EPRP was faced with a pragmatic problem that required it to appreciate its subordinate position to Eritrean People's Liberation Front (EPLF) and Eritrean Liberation Front (ELF) if it ever was going to leverage the national question. It was also faced with an ideological problem that had to be reconciled to its dogma that EPRP was the vanguard organization that was to mobilize all the progressive organizations under its wing. Under this ideological construct, EPRP was to lead EPLF and ELF, not the other way around, if one was just to follow the dictates of the ideology. The reality was of course different. With the land issue gone and the national question being spearheaded by groups who did not accept the national question per se but saw it as a colonial question, EPRP was left to focus more on the urban struggle to overthrow the regime.

At this point, there was little information available to us about EPRP's armed wing, EPRA, which was ostensibly operating in Assimba, Tigray. While little was known about this wing to us, the idea was to wage a classic armed struggle by organizing the poor peasantry just like the Communist Party of China. The only problem was that EPRP's army was in Tigray where there were many poor peasants but not a land tenure system, which put the poor peasants at loggerheads with the land-owning feudal owners. In a classic guerilla warfare scenario, you can't organize the peasants against a hated and local enemy in these areas. This would have made more sense in areas of the south, where you could always organize the poor peasants against hated, ethnically alien landed gentry that was culturally abusive and economically exploitative of landless tenants. For reasons that have never been officially told, EPRP chose Tigray. Maybe the first leaders of this army that never became effective enough to threaten the Derg included many from the area and knew the population and the country better. Maybe because it was adjacent to Eritrea and the leaders knew that if they were ever to become militarily powerful they needed the support and training from the Eritrean fronts. All these may have been factors in the initial decision to start a guerilla war in Tigray. It may also be because the land terrain of Tigray was considered more hospitable to a small group of mobile fighters while it was difficult for a modern, highly mechanized army the government had. I know there are alternative explanations for this also; I will leave that to historians.

The Land Proclamation Act could not, but it had raised a very serious question about mobilizing the peasantry to fight the government. Whatever slogans, policies that EPRP or EPRA were to use, the Derg was effectively using it to organize peasants. In fact, the language, the rhetoric, and everything about the Derg was slowly becoming indistinguishable from EPRP and other leftist groups. These groups were barely distinguishable from one another even among the most educated people. For the peasantry, none of it made any sense anyway. Nonetheless, EPRP, in what may be seen as a big strategic mistake, did not make any changes in its position and was now beginning to singlehandedly oppose the government.

While the ideological lines, no matter how blurred, were being drawn between EPRP and the Derg, there was no violent conflict yet at this time. Most underground cells operated well and EPRP was gaining popularity within elements of the labor union, students, and the teachers. This was because EPRP had won the leadership of these organizations earlier. EPRP was also buoyant about its successes, especially in the Confederation of the Ethiopian Labor Union (CELU), where its members held key positions both in the national organization and in the member organizations in and outside Addis Abeba. EPRP members, Girmachew and Kiflu Tadesse served the organization as legal counselor and education program director respectively. EPRP definitely had CELU under its wing very early.

Our cell began to assume more aggressive role in the distribution of leaflets in plants, schools, and other areas. At the same time, we continued to read Marxism-Leninism and acquire the social ills of frequent drinking and *khat* chewing. In our cell, Mesfin began to emerge as the leader, receiving more sensitive information from Birhanu. I was beginning to delve more and more into revolutionary activities although I was never resolved about completely committing for it. I was very ambivalent and made that known to Mesfin and Sahle. Mesfin said that I should forget about my family and commit myself to the revolution. Sahle was more understanding and expressed sympathy with my dilemma.

Working as a CELU Cadre

That summer of 1975, Mohamed and I were told to go to Wonji Sugar Factory and instruct the members of the workers union about socialism, the history of international workers' movements, and other topics. The Wonji Sugar Factory's union, which was one of the strongest and best organized, had requested the Confederation of Ethiopian Labor Union (CELU) to send instructors who would introduce the basic tenets of socialism to its union members. Apparently, the management of the factory, which was not fully nationalized but was minority owned by the government, was not opposed to it. Mohamed and I were told to go to CELU and receive our instructions from the leadership. When we came into the building, we were received by Kiflu Tadesse (who was in charge of education) rather than by Girmachew, the man we were scheduled to see. Girmachew, the legal counsel for CELU, appeared to be tied up with other issues. Instead, Kiflu Tadesse gave us a brief orientation of what was expected of us, where we were to stay, and how long the program would last. Our accommodation was arranged to be at a guest house with the consent of the management. We were to provide evening classes to foremen, workers, and also to some who were daily laborers. Kiflu said that details would be worked out between us and the union leadership.

We first went to Wonji and were assigned to stay in the guest house as agreed between the management and the union. The schedule was prepared by the union. The union offered us a van, with a chauffeur to take us to our classes and bring us back to the guest house every night. We were assigned one class each. These classes were away from the main plant and the guest house; they were located near the residential quarters, which were segregated by one's position in the factory, depending on whether one is a foreman, a skilled worker, a laborer, etc.

The Wonji experience was quite extraordinary for me. Wonji had many highly skilled engineers and foreign workers from Holland. The plant and the sugar plantation were now partly owned by the government and partly owned by a foreign firm following the government's nationalization decree. I thought government was a minority holder. Because of the importance of the plant to the Ethiopian economy and the requirement for technical and managerial skills, the government was deterred from fully nationalizing the factory. The factory was impressive.

Wonji neighborhoods, I came to realize, were highly segregated based on one's position in the plant. Whites (mostly Dutch) and foreigners, including Ethiopians in the management positions, lived in a nice subdivision, where the guest house was located. Most of the engineers lived in an area of the town that, to me, looked like a European neighborhood, meaning the ones that I have seen in movies. These houses were provided by the company and were well kept, with immaculate lawns. There were many university graduates, chemists, and engineers who lived in this area. The guest house was in the midst of this neighborhood and had all the amenities of a luxury hotel. We were provided with excellent food, different every day. It was here for the first time that I had cereal for breakfast. It was a lovely accommodation, which made me envy the people who lived there.

The next tier of housing located near the plantation was also very good and pleasant, to my astonishment. Here lived the foremen, other skilled employees. These houses had their own backyard, were of different sizes. The roads were paved, with trees lining the sides. The quality drastically falls as you go down the tier to the daily laborers' sections, which were more crowded and less attractive. But you could not see the abject poverty you see everywhere else in the country, and I thought life was reasonably well here. However, I saw very little of the housing where the daily laborers or the seasonal workers lived. I also remember seeing many employees with hunched backs. This, I learned later, was caused by the water. People who were exposed to the drinking water in the factory town over an extended period developed serious health problems. I remember seeing many people with highly stained teeth, which was again attributed to the drinking water.

We had a wonderful time in Wonji, preaching socialism while enjoying the life of a petty bourgeois. The irony of this situation was lost to us. We had a taste of the bourgeois life that we were so opposed to. In the morning, when we woke up we would be served breakfast at the cafeteria. We had cereal, different kinds of eggs, and toasted bread with margarine and jelly. For lunch, we were served roasted beef, broiled chicken, spaghetti, or lasagna. To this day, I remember with pleasure the two to three months I spent in Wonji and Metehara.

The teaching went very well and I became very popular with the employees. What we taught was general theoretical material that said nothing about the existing political situation. For individuals who knew about the shades of political differences that existed between Meison, the Derg, and EPRP though, it was clear that we were on EPRP's side. We definitely pushed EPRP's version of the revolution by saying that neither the agrarian land reform nor the urban land nationalization would work unless implemented by a truly working-class party. We declared that under another leadership the changes could only be instruments of oppression. This nuanced position was really hard to grasp in reality, but we tried to articulate it.

We used the term "*lab-ader*" as opposed to "*woz-ader*" for the proletariat, which was the preferred term of Meison and later the Derg. These terms later were so important that neither side would use the other's term, in the process exposing many EPRP members to easy identification. The difference was the prefix "*woz*" (pronounced "was") implied the sweat of the rich, while "*lab*" implied the actual sweat of working people. "*Lab*" translates in English into *sweat*. *Woz*, however, translates into *facial glow*. In retrospect, it is amazing why each organization so stubbornly held to its term. For Meison, it was advantageous to do so. EPRP could have been more tactical in its use of the term, and that may have probably saved a few lives whose only crime was probably using the wrong prefix.

We taught at night and read during the day. We smuggled *khat* into the guest house daily and discussed the curriculum. We were also ordered to prepare a manual of what we presented so it could be used by our trainees to teach others. We started preparing a small booklet of the material covered in the teaching for future use. We split up the topics, but I wrote most of material. At this time, Mohamed and I began to develop differences over many issues, such as who should write what and who should have an editorial say. Our biggest difference was over another individual who was also staying in the guest house. This individual, Italian in origin and probably in citizenship, owned a firm that was prospecting for water for the plant and its employees. As said earlier, many old employees had developed hunched backs, and it was said at that time the Dutch firm was being sued by as many as seventy employees who suffered. The Italian firm was testing water levels for fluoride, and the engineer whose firm was doing the digging was confident that he would be able to drill good drinking water from areas in the city by digging for water deeper.

This engineer and I liked each other. He was an unabashedly bourgeois and he liked to flaunt it. He knew what we were doing but fraternized with us. He bought us beer from the guest house and joked about us taking advantage of money exploited from the masses. He was young, easy going, and very fun loving. We talked about politics, revolution, and music. I really enjoyed the discussions and liked his bourgeoisie taste. Theoretically, there was nothing that I have read that told me not to fraternize with similar personalities. He was a capitalist and the capitalist class is an ally of the proletariat in the bourgeoisie democratic revolution. That, of course, meant the local capitalist class, and this guy was a foreign capitalist, which meant he was an imperialist and hence by definition a class enemy. Somehow that did not bother me, but made Mohamed uneasy about me and about him. For me he was just a good-natured man and very intelligent, which made him very likeable. He also brushed off our harsh rhetoric about class warfare, exploitation of the blood and sweat of the working class, and things of that nature we sometimes brought to the discussion.

I always remember what he told me about Beethoven, the musical genius, and what he could have achieved if he had not died young. One night he told me how Beethoven tried to translate a spectacular sunset into musical notes, which at that time intrigued me. To this day, I remember what this engineer said every time I listen to classical music or watch the sunset over the ocean or beyond the horizon.

Also, near the guest house was a fully equipped movie theater for the exclusive use of the people who lived in the section of Wonji. The fee was a nominal amount and the patrons could bring beer and snacks to the movie theater. Mohamed and I were able to get into the movies and enjoy a number of beautiful movies in a very luxurious atmosphere. I remember watching the *Planet of the Apes*, *Shangri-La*, and a John Wayne movie that showed American GIs snatching a POW from a North Vietnamese prison. We enjoyed the action but realized it was a propaganda piece since we were on the side of the Vietnamese struggle.

Mohamed and the engineer also used the swimming pool. I tried to learn swimming one day and nearly sank. Terrorized, I gave up and had to wait until I made it to Djibouti to learn how to swim.

After our teaching in Wonji was over, we were sent to Metahara, another sugar manufacturing plant owned by the same company. We had the same quality level of accommodation in a guest house. Here we were introduced to individuals who we suspected were EPRP members. We chewed *khat*, drank, and fraternized with them. We were told that they would find us employment if we could stay, helping the union and teaching socialist ideology.

In Metahara, while we were sitting outside in a bar and enjoying a cold beer in a hot and humid day, we heard the announcement on the radio of the passing away of the emperor. I don't think it was major news for the people around. Nobody seemed to pay any particular attention to it. Mohamed and

I might have discussed the possibility of the emperor's murder. So much had changed in such a short time that the death of the Emperor who had ruled Ethiopia for so long and introduced some level of modernization did not stir any feeling of nostalgia. The announcement said that the emperor was given full medical care by his doctors and died peacefully. We did not care.

While in Methara, I used to read *Newsweek* and *Time* at the guest house. I remember reading an issue of *Newsweek* that featured Iran's military strength in the region when it was both a friend of America and Israel. Among the pictures was an impressive display of Iranian armed forces, navy and air force, with a caption that read "the best in the region except for Israel's" and they "don't smoke pot." A few years later, when I came to Djibouti, Iran was engulfed in a massive revolution. The army stayed neutral but the *shah* was overthrown, just like the emperor, who at one point was a close friend of Haile Selassie.

The security situation for us in Methara was also not very good. I somehow felt that we were identified with EPRP and it was a matter of time before the government moved against us. After we left, Birhanu asked if I wanted to stay in Methara and work since the people there had expressed interest in keeping me. I said I was too well known there to stay and do any meaningful work. Mohammed, to my surprise, also said the same thing. It was obvious that we could be arrested if we stayed. Birhanu withdrew his offer.

By this time, every one of the members in our cell was very much engaged in underground work. The group now lived in a big house south of the Ethiopian Electric Company. The house was rented by Mesfin, who worked for *Goh* magazine. This house had become one of the main production centers of *Democracia* and *Red Star*, the theoretical journal of the party, which appeared intermittently. This became a busy center with unknown and hooded party members coming in and going out with stacks of *Democracia* that was laboriously printed by the people in this house. Birhanu would bring the manuscripts for us to print and then bring a car to take it back once it was produced. I don't know how many we produced, but I don't think it was more than a few hundred. But we were told that our house was one of the many centers in Addis where the paper was produced. About seven to eight people stayed or slept here every day. The house had its own compound and was surrounded by a fence, which allowed us some privacy. This was a relatively peaceful time and the neighbors probably never suspected what was going on. We stayed in the house most of the time and went out to the neighborhood joints at night for our usual drinking binge.

This was where Mohamed and I stayed when we came from Wonji for the weekend. Occasionally, Birhanu and Mezy would sleep in this house too. One day, it must have been on a weekend, we had some discussion about the impending EPRP program that was to be launched. We discussed the name of the party. I don't remember what names were suggested by us. What I remember was a question/suggestion by Birhanu to call the party the Ethiopian Communist Party, which struck me as odd at that time. Birhanu seemed ahead of the curve as usual. I argued against using the "communist" term for being untimely, adding that it would be rather confusing to the public. I think the others may have also said the party could stay Marxist-Leninist but be given a different name.

Another time, after a day filled with eating *khat* and drinking a highly potent *areke* brought from Gojjam (it was called *dagim*), I remember us singing EPRP's party anthem as we lay down to sleep. Mesfin must have started it, and then one by one all of us followed and sang it all together in a subdued voice.

I could sense some of them really got emotional about this and meant it. As I lay down on the floor, staring at the ceiling, I wondered to myself if I had what it takes to take up arms. I instinctively reacted negatively to the concept of armed struggle. I did not really want to commit my life for the cause, not yet.

Sometimes, when I was lonely and depressed, I would hum a patriotic song with pacifist lyrics. As if unconsciously replying to my dilemma, I would sing:

ጦር ይምጣ ጦር ይምጣ
ለምን ትላላችሁ
ደህና ደህና ነበዝ ታስወስዳላችሁ

Why do you seek war, or call for war, for you might lose guys who are irreplaceable.

I would sing it loudly for everyone to hear that Mesfin one day said that song is for cowards. I did not really agree, but did not make my point either.

It was also here in this house that Birhanu and Mezy told us of the national congress of EPRP, which declared the party. They told us tidbits from the congress. For some reason, I really believed it was a big conference involving a large number of people, which of course would have been difficult to organize. We were told the meeting was guarded by EPRA fighters. We heard that Berhane Meskel attended the congress protected by bodyguards. These stories assumed epic proportions in our imagination. *Democracia* later bragged that the congress was held under the Derg's nose to declare the party.

Most nights we would go to the many bars around this area and break the *khat* effect. If we had more money, we would usually go to the relatively nicer place. There was one where we used to go and listen to English songs.

Most of the girls in this bar seemed to be high school dropouts, and some may have been *Zemecha* (a national program that deployed high school and college student to rural Ethiopia) *refusniks*. We could talk to these girls, listen to music, and stagger back to our place completely inebriated. When we didn't have enough money, we went to the seedier section of the neighborhood for *areke*, which was cheaper and deadlier. For me, the hangover was always debilitating. In the morning, I get a real throbbing headache, which I could only get rid of with more *khat* and alcohol. I realized how much damage I had done to myself later when I came to the United States.

For some time, while we lived in this house most of us worked. Mesfin and I worked for *Goh*. Kassaye, Mohamed, and Abraham worked for CADU in Arsi. After we all lost our jobs and went "underground," we were occasionally paid forty birr as a stipend from the party intermittently. We used the money mostly for entertainment. For food, we always went to our relatives' places and ate. Although we did not see it as such, it was not a dignified existence. Mohamed had a sister who provided food and occasional pocket money. Abraham's family lived in Addis, so he could go there and eat when he needed. Aya also went to his house for food and when he needed money. I also had a cousin and second cousins where I could go and eat food as often as I needed to. I also had friends from Dessie where I could go for an occasional meal.

Toward the end of summer when we were in Metahara, EPRP officially declared itself a party and distributed its programs. We had discussed the program in our cell although not as extensively as one would expect. I remember us discussing something about the right of nations, which was a very difficult issue in principle, but even more complicated when viewed in the light of a political program. We offered some suggestions about an official language, out of which nothing came. We were not bothered that we did not discuss it. Many copies of the program were printed in the house although Mohamed and I were out of town and did not help.

Throughout this period, young people who were in the eleventh and twelfth grades and the colleges and universities were being mobilized and sent to rural Ethiopia. There was enormous opposition from EPRP and its members, but Meison was behind the *Zemecha*. While EPRP officially was opposed to it and saw it as a scheme to get rid of students from towns, it also made attempts to organize the students that were being dispatched. Teenagers who belonged to the youth wing were given orders to infiltrate the peasant associations that were being formed and foster opposition to the government. Many students in the south were particularly radicalizing the peasantry into taking the implementation of the proclamation of the new land tenure system in their own hands. There were chaotic peasant revolts and looting in parts of Sidamo. Elements in the party saw this as a positive step and encouraged it. Some even thought they might be able to raise a rural army in this way. In Wollayta and Kembata, peasants and *Zemecha* students invaded towns, murdered absentee landlords, and looted many stores. We were high on these independent actions, which were infuriating the Derg. One of these rebellious youth from Sidamo stayed with us for a while to avoid arrest following incitement of peasants.

The Derg, as it turned out, had no opposition to the organization of the peasants except that it wanted to do it so it could exercise control over the organizations. What EPRP was doing was more of a disruptive effort than a systematic attempt at controlling the associations. Many of these students were doing this on their own initiative. For many this was somewhat of an adventure.

Zemecha was a disaster right from its inception. It was hastily organized, never well-planned or thought out. It was a waste of money and human resources, although it may be argued that students were not doing anything anyway by remaining in the cities. For many students, especially girls, it became a turning point in their life. Discipline in the *Zemecha* areas was a serious problem. Students in many areas were just sitting idly and being fed. Accommodation was never well organized and was a drain on the resources of the community. A lot of the students turned to alcohol and sex. Many people, to this day, say that *Zemecha* was a turning point for many Ethiopian girls. They broke with traditions, got rid of the control of their life by parents and engaged in what could not by any means be considered healthy or positive behavior.

I was assigned to go to Bichena, Gojjam. Bichena was not completely "cleaned" from "reactionary" elements and the Derg did not want to send us to this district. When I was in Wonji, I knew of my assignment, but our departure was never posted. While waiting for my assignment, I was very conflicted as to whether to participate in *Zemecha* or not. On the one hand, I thought it would give me some freedom, away from the ever presence of EPRP in my life. I thought if I stayed outside Addis, since nobody knew who I was, I could manage to live my life without being sucked deeper into underground politics. After I returned from my stint as a CELU cadre, while waiting and internally debating this situation, Mezy told me that I could work for *Goh* Magazine. Without much enthusiasm, I decided to accept this job, which paid 150 or 200 birr a month and sounded prestigious on paper. With this decision, I gave up the idea of going on the *Zemecha*, even if they changed my assignment to another district. I became AWOL.

WRITING FOR GOH

Goh came into being right after the February revolution. It was founded by two enterprising women, Sara and Mulu. Sara was in charge of the operation and Mulu was in charge of advertising. None of them had any political interest, although Sarah was always quick to learn and became conversant in the politics of the time. Mulu was more of a traditional lady, who seemed to be preoccupied with her looks and fashion. I assumed that she came from a well-to-do family and saw this as a fledgling business. She wanted to make money and a name for herself. They were, at this time, trying get into television advertising and had even made one or two commercials. Their biggest account was a quasi-government enterprise that was selling cars built in the Soviet Union in Ethiopia.

The marketing strategy behind the magazine was to take readers away from *Tseday*, which was the more established general-news magazine at that time after it came into existence following the February uprising. Another magazine called *Koum Neger* which was edited by Debebe Eshetu, the actor who had a minor role in the movie *Shaft in Africa*, appeared on and off and never regularly. It did not seem to have heavy political content. I remember *Koum Neger* because of the other editor that Debebe Eshetu had hired. Hassen Abegaz was a fashionable and handsome young man who graduated from Woziero Siheen and was a year behind me in class. He was bright, extremely self-confident, and was always impeccably dressed. I did not know he was in EPRP. All I remember was the last time I talked to him he sound contrarian, questioning all the movements at that time. For reasons I have never been able to figure out, he was arrested early on and disappeared in prison. I ran into his brother when I first went back to Dessie after the Derg fell. He told me that no one would ever tell him what happened to his brother. It must have been heartbreaking to wait for so many years, not knowing whether or not your brother was dead or alive and hoping against hope, expecting him to walk into his parents' house one day. It was one of the saddest stories I ever heard.

To go back to the *Goh* story, Mezy, while trying to find work after the withdrawal from the university, found out about a new advertising agency that was also venturing into the publishing business, got an interview, and landed herself a job at *Goh*. Quickly she became its main editor and started writing a series of articles that became extremely popular. One of her first was "Jollyjacksim," a critique of the western culture that was very much evident within the urban youth in Ethiopia. This article was an instant hit and garnered enormous readership. Mezy, who was daring, smart, and shrewd, decided to write about Tilahun Gizaw, a victim of a Haile Selassie's security apparatus and a popular hero among students. That article, which I then thought was brilliantly written, became very famous and established the magazine nationally. Soon, Mezy interviewed Tsegaye Gebre Medhin, the playwright. The interview was unusual in that the style was very confrontational, a style she had adopted from the Italian journalist Oriana Fallaci. This and a series of other leftist articles, spiced with popular but acceptable topics catapulted the magazine into the number one monthly in the country. *Goh* became the magazine of choice for *Zemacha* students, teachers, workers, and the most educated section of the population.

Sometime after Mezy popularized the magazine, Mesfin was hired as a writer and reporter. Mesfin added a sports section, wrote mostly the editorial section and some political pieces that were particularly eye-catching. The sports section debuted with an interview with Solomon, a national soccer star and player for the Ethiopian Airline Club.

Goh had to pass government censorship to be published. While the situation was relatively liberal at this time, no one could write anything that was openly critical of the government. *Goh*, under the editorial guidance of Mezy, was pushing the envelope and testing the limits of the available freedom by writing more and more radical pieces that would have been unthinkable in previous periods. In this, she was helped by the excellent relationships that both Mulu and Sarah enjoyed with bureaucrats at the Ministry of Information, who had to review every edition and make changes before the magazine goes to print and to the public. Whenever they run into an iron wall at the ministry, Mulu would take the article directly to major Fisseha Geda, a Derg member, and plead with him so it would pass. So *Goh* sort of signaled the extent to which press freedom was to be allowed by the Derg at this point.

As the paper became known at least in the major cities outside Addis, I joined the editorial staff, again at the recommendation of Mezy, who seemed to do pretty much what she wanted to as far as staffing and editorial work was concerned. When I first joined the *Goh* staff, the paper was running again into a serious censorship problem. Many of the articles that were sent for censors could not pass. Sarah and Mulu were in a bad mood. The *Goh* office at this time was in a suite at the Addis Abeba municipality building overlooking Churchill Road. The first article that I wrote appeared in one of the skimpiest issues we had ever printed. I wrote the lead article about coffee and the Ethiopian economy. I came up with a catchy subtitle that I thought would attract readers: *And Yalat Enkilf Yelat*, an Amharic proverb that literately translates as "she who owns only one (child) will never be able to sleep." The magazine sold, but because people expected it to be like the previous issues, not because it was that interesting.

Thanks to Mezy, who seemed to have a knack for what would sell and what people would love to read, *Goh* continued to grow. Our strategy was to focus on materials that would attract people but would also not be too irksome to raise the ire of the censors. Talking about Marxism was acceptable as long as we did not say who the correct Marxist was and who was not. We found a way to do that. Following a profile of Tilahn Gizaw, Mezy wanted to write an article about Wallelegne, the leader of the group that died while trying to hijack a plane outside the country. That would not pass. Her article about Leila Khaled sold very well. Then she wrote an interesting but a little critical article about Stalin that people enjoyed. We received criticism for being Trotskyites. Mesfin wrote a portrait of Lenin that was warmly welcomed.

My first feature and lead article was about Angela Davis, the American Communist Party leader. I knew something about her and I thought she might be an interesting person to write about. I went to the Haile Selassie University library and read magazine articles about her life, education, and membership in the Communist party. I gave relatively more space to her trial and her criticism of the American justice system. The article aroused some curiosity and criticism. The criticism focused on her revisionist Marxist ideology, which then meant that she was a supporter of the Soviet Union. Many of the Ethiopian left then leaned toward Beijing than Moscow. Moscow was deviating from Marxism-Leninism, while Mao Tse Tung thought developed to reflect the realities of the Third World, or so we thought.

For the "February Revolution" anniversary issue, I wrote a poem entitled "*Yekatit* (January." It was not as good a piece as some of the poems that we were now beginning to get published in the magazine. I realized I was not good at writing poetry that had political content. We then published a poem by Esatu Tsema (an apparent pen name) entitled "*Tsegaye BiErih Yemut*," which literally translates as "Tsegye, Let Your Pen Die." It created a big stir in our readership. This article was triggered by Mezy's hard-hitting interview with the poet and playwright, the late Tsegaye Gebre Medhin. This was more or less an invective on a prolific and famous writer who in our view happened to be on the wrong side of the politics of the country. The morning the poem appeared, I saw Tsegaye Gebre Medhin sitting in his car outside *Goh's* office. I don't know what he was doing there, but it seemed like he was trying to see the writers of this magazine who were responsible for the diatribe against him. He left after lingering around for a while. But the magazine sold, and judging by the readership and letters we received, the readers loved the poem.

We received many other poems by Esatu Tesema and published them unless the censors refused otherwise. He became extremely valuable for selling our magazine. He wrote nice poems that rhymed well and seemed to have a first-rate command of the Amharic vocabulary, which he used very artfully. One of his poems spoke of the struggle between the proletariat and his enemies, in which he depicted the struggle in a very graphic, almost cannibalistic form. Another poet named Jale Bia (pen name) later commented to me that this particular poem made the proletariat very inhuman. However, whatever Esatu wrote was warmly welcomed by the readership that we even invited him to come to the office and meet Wolde Ab (the other editor) and me. I found him to be very security conscious and avoided meeting him, although I was able to get a glimpse of him that I have never forgotten. Years later, in the early 1980s, I ran into him in Washington, D.C., and introduced myself to him. He told me that he did not know me, but I reminded him of where I saw him. He was strangely secretive and visibly uncomfortable with the content of our discussion. I stopped my prodding.

Wolde Abe and I also interviewed the artist Afework Tekle, one of the most celebrated artists in Africa, famous for his stained-glass paintings at the headquarters of the Organization of African Unity OAU. Afework invited us to his beautiful house, Villa Alfa, modeled on the Gondar Palace. He showed us his awards and pictures that he took with African leaders, including his admirer, the late Sedar Senghor, the Senegalese statesman, writer, and poet. Steeped in deep Ethiopian culture, the artist was the embodiment of *chewanet* (civility) to a fault.

We conducted the interview on tape in his studio surrounded by great works of art. The interview was tough and at times confrontational, although neither Wolde Abe nor I was that abrasive in temperament. We could not have been too abrasive if we had wanted to as we were completely disarmed by the artist's charisma. Again, the purpose was not to feature the great artist's accomplishments but to expose his "bourgeois" mentality. I even asked him if his artwork the "Ethiopian" was not a composite of the "dominant" persona and not necessarily reflective of the cultural heritage of many minorities in Ethiopia. We asked him about what seemed to be his ostentatious lifestyle. He confronted the question head-on and declared without a hint of defensiveness that he preferred not to live like a poor man. When the interview was published, we included a picture of his architecturally unique and famous Villa Alfa with a sensational caption, "I prefer not to live like a poor man." I chose the caption.

In addition to poems, we also printed short stories that became popular. A three-part short story entitled "*Tulu Forsa*" depicted the life and struggle of a fictional laborer. This was written by an individual who had a degree from Addis Abeba University and worked in a management position in one of the plants in the industrial suburb of Akaki. I loved this short story. The language was simple and expressive of a great deal of realism. We had difficulty with the second and third parts of the short story from the censors, who considered its political lines as unacceptable.

I wrote two short stories that never made it through the censors. When we ran into heavy censorship, which seemed to occur randomly and arbitrarily, our tactic was to emphasize literature, poetry, and translation. I translated Maxim Gorky's *Twenty-Six Men and a Girl* for one of the issues. I remember Birhanu saying something good about it, but otherwise my translation was not at all appreciated. I tried to remain true to the English translation and was so literal that reading it became very difficult for the average Amharic speaker. Many did not appreciate Gorky's brilliant depiction of alienation in the workplace in pre-Soviet Russia. In retrospect, this effort flopped, but we never hesitated from translating any short stories that we thought would be popular with the readers.

Aside from this, I wrote a three-part article about the Chinese Revolution. I also wrote an article about the Chinese revolutionary general Chu Teh. This was actually an article abbreviated from a book by Agnes Smidely, an American author. *The Great Road: The Life and Times of Chu Teh* depicted an impressive and colorful military general who was one of the finest in Chinese revolutionary history. I knew people were interested in guerrilla warfare. I also knew that Chu Teh, unlike Lin Biao, had not fallen out of grace in China during the Cultural Revolution. That was good enough reason for me to feature him. I may also have done it because I happened to be reading the book and must have loved it. I was especially fascinated by how a person with barely elementary education could outfox "enemy" generals that were educated in the finest western military academies.

Mezy, by this time, was a part-time employee of the magazine, having left the day-to-day editorial work to the three of us, Wolde Abe, Mesfin, and me. She was very active in a legal organization that was trying to form a national women's organization. The group, whose leadership included women from both Meison and EPRP, was able to hold the first Women's Day in Ethiopia. These activities were said to have exposed her to government security, and so she was making an effort to stay not too visible. However, she contributed articles regularly, had editorial say, and was paid for her services. In her place was hired Wolde Ab Haile, a decent guy of Eritrean origin who grew up in Addis. He came through Mezy, so it was obvious he was a member of EPRP too. By this time, the party had very much control of the magazine through the four of us. Neither Sara nor Mulu was ever bothered by what was now becoming an obvious association of the paper with EPRP, or if they did, they did not raise any objection.

I think Sarah knew fully what was going on and supported it. *Goh* could not have been such a useful instrument of EPRP without her willingness to make it happen. Sarah even allowed the *Goh* vehicle to be used for underground activities. And for this she paid dearly as she was rounded up in her office and put in prison for nearly a decade.

Mesfin, Mezy, and Sarah covered the 1976 May demonstration. They were taking pictures of the parade when the police arrested them all and took them to the Central Security Prison (*Makelawi*). It so happened at that time, Lieutenant Omar Mohammed, a police officer in Gondar, was in Addis for political orientation given by the government. Omar knew many of the police officers who graduated from Abadina Police College and pleaded on their behalf to get them released. I think their arrest would have been detrimental had he not happened to be there at that time and used his influence to get them released before the investigation went further. They probably had *Democracia* in the trunk of the car that was going to be distributed to the parade participants. This could not have happened without Sara's awareness. Luckily for all of them, they were all released.

THE ARREST OF AYA

I was beginning to enjoy my life as a journalist and the very much undeserved notoriety *Goh* had earned, when the first major crisis of our group exploded in our face. Aya, like me, a reluctant cell member, was caught with some other members while duplicating *Democracia* in a different neighborhood. Probably for safety reasons and because our house was thought to be so valuable for meetings, it was no longer being used for producing *Democracia*. Aya was assigned this dangerous work, which required regularly going to different places and helping with the duplication of *Democracia* by Mesfin. Mesfin may have done this a couple of times before he transferred it to Aya. Aya reluctantly obeyed. He and Bezabeh were the only two members who were not employed and had to help with underground activities. Bezabeh was famously reckless and had somehow made a name for himself for taking dangerous actions in demonstrations. EPRP at this time had not started the urban armed struggle in which I suspect Bezabeh took part later on. He was finally caught and died in prison, but I don't remember how and when. Aya, on the other hand, never gave anyone any impression of being serious about the revolution. He lived with his mother, who used to own some houses that rented and made enough money to live by before the nationalization of urban dwelling places. He was not a rich kid by any means even by Ethiopian standards, but had some money that he reluctantly shared with us. He was often chided for not being generous enough with his money and spending it sometimes only on himself. In a sense, he was the odd man out. He was not very much liked either. Aya was a high school dropout and his understanding of the ideology was neither good nor inspired.

I had long observed that Aya was not happy with what he was doing. Every time he had to go, I could see his subdued emotion and the tension on his face. I saw a plea for help with Mesfin to relieve him of this responsibility. I never saw him refuse, probably for fear of being labeled a coward, but his disposition said as much. Time and again I had observed the terror in his face, but never did anything about it.

Mohamed, Kassaye, and Abraham, on the other hand, were all working in the Chilalo Agricultural Development Unit (CADU). They had a respectable job and were making good money, out of which they paid their contribution for EPRP. They got their job through Tekalegne, nicknamed Shimagelew, a member of the so-called Crocodile Group and presumably one of the founders of EPRP. Tekalegne had a management position in CADU. CADU for a long time was thought to be EPRP's stronghold. The three were trying to organize peasants through CADU's extension programs while working to influence the technical employees to take favorable positions toward EPRP.

Not that it would have made any difference, some of the individuals who were working in this production center were probably armed, but there was no fighting and all the members were captured. We had some sense of what may follow. Under torture, Aya was going to spill his guts out and tell who is who in our group. We feared that Aya would tell his captors who his friends are and where they lived. Apparently Aya did all of that. According to the security people that were doing the interrogation, he gave the name of the three in CADU and Mesfin and mysteriously left me and Bezabeh out. I suspected because I was always nice to him and did not have a say in his assignment, although I did not protest against it. Mesfin was rounded up while in his office, but the others escaped before the police arrived. We abandoned the house in haste. We left a number of things and later another person that I don't remember and I were ordered to go and get out whatever could be salvaged from the house. We did as ordered and we made sure that nothing suspicious stayed around. I don't remember if the house was ever searched by the security people. If it did not, it was because probably Aya did not tell them where he lived. I suspect he did that not to create trouble for me and Bezabeh who lived with us and toward whom he did not have any bitterness. I really never found out what happened to the house anyway. It was too risky for anybody to stay in the house although that particular *kebele* was not considered anti-EPRP at that time. There were *kebeles* like this that looked the other way when they saw suspicious activities in the neighborhood. There were also many *kebeles* whose leadership was loosely associated with EPRP. This situation changed drastically in favor of the organizations allied with the Derg. For some reasons, of all the places that I lived I have fond memories of this house and the house by Yared Music School. Even now, I remember it vividly. We took pictures of us and of Birhanu in the compound. I remember the image of Birhanu wearing a London Fog type overcoat and smarting a Bolshevik look. He was temperamentally suited to this kind of life. For the most part, once we left this house our living arrangement was never that stable.

This episode was very educational to me. I saw clearly the unfairness of the situation for Aya. It may be said that Aya was a member of the party and as such had to serve the party where he was needed. But Aya never became a member of his own volition. He was in a sense like me, railroaded into becoming a member by the group he belonged to and identified with. I wonder if he was told what membership in the party entailed or if he was individually asked whether or not he wanted to become a member of the party if he would have said "yes." When we joined the party, there was no way of knowing what was coming up, although people like me have no reason to blame the party but their own weakness. I had no illusion about what could happen to us, but was slowly being dragged, partly because it seemed a heroic thing to do, and mainly because, in my case, I was too weak to resist and too naive to believe in the goodness of our cause for our country. Aya, on the other hand, had now become dependent on the group and on the subsidy of the party for his sustenance after his mother's houses were expropriated by the government. It was a more difficult situation for him. He was chided for being a coward in a group whose members, except for me and Abraham, seemed calmly resigned to their fate. It is hard for me to judge character and I refused to openly do that. After he was caught, he was despised, was called a traitor, and had nobody to visit him or take food for him, except probably his mother. Aya perished in prison.

It was a relief for me when I heard Aya had not told the security people about me and where I work. The news came through Wolde Ab, but he advised me not to come to work just in case. I was very depressed about the situation and about the fact that I had now been stripped of all legal cover, not to mention the salary that I was receiving. In retrospect, I should have been happy that I was not caught and was still free, but I could not reconcile myself to the fact that I would not be able to have any money. This salary was not enough for living in Addis given our lifestyle. We ate outside all the time and visited the bars almost daily as long as there was some money left. In fact, we took advances from our salary and always spent it before we received our pay; the salary was usually consumed in the first week of the month.

Mesfin was quickly transferred to the main prison from the much feared security place called the Third Prison (Central Security Prison). Here, prisoners were often tortured and many lost their lives. After he was transferred, Sarah and Mulu visited him, took food to him regularly, and did everything they could to help him. I also went to visit him once and he advised me to be careful. He told me that my name did not come up in the investigation, which confirmed to me that they may not be looking for me after all. However, I was too anxious to go back despite my fear that I could meet the fate of Mesfin. I started working from home and receiving money for a while. Later, I eased myself back to the office despite the daily terror of getting captured.

Goh's office was on the fourth floor of what was called the Artistic Building, on the road from Piassa to Arat Kilo. From the fourth floor of the building, we could go up to the rooftop and see what was going on around the building and on the street below. We had an excellent view of the surrounding area on all four corners and tried to watch for suspicious activities and monitor the situation most of the time.

After this fiasco, the party rented us a beautiful secluded villa near Bole. The only problem was most people who lived here were families, professionals, and diplomats, and we did not fit that mold. We were young, did not have cars except for a few that come at night, and we were living in groups. The *kebeles* were not strong yet at this point. We tried to stay inside during the day and get out in the evening, which usually meant going out to drink. This activity served to ease the tension that all of us to some degree really felt and experienced.

Covering the 10th African Soccer Cup

One of the most memorable things that happened to me at this time was covering the tenth African Soccer Cup with Wolde Ab. Through *Goh*, I received a pass that gave me a premium seat at the section of the stadium assigned for press and other dignitaries. I sat in this section to cover the games. Every now and then I sat with other journalists, but generally avoided the section in case the security people were trying to capture me. I was extremely security conscious, although in retrospect what I was doing was definitely foolish. In spite of the tension and the occasional suspicious looks of individuals, I enjoyed the games and did what I consider my best work as a journalist for *Goh*. This was nothing that I took from books. Unlike the political writings, I did not worry about making ideological mistakes. Writing political materials, we all wanted to make sure that no ideological blasphemy was committed. To avoid committing ideological blunders, Marxist political writers are extra cautious. Their writing is done in the context of their understanding of the icons, which made the writing dull, devoid of creativity and independent thinking. We felt we had to stay true to the ideology, and that always meant what I wrote was pedantic, dry, and as close to the books as I could understand and reference it.

But writing the Africa soccer tournament report was different. I love soccer and was confident that I knew the game as well as anybody. With my newly won confidence as a journalist, I now decided to call the game independently as I saw it. Actually I made it a point to give the game a different kind of coverage than the readers of the government papers were used to. I came hard on the national team, which was outclassed by most of the teams and barely won a fourth place. Since the players also behaved so abominably especially when they played Guinea and Egypt, I was very much pissed off. Morocco and Egypt were brilliant. I did not like the style of the Guinea team. It was tough, physically quick, and it outran and outperformed our players. I praised it. Ethiopia had won the championships when the sixth tournament was held in its territory and it was widely anticipated to win the tenth tournament. This situation made for a lot of drama and frustration in and outside the game. The weak Ethiopian team felt like it was entitled to the championship and could not stand it when the other team played better. Using its home-court advantage and a wildly cheering crowd, it played rough and dirty. In one of these tough games, a brawl erupted and one of the Ethiopian players had to run for his life, much to the dismay of some chauvinist fans. I wrote all of these and my impression of the tournament. I loved what I wrote and got a couple of good comments. Although the article came out with enormous amounts of typographical errors for which my bad handwriting was to blame, I was very proud of what I did; the reaction did not even matter.

Slowly and very cautiously, I eased back into my job. The situation at this time frequently fluctuated between bad and good. There was a two- or three-month window of freedom when the regime allowed unprecedented freedom of the press and a very vigorous debate raged between Meison and EPRP. Both sides wrote articles using pen names. The government papers printed articles that were boldly antigovernment and people read them. For that period, *Goh* became secondary to the official press, which was printing materials that included terms like *fascism* and *provisional government* and everything that separated EPRP from Meison, Woz League, Malerid, and others.

The strategic differences between Meison, Woz League, and Malerid on the one hand and EPRP on the other were openly discussed. The three organizations had differences within, but they all agreed to support the "revolutionary" actions of the Derg, while trying to maintain their independence. Meison's argument was that no organization had enough popular support at that time to claim any leadership role. So they said that the workers, the poor town dwellers, and the peasants must be reorganized within their new associations. They saw in this the opportunity to take control over the leadership of the mass organizations that were being formed and strengthened. On the other hand, EPRP felt that it had enough support within the labor unions, teachers, and the youth and that it would continue to keep organizing these groups clandestinely while fighting the regime.

EPRP now began to see Derg's and these groups' efforts to organize these associations in the absence of freedom of speech, writing, and association as fascism. Slowly its organs began to say that the regime is a fascist regime and its civilian supporters were *bandas*. The latter term used during the Italian invasion against collaborators was catchy and provocative but very confusing. The others called EPRP anarchist, opposed to the organization of the people. They alternatively called EPRP *Trotskyite, left adventurist,* and any other term found in the Marxist lexicon. Later, EPRP members were castigated as hired assassins.

At this point, EPRP looked like it had the upper hand because its members were more militant, more educated, and dominated all the independent organizations in the labor union, teachers union, and more noticeably in the youth organizations. It was even successful in having its sympathizers or members selected in many of the *kebeles* that became a crucial organ of power. The early elections were very democratic, and EPRP succeeded in having a sizeable number of the chairperson positions through the tireless and self-sacrificing efforts of its youth members. Derg and Meison of course knew this, but did not take any action. They were bent on having the structure set up in place than in trying to ensure that only individuals that were anti-EPRP got selected. That, they correctly reasoned, would come later either through coercion, enticement, and/or other means. However, they made sure that the danger of infiltration by "anarchists" was known by the people, and vigorously and cleverly prepared the population for this. This was a precursor of the purge of *kebeles* and reelections that would come as the Derg and its supporters felt that they cannot let any *kebele* fall out of their control. Even more important was the militia wing of these associations, which were now being formed to defend the association. Arming these units came after intense political work to ensure that only reliable elements had the weapons and could use them against EPRP elements when asked.

These spelled disaster for EPRP. Whether EPRP's leadership saw the significance of these or not is dubious to this day. The Land Proclamation Act deprived the party of any economic and political rallying point to organize the peasantry against the Derg. Now these changes in the cities and the political and military structures that were being formed by its enemies were going to deny it any foothold in the big cities, where it had considerable leverage in the beginning. EPRP was facing disaster on both fronts, but it was going to commit its most valuable resources to the struggle in Addis. The struggle in Addis was fierce and vicious. It pitted EPRPs' ill-trained and ill-equipped individual fighters against a determined enemy that would go to any extent to assert its power. EPRP never had a chance.

It was obvious that the rural armed struggle was not going anywhere either given the changed economic and political relationship in the countryside. Although it was not known by us at that time, EPRA was not in any sense active in the Tigray areas, despite strange and unsubstantiated news of heroic battles and exploits that were being rumored in Addis. The party also had half-baked plans to initiate some sort of armed struggle in Sidamo, Kaffa, and later in Harrerghe. None of these were carefully planned and in retrospect seemed unbelievably stupid. The individuals who were sent to these areas were people like Birhanu in Sidamo and another activist who grew up in the Teklehaymanot area in Keffa. These individuals did not know the area they were sent to operate in, nor did they speak the language. Both of these guys were later either captured or killed.

It seemed like EPRP banked on differences within the Derg to help it forestall the coming storm of political persecution. While Mengistu was now emerging as a powerful figure in the inner core of the Derg leadership, there were individuals within who were trying to reorganize the different committees of the Derg and wrestle some power from him. These were called Derg Democrats by EPRP, and if there was to be a provisional government like EPRP wanted, these people were going to represent the Derg in the popular government. EPRP leaders or members probably worked with this group, and for a brief period these individuals seemed on the ascendancy. While there was no official statement I have read, it is obvious the party hoped this division within the Derg would evolve in its favor. When it started its armed struggle in September 1976, it was trying to intensify this division and help the so-called Derg Democrats ascend. If the planned mass strike had also materialized in September, EPRP would have attempted something akin to armed insurrection.

This division within the Derg (September to December 1976) was responsible for the random policy fluctuations that were apparent vis-à-vis the mass media, the political arrests and releases and the confusion that some organs of the government were displaying in those days. This was after the second anniversary of the overthrow of Haile Selassie, and the party's silly declaration that it was ready to fight arms with arms and terror with terror. This was months after the attempt on Mengistu's life, which signaled EPRP's much ballyhooed entry into the armed struggle that fascinated us all naive members and caused the destruction of the Ethiopian youth.

HAILE FIDA VS. YOHANNES

Early in 1976, Birhanu was captured while walking on the road between Piassa and Arat Kilo. It was not known why he was captured, but we suspected that it had to do with his involvement in the teachers union. That was another shocker, but nothing happened. He was not investigated; he was not tortured and was just kept in prison. Before his arrest, Birhanu had written a criticism of the book that Haile Fida, Meison's leader, had written on the subject of dialectical and historical materialism. This was a hastily written book to help with the spread of the ideology and for use as a manual in the cadre school in which Meison members were in control. Under normal circumstances, this would have been a philosophical book by someone who at best was considered a revolutionary and at worst a revisionist. But Marxists know the feud between Plekhanov and Lenin, and any ideological differences, especially by individuals who are standing on real or perceived opposite sides of the political issues, must be fought to the finish. It was in this spirit that Birhanu wrote the article at the insistence of Mesfin. The purpose was to show that Haile Fida was not a true Marxist.

Birhanu wrote the article under the pen name *Addefresse*, which literally means someone who stirs and muddies the water. Haile Fida responded to the criticism but did not make any mileage out of the name, although he alluded to it in his rebuttal. The first article by Birhanu was not that remarkable but the controversy that it ignited became a focal point of debates between individuals who supported EPRP and Meison. Letters received by *Goh* were disproportionately pro-Addefresse, although we were accused of clear bias against the author. We published the letters in proportion to what we received. Additionally—this was probably where our bias showed—we printed poems that came against Haile Fida, giving suspicion of our tilt toward Adefresse.

Since Birhanu was arrested and could not respond to Haile's rebuttal, Yohannese, who I suspected was *Democracia's* main editor, responded. I have known Yohannes since my trip to Harar to collect my last paycheck as a teacher, and I had also seen him in Birhanu's house many times. Yohannes was a first-rate writer with unmatched ability to translate foreign terms and ideas into Amharic concepts. To do that, he did not resort to *geez* terms or all these peculiar combination of terms that most of us employed. In an article entitled *"Kedetu Wode Matu-Ye Haile Fida Tengertawe Zektet,"* which translates as "From the Fire to the Frying Pan: the Amazing Fall of Haile Fida," he laid bare Haile Fida's contradictions. He made him look silly, with a clumsy grasp of Marxism-Leninism. By contrast, Yohannes looked like a Marxist-Leninist with depth and unbelievable sophistication. On top of that, Yohannese wrote Amharic prose with such grace and beauty compared to the pedantic and dry sentences of Haile Fida, that fight seemed hardly a contest of equals.

I concluded rather hastily that Haile Fida was finished as a Marxist ideologue. Of course, later I began to see the leaders of Meison were much more politically sophisticated than the leaders of EPRP, who I still believe knew the books better. Haile Fida never responded, and given the overwhelmingly favorable response to Addefresse that we received, the latter had convincingly won the contest. Translated into the political terms of that time, EPRP was a better Marxist and hence a more credible revolutionary organization. Little did we know that victories were not won by how much and how well one knew Marxism-Leninism or any other books for that matter, but by organizations that have the correct strategy given the prevailing alignment of forces. EPRP, as I will show later, failed to grasp this reality and fought a war that it was ill-equipped to win. It never even made a sensible retreat when it was clear what kind of political and military forces were arrayed against its minuscule power. Instead, in one of the most memorable issues of *Democracia,* it declared that it could wipe out its enemies without leaving anyone to tell their story to posterity. Little did these amazing individuals with so much intelligence and sophistication realize that what they so boldly broadcasted in *Democracia* was their own epitaph and not that of their enemies. This statement by *Democracia* captures the mentality in the party that may have been responsible for the destruction of the organization. It defines the organization. That is why I chose *"Wore Negari,"* the term used by *Democracia,* for the title of this book.

While the security danger that I faced because of Aya's arrest never left me, I continued to work at *Goh.* When the general political atmosphere improved due to the tensions within the Derg, I began to go to my office and even spend the day there. Soon, I was used to the idea that the danger for me was over, and it was, if only for the time being.

COVERING THE
OAU EXTRAORDINARY
SUMMIT ON ANGOLA

Early in 1976, there was the OAU extraordinary session on Angolan independence. Wolde Ab and I were assigned to cover the session for *Goh*. This was a good experience for me. The only problem was that I lacked the proper attire to minimally look like a journalist or a professional of some sort. I felt a little bit awkward and out of place with my cheap shirt and old pants. Wolde Ab, on the other hand, wore better clothes and looked like he fitted in the crowd.

The OAU chairman at this time was Idi Amin of Uganda. Many journalists from all over the world were in Addis and were having a field day covering Idi Amin and the emergency session. In the opening session, I sat near Andrew Jaffe of *Newsweek*, who sat with another Western journalist, poking jokes at almost every African ruler. Andrew said these jokes were made often even by other African journalists like Peter Enahoru of *Africa Magazine*. When the then Kamuzu Banda entered, Mr. Jaffe said, "Look at the medals on his chest." The other journalist commented, "Banda is vulgarly fond of decorations," which was something that I had read before. However, I was pissed off at their remarks and saw it as racist. When the ruler of Mozambique, Samora Machel, entered the hall, I said, "Here comes a hero," itching for a fight and to preempt their remarks. They said something nasty about him too and I felt angry. Andrew told me that he was in the capital of Mozambique the week before and had found the city a big mess. I was not in the mood to listen to all of that but only wanted to register my displeasure with what they were saying. Andrew told me his favorite leader was Idi Amin because he made news and people loved to read about him. He was able to interview him in the swimming pool of the Hilton Hotel that morning. He said it was very common for journalists to poke fun at leaders as they did that all the time in America too. I was not appeased and kept haranguing him for what seemed to me contemptuous and racist remarks. He ignored me.

That night, Wolde Ab and I received EPRP's official statement on the Angolan Crisis to distribute among the journalists. I accepted the assignment, calculating that there would be little risk in doing it. The only problem was taking in the paper through the checkpoint. We stuffed the one-or two-page statement under our shirts in the back, and carried some along with newspapers. We managed to take this information at the last day of the conference. Wolde Ab did his part, although I am not sure who he gave it to. The first journalist I gave the statement to was Peter Enahoru. I pulled Peter out of the hallway and told him that I had something that might be of interest to him. He suspected what I was up to and said, "Let us go to the bookstore and we could talk there while browsing." I said, "I have a statement on EPRP's position on the Angolan crisis." Peter misunderstood what I said and thought that I had some leaflets from Ethiopian students. In any case, I gave him a few copies. I felt braver now and wanted to give some more. I could not give Andrew Jaffe because he avoided me. I pinned a tall, slender, and nervous black American journalist in one of the hallways and asked if she would mind taking some paper from me. She was very uneasy and said that she writes for a small local newspaper and has no use for materials of that kind. I gave copies to a journalist from Somalia, which was a risky thing to do.

At the OAU extraordinary session, there was a police lieutenant, a graduate of Abadina Police College from the same cadet class as Omar, that I knew from high school. He was in civilian clothes, and Wolde Ab and I knew he was one of security people assigned to the occasion. He was half-Arab from Dessie. Although I knew him and had spoken to him before, I did not say hello at the OAU summit. In fact, both Wolde Ab and I made every effort to avoid him. Since I knew him a little, I was once asked by Yohannes about him and told him Mohammed seemed to be very sexist but I did not know much about him. As it turned out, Lieutenant Mohammed was a member of the party. Apparently, both Mohammed and another intrepid fellow named Ahimed Abetew, who also worked for the Ethiopian security system and was a friend of Mohammed, were both being handled by EPRP. I just happened to know Ahimed Abetew because he lived near my cousin in Merkato. These EPRP moles functioning deep within the government security apparatus and providing crucial information were finally exposed and lost their lives early on. Both apparently resisted much torture and died without doing much damage to their handlers.

Outside OAU, at the end of the sessions I saw two journalists taking a taxi to the airport. I dropped EPRP's statement inside the taxi. I felt high at what I had accomplished that day.

One of the highlights of this session was a press conference where the Movement for the Liberation of Angola (MPLA) showed the international media white South African troops captured in the battlefield. African nations were divided on Angola, but most favored MPLA despite intense pressure from the United States. This conflict took place within the broad Cold War and was considered part of the proxy wars fought between the US and the Soviet Union. MPLA paraded young and scared-looking troops in front of the foreign journalists. I remember a journalist who was from one of the African countries asking these soldiers, "How many of my African brothers have you killed?" Many of the European journalists jeered the questioner and retorted, "Unfair! Unfair!" Others asked where they were captured and if they were captured by Cubans or MPLA troops. The other Angolan group, UNITA, which claimed to have captured Cuban troops, was refused entry into the OAU sessions and did not have a place to hold the conference. The West and a few African countries supported UNITA, but the majority of African countries and the Eastern Block were clearly in favor of MPLA. Most of the African countries supported MPLA because of South African intervention against MPLA. The whole session was one of the most divisive in the continent, which threatened the very existence of the OAU. The Soviet Union, at this time, came out, as was the case in those days, on the winning side. The Soviet Union was in its most aggressive posture in the continent, while America was seen to be retreating in the face of nationalist movements that tended to be left leaning. Both America and China supported UNITA, which was routed by the MPLA and supported by Cuban troops.

The Soviet press was in Addis en force. They distributed communiqués, entertained the foreign press, and hosted the MPLA delegates. The Addis Abeba representative of Novosty Press, whom I knew through Sarah and Mulu and had drunk vodka with before, smelled of alcohol at the press conference where South African troops were being displayed. Later, while taking a taxi with a Chinese journalist whom I was eager to know and talk with, I said, "Did you see the Soviet journalist? He was smashed." The Chinese behaved like he did not understand what I was talking about and I kept quiet.

EPRP's position, which I thought was good, was hastily conceived and poorly written even by its own standard. Apparently it received a lot of flak among the Ethiopian students in the USA who were generally supportive of EPRP's political position. The statement declared, "Angola is the acid test," which did not make sense since most of the African countries, including the Ethiopian government, supported MPLA's position anyway.

Weeks later, I was eating *khat* with some friends who were not party members when I heard one of them say that EPRP was able to put leaflets under the mattress of every OAU leader in Hilton Hotel. I knew I was the only one who distributed the paper, but I could not rule out others may have been involved. Of course, there was no reason to put that much effort for EPRP to distribute its position to African leaders. In any case, this was typical of the false stories and myths that people were building about the party. It is amazing how these stories were believed even by people like me when a little bit of critical thinking and fact checking could have uncovered the fabrication behind many of these stories. Had the party been stronger, it would have been in a position to control such self-destructive narrative that could not have done anything but damage the party's reputation. These stories reached an epic proportion once EPRP started the armed struggle in Addis and other cities.

Nothing came out of EPRP's statements we distributed at the OAU meeting except the mention of the name of the party in a short sentence in Peter Enahouru's article about the session—a letdown for my uncharacteristically bold effort. Peter mentioned EPRP was as one of the civilian organizations opposed to the new government. It was one sentence inserted in passing and as an afterthought. It was very obvious that one of the most veteran journalists of Africa did not take EPRP seriously enough to say anything more than a sentence in a one-page article. The truth was probably that one sentence was not even deserved. That was a lesson to be learned, but my eyes were not yet open.

PART II

Swept Away by the Whirlwind

Sinking Deep in the Quagmire

As I briefly mentioned above, I was still working for *Goh* when Birhanu Ejigu was arrested while walking to his apartment. At this time, Birhanu and Mezy lived in a high-rise apartment near what used to be called Ras Makonnen Bridge behind the Ethiopian Press Club. Nobody knew why he was arrested but it was believed to be connected to his activities in the Addis Abeba branch of the National Association of Ethiopian Teachers Union. The Addis Abeba Branch was the most radical and militant group that spearheaded the efforts of the National organization's participation in Ethiopian politics.

Just before he was arrested, Birhanu asked me if I would like to be a member of the editorial board of *Lab Ader* (the Proletariat), known among party members as the labor organ of EPRP. *Lab Ader* was no *Democracia*, which was the party's organ and was generally well written and extremely influential. On the other hand, *Lab Ader's* editions were less regular and had narrower focus. It was, however, the second most important paper of the party.

There was an interesting history behind the two publications. The two organizations that formed EPRP were separately organized around two publications: *Democracia* and *Abeyot*. The *Abeyot* group, founded by Getachew Maru, was rumored to be the smaller and the more militant part of the two organizations. When the two organizations merged, they agreed that *Democracia* would be the main organ of the party and *Lab Ader* (instead of *Abeyot*) would be the organ of labor. At this time, many of the union organizations had small underground papers that dealt with specific local union issues. *Lab Ader* was intended to be a national paper that would address labor's political and economic struggle from its own angle. I doubt the paper circulated outside some labor unions and party members.

When Birhanu informed me of this, I was obviously flattered. For once I might have even fantasized about greatness, for which I must have had some hidden yearning. Mezy also mentioned to me that my selection was approved by the central committee, which added to the air of importance that I assumed. I was surprised that the central committee met and approved what might have looked like an important assignment, and that I was a candidate for this position. I certainly have neither lobbied for nor sought the position. I did not even believe I was qualified for it. Soon after I realized that Wolde Ab, who was working with me for *Goh*, was also one of the editors. Wolde Ab probably was one of the founders or original members of the *Abeyot* group. Wolde Ab, I, and a third person who held a management position in one of the nationalized factories made up the editorial committee. To help us with news from factories and unions and to give the article a workers' perspective, a former union leader in one of the transportation companies who had lost his job following one of the unsuccessful strikes called by CELU was included. He was a militant worker and a leader at one point in the Ethiopian Transportation Workers Union. He lived underground following one of the abortive EPRP-instigated strikes that helped the regime systematically root out EPRP sympathizers from labor unions. All three of us respected him. He was smart, highly disciplined, and very militant. Because of our own ideological predilection then, we used to say that we wished the party had more people like him than petty bourgeois intellectuals like us. But we were the "vanguard" elements with the "historical responsibility" of bringing Marxism-Leninism to the working class and providing leadership by sacrificing our class interest. That was what the theory says and that is what members of EPRP, the so-called most advanced elements of society, stood for: to provide leadership for the proletariat, which was the only class capable of leading society, or so we believed. Now, after the disaster of the Ethiopian left and the collapse of the Soviet Union, one is amazed at how reasonably intelligent people would believe such nonsense and risk their life for it. But believe it we did.

How I was selected from the many others in the party, I never knew, nor did I care to ask. It certainly had something to do with my friendship with Birhanu and Mezy. My friends may have thought that I would be more useful to the party in this area. It also might have come right after my encounter with journalists at the OAU meeting in which I distributed the EPRP position. By that action I had demonstrated some potential as a reliable party person who could be counted on to perform assigned tasks. My work with *Goh* may have been the most important factor. Later, I came to realize how these seemingly important positions with big titles, while they never meant what they promised, really made people believe in their self-importance. Individuals were called *squad leaders* or *zone leaders*, which came with some power and an exaggerated sense of one's own worth. These titles were effective tools for what they were intended to do. I began to believe later that this must have been one of the techniques employed by EPRP in using young people for difficult underground work. What made these titles phony but otherwise useful recruitment tools was that people were made to feel like generals although they knew they did not have the army to command. This may sound like an unfair characterization by a disgruntled former party member. Many members were hardened revolutionaries who were in it for the ideals of the revolution than for what good may come out of it for them personally.

With this new responsibility, I was now in the agitprop section of the party. Organizationally my position would be a senior position, although I never sensed it that way. I also reasoned to myself that if I had to fulfill my responsibilities as a party member, it was better that I did it in this area. I figured this should be the least risky position for underground work. I was very clear about not wanting to work in the organizing side, for which I thought I was not fit. My discipline was never good, I admitted. I never felt comfortable with doing things secretly. When I lived in the different houses and was told to stay in a room so others would not have to see or know me and vice versa for security reasons, I intentionally disobeyed. I met many of these people and befriended them. I never used the term *comrade* to refer to party members even at the editorial board of *Lab Ader*. For anyone with any sense of party discipline, it was clear I did not hack it. But nobody mentioned that to me, and worst of all, I kept on masquerading as if I belonged. When I finally came to my senses, it was finally too late.

I told many friends what I did when I was a member of EPRP, but I never mentioned that I was a member of the editorial committee of the *Lab Ader*. One reason was that I was very angry with the party and was ashamed of my membership in it. I was never proud of what I did for the paper even from a professional development point of view. By comparison, I think I learned from my work as a writer for *Goh*. What I wrote was dry, hyperbolic, and plagiarized, but still had some merit as far as my self-development was concerned. On the other hand, I knew nothing about the life of the Ethiopian proletariat, whether as an individual or a union member. What I knew consisted of what I learned, which was very little, when I worked in Metahara and Wonji as a political instructor. That group was one of the best organized and powerful unions in the country with very large membership. It was led by individuals who had technical skills and had gone on to specialized training. These leaders were as petty bourgeoisie (or middle class, as we say now) as the leaders of the teachers unions or the leaders of the employees of the Ethiopian Airlines were. Because they worked in a factory, we assumed that they were revolutionary and capable of leading the Ethiopian revolution. One can't be more dogmatic than this. It was the theory superimposed on reality—a mindless application of revolutionary theory if there ever was one.

My lack of understanding of the condition of the working class began to show in my writing for the *Lab Ader*. What I wrote mostly was the usual soliloquy of the proletariat that Lenin, Marx, and others have written. To this I added how EPRP, the Leninist party of the proletariat, was leading the struggle to establish its dictatorship. One can write one or two issues about this, but after a while it becomes redundant. It became tiresome to me and it took hours and hours of frustrating exertion to finish two to three paragraphs.

I wrote a very laudatory article of the May Day Demonstration in a special issue. The 1976 May Day was the last May celebration that EPRP looked like it still had some roots in the different labor unions. In spite of the very careful efforts of the government to control the slogans and the placards of these rallies, EPRP's slogans were carried by the youth and many members of labor right in front of Mengistu, who was reviewing the parade. The government and the other organizations had their placards and slogans carried too. But EPRP convinced itself of how strong an organization it had become in a matter of a few years.

It was easier to write about this issue than anything else at this time. There was sufficient material for a special issue. There was a great deal of defiance displayed on the streets by workers and students. This was particularly true of the more educated working-class units like members of the Ethiopian Airlines Union, Addis Goma, and others. However, it was also clear that the regime had made headway in its efforts to get into the labor organizations. I ignored that. I convinced myself that that was the right thing to do in a propaganda piece. I wrote of the heroism and the sacrifice of the different organizations of Ethiopian workers under the leadership of EPRP. I added some news from other cities to illustrate the national significance of EPRP. It was mostly about sacrifices made in Wonji, Akaki, and other labor areas. I was never pleased with it, and I do not know if anyone was.

Wolde Ab was more comfortable with his work, and he wrote many of the issues. Wolde Ab was an easy-going person who did not agonize over what has to be written. I never knew how many copies were printed. I was not also sure if it reached any number of workers other than the ones who were party members.

ADDIS ABEBA SPRING

In the spring of 1976, there was a sudden burst of freedom in the government-controlled media, especially *Addis Zemen*. For a brief, very memorable period, the population enjoyed a debate among the different political positions in the country to a degree hitherto unknown. Although a disproportionate amount of the space was given to the groups on the Derg's side, EPRP's position was openly written and discussed. The papers sold like hotcakes. People carried *Addis Zemen* and read it in cafés, while getting their shoes shined, and in their homes. Some days it was hard to get *Addis Zemen* as it was sold out early. Everyone who was literate proudly carried *Addis Zemen*. People looked happy and relaxed. It was one of the most memorable and liberal periods in Addis, to which I sometimes refer as the "Addis Abeba Spring."

EPRP members wrote under pen names, as did Meison members and others. This was the only time I remember that the pros and cons of the provisional popular government—the most significant issue that separated EPRP from Meison—was openly and intellectually discussed in front of the nation without censorship.

During this period, while Birhanu was still in prison, I was called for a meeting with Yohannes. He told me that an ad hoc committee that included me had been formed to legally respond to the newspaper articles that affected EPRP. Other party members had been doing that very diligently as far as I could tell. Although she did not tell me, Mezy was also an active participant under the pen name Martha Wallelgn. I suspect Yohannes wrote some of the most important pieces at that time. However, the feeling was that these responses have to be organized and coordinated. There were three of us in the committee. One of them, I came to recognize from his handwriting and style, was the author of "Tulu Forsa," a series of short stories that appeared in *Goh*. Yohannese told us what the "directive of the politburo" was: the three of us were to function as an ad hoc committee and respond to all the newspaper articles concerning EPRP.

This was another big surprise to me. On the one hand, my perception of EPRP was that of a strong organization with considerable political clout that could command the resources of a wide array of intellectuals. This meant that I was now definitely becoming a very important person in the party structure. I felt I was getting close to the leadership. On the other hand, this reinforced my doubt as to whether the party was as strong as we all believed it was. If these were the individuals who were in leadership positions and I could see who they are, the party may not be as mysteriously strong as I thought it was. By now I have heard the central committee and the politburo mentioned in connection with my assignment; it gave me a sense of importance, mixed with doubts about how strong the party actually was. Our committee functioned briefly. We might have sent one or two pieces, none of which was written by me. None of our submissions was published. Just like it started, this period of intense and open political debate among the political protagonists abruptly ended, much to the frustration of everyone concerned. I don't remember how long it lasted. It was about three to four months. Rumor had it that Senai Leke was the person who ordered the end of this exercise. He was reported to have said that it did not make any political sense to have this freedom available to *anarchists*, as members of EPRP were called. *Addis Zemen* declared that "EPRP was completely defeated ideologically." It was not true. However, it was conceivable then that the weakness in EPRP's position would have been more apparent had they let this debate go on for some time. I personally was beginning to understand the rationale behind Meison's position on the provisional government. I appreciated the political pragmatism in it, although I probably still felt that their position drove from their opportunistic political stand. It was later on that I really felt Meison's position was not only principled but also realistic, and that it should have been better appreciated by us. But given time and more interaction, I could even have been persuaded. But the purpose behind the whole exercise was not to win over EPRP in an open political debate, but to expose, and by using the repressive power of the regime, to wipe out EPRP. We were heading for a major showdown.

*   *   *

During this period also I helped the party buy a truckload of duplicating papers from a businessman I knew in Merkato. However, after Birhanu was arrested we had difficulty finding individuals who would come with a truck and transport it. It was stored in a warehouse near Tekle Haymanot, and I was under intense pressure to remove it very fast. Yohannes was finally able to send me some individuals with a truck. We loaded the truck and removed the material, but I noticed that removing the material was not as easy as I thought it would be. There were sufficient signs for me to know how weak EPRP was even at this time.

A House in My Name

As unexpectedly as he was arrested, Birhanu was surprisingly released from prison. Apparently there was no serious case against him. The party must have also used its connections, which were good then, to get him out. After his release, he and Mezy left the high-rise apartment near Piassa for security reasons and moved to a bigger house. Finding housing was becoming increasingly difficult following the nationalization of urban dwellings, but this was obtained through a teacher who was also a chairman in the *kebele* where the house was located and was probably a party member. Since I had legal employment with *Goh*, I was told to rent this house in my name. I did so as ordered, although the thought of refusing to do so indeed occurred to me many times. I could not easily get out of this now that most of the people that I started with were engaged in very serious and risky revolutionary activities. I rented the house, but I knew there and then that this was going to create the sort of problem that I could not anticipate and control. Things were getting out of my control. I realized the impending catastrophe but deluded myself into believing that it won't happen. I began to feel that this may be a turning point in my life over which I was slowly losing control. I resented this imposition from Birhanu and began to avoid both Mezy and Birhanu. I started developing parallel relationships with other EPRP members with whom I felt at ease, like Wolde Ab and the poet Jale Beya.

This was a large house with a big front yard surrounded by a fence; it was located in a sparsely populated part of Addis—an ideal place to house underground activities. I soon found out this became one of EPRP's most important nests of revolutionary activity. Many of the most senior leaders of the party—Girmachew, Tesfaye Debessaye, Yohannes, and many others—came to the house regularly. I visited the house a few times.

HEALTH PROBLEMS

The tension of underground life, my ambivalent position toward the party, the illegal activities, and the impending danger that I very well sensed but never spoke about began to take their toll on me. I began to experience problems with my sleep. I also felt a burning sensation on the surface of my head and began to have difficulty focusing. I was experiencing problems with my balance. I could not sleep for many days in a row. I never had such a severe sleeping disorder before. Strangely enough, I did not feel like I had not slept. *Khat* began to affect my memory. I looked very distracted every time I abused *khat*, and this was noticed by my friends. I became anxious about my life, my safety, and my sanity in an environment that was anything but sane.

A friend of mine, who was not a party member but who stayed and slept sometimes in our apartment, suggested that I put a big chunk of raw and untreated butter on my head, tie it, and sleep on it. This is traditional medicine for headache, and my friend convinced me that he himself had found it helpful. I did as I was told. I was supposed to keep it on for more than a day. However, I could not stay in this position for a long time because of the pungent and nauseating smell it creates a few hours later. I went to Fil Wuha, a hotel complex in Addis with a natural hot spring bath, and washed it off the next day. It did not work. At the urging of Sarah, the *Goh* owner, I decided to go to Amanuel Hospital, the hospital for the mentally ill.

I was examined by a Russian doctor. I told the doctor through a translator what my symptoms were. The examination seemed rather routine and simple. The doctor gave me some tablets and told me not to take alcohol until I had used the medicine. I took the medicine but never completely gave up alcohol. My situation slightly improved and Sarah and Mulu advised me to take a vacation. I went to Dessie, stayed with my family, mostly sleeping in a friend's house. I only remember few details of my stay except I never ceased to abuse *khat* and alcohol. My family must have really seen the dramatic change in me. Before I went, I had borrowed about five hundred dollars from *Goh* to give to my family. Instead of giving it to them, I used some of it to buy a Seiko watch, which proved to be useful later, some to entertain myself, and left the remaining amount, which was not much, to my family. Unlike in the past, I refused to look at my family's problems and my siblings' eyes and question myself whether what I was doing made sense or not. I ignored the family reality completely. I must have felt that I have gone too far to do anything about it now anyway. Besides, there was nothing I could do. I could not work, nor could I go back to the university, because it was still closed. I sensed that my life was irrevocably set on a very destructive course and that I was too weak or too stupid to do anything about it.

When I returned to Addis, I brought about thirty pistol bullets purchased by a mutual friend of Birhanu and me. Birhanu had asked the guy to buy them in the black market in Dessie. These were very small bullets and did not seem to weigh that much. I put them in a few Palmolive soap boxes so they looked like bars of soap for the soldiers at the checkpoints. I also put them in a different bag, separate from my clothes, so I could disclaim the bag in case the bullets were discovered. When I returned to Addis, I called Birhanu and told him that I am back in Addis. We talked about our mutual friend, who was a good financial backer of Birhanu throughout high school and at that time. I did not want to tell him over the phone that I had brought the bullets. His reaction was immediate, "You could not possibly have forgotten the bullets now that the party is moving into a higher phase of struggle: armed struggle."

Urban Guerrilla Warfare: EPRP's Unraveling

When the production unit that Aya participated in was captured, Yohannes said to me, "You know, I do not know why we are feeding armed people who are not doing anything in Addis at this time. It is time that we used them." Later, when the debate raged as to whether EPRP should have started the urban armed struggle in Addis, I remembered this statement again and again. I never understood the policy implications of his statement. When the party started assassinating individuals who were thought to be dangerous, I though it simply meant that it was the right terror tactic to use in self-defense.

We had always heard that there were units of EPRA, the so-called urban wing, who could be deployed anytime if the party wanted to use them. It was said that some high-level committee meetings were now being held under armed guards. I believed all of that. I was also told that the First Congress that declared the party was guarded by EPRA units. Berhane Meskel, who had amassed an enormous reputation not matched by his actions as a fighter and leader of the EPRA in Tigray, was said to have attended the meeting flanked by bodyguards. Such anecdotes intentionally, though not maliciously, spread for propaganda purposes, came from people like Mezy and Birhanu, who I suspected, although I had no proof of it, participated in these meetings. To many of us, this was an incredible and fascinating story. These individuals, especially the ones that were carrying arms to fight the regime, assumed a larger-than-life existence in our imaginations.

I have also heard anecdotes of differences within the leadership in the First Congress, but never pursued it. Later, *Democracia* bragged that the congress was held right in front of the nose of the regime, which convinced me that the strength of the party was for real.

When Yohannes asked rhetorically when the party was going to stop just feeding its army and begin to use it, I never analyzed the full implications of his statement. That meant the party was going to go to war—a different and dangerous phase of struggle for any organization—and in the urban areas no less. Surely the party was sailing in uncharted waters. He spoke so casually about such a grave decision, leaving me to wonder if the party had really planned this out as would be expected. Sometimes I wondered if the party was not dragged into it deeper and deeper once it crossed the Rubicon, which I believe was the attempt to assassinate Colonel Mengistu.

I realized very early that such actions follow their own logic, irrespective of what the plan was. When the party decided "to fight terror with terror," it unleashed a series of actions that began to follow their own inner logic. For a while also these actions seemed to work in deterring some *kebele* leaders from taking unprovoked actions against suspected EPRP members. But soon the *kebeles* began to feel that they had no choice but to fight, and they became emboldened. They realized that EPRP was no match for their organization, weapons, and state power. If they were scared at first, they became emboldened when they saw that EPRP fighters were not the seasoned warriors that we made them out to be, but very green fighters who had neither the training nor the motivation to take on a force that was a thousand times stronger. Many of these fighters when caught looked frightened and nervous, just as one would expect of them. Many, to be sure, had guts and stood up in an unfavorable environment. But many were cut short before they made any sense of it all.

Some people say now if only the party had managed to get many of these youth out of Addis in time it would not have suffered such a crushing defeat in Tigray by the TPLF. I am not sure about that either. From the start, the TPLF fighters were recruited from peasants, who it seems to me are more suited to discipline and to guerilla warfare. TPLF was organic to Tirgrai society; EPRA was a transplant struggling to develop roots. It appeared that Asimba was an outpost woefully isolated from the people. When EPRA disbanded, it was not because it lacked a sufficient number of fighters under arms, but because the people it had were not willing to go on fighting for a lost cause. Sahle also said many, including himself, left because they lost faith in the party's leadership. After he escaped to Kenya, Sahle wrote me a letter describing his journey and concluded with an apt Amharic proverb that captures in a nutshell what our experience with EPRP was about.

Chewata ferese dabo tekorese. Game over. Time to break the bread. Or it may be figuratively stated as "let us call it a game and start the party."

Many of these young people saw that if they could leave the area, they might be able not only to save their lives, but also to make a decent living for themselves. They were aware of people who had migrated to the United States and other areas. They knew they could make it, and that is exactly what they did. Of course, the situation in Tigray had become inhospitable, but they could have probably stayed in other areas like Gondar, Northern Wollo, etc. A sizeable portion of the army went to Gondar through Eritrea, although they never made any headway in expanding its hold in Northern Ethiopia.

In preparation for the armed struggle, the party began to "liberate" money from banks and government agencies. It was also beginning to buy and store weapons, especially weapons that were just being distributed to the newly formed *kebele* militia. One night, I stopped by the house; Mezy proudly displayed a weapons catch that looked formidable to me. There were what looked like Uzis, Thompsons, and other semiautomatic weapons all over the floor. Later, I heard Tesfaye Debessai was there in another room, but I did not make an effort to see him. I also remember seeing birr notes all over the floor. There was pride and pleasure in Mezy's eyes. I felt this was an ominous sign, but was very impressed by these people, who seemed ready to lay down their lives for a cause they believed while I was perennially ambivalent about the whole mission.

Mezy always thought highly of Tesfaye Debessai. I often asked her if Tesfaye was as good as Girmachew. Girmachew had been a fixation on my mind as a revolutionary leader of the first order since I heard his speech at the university. Whatever I heard about him later also reinforced my belief. Mezy told me that she had seen the two argue. While no one had the oratorical command of Girmachew, she felt Tesfaye was a born leader. In these debates, Tesfaye would often respond to Girmachew by saying, "Comrade, stripped of the jargon, what you just said amounts to this . . ." and then would show Girmachew's contradiction and the fallacy in his argument. Tesfaye, it was also said, was not only brave, totally selfless, and dedicated, but also extremely disciplined. He did not eat *khat*, did not take alcohol, which if true made him stand above everyone else. The same was also said about Getachew Maru, who was later accused of having formed a faction within the party and was murdered in cold blood in the intra-party fight.

What I heard about Tesfaye and later his death by jumping from a building, gave me a picture of a leader who was calm under fire and very courageous. I was told he often walked from Merkato to the house I rented on foot to save money, which in retrospect seemed meaningless. He was dressed like a Muslim priest (so was Yohannes). During the first *assessa*, I was told that he made sure that people left Addis and personally saw many of them off at the bus station. He himself, for some reason, stayed or was not ready yet to leave, for which mistake he paid with his life. Tesfaye died by jumping from a high-rise than risk being captured.

The only senior leader other than Birhanu that I have come to know and had conversation with was Yohannes. I was often told that Yohannes was brilliant. He double-majored in geography and geology, in which, it was said, his grades were well above anyone in the department. When the revolution broke and before he went underground, he was a high school teacher. He had been a friend of Mezy and Birhanu since the two came to Addis. I was impressed by his sophistication and urbane persona. His nickname was *Arabu*, presumably because of his Arab or Greek features. He spoke fast, was enormously self-confident, and was said to know Marxism better than anyone. He also had a highly developed sense of humor, made jokes practically at anyone, twisted people's statements. He was a womanizer who made no bones about it and spoke openly and uninhibitedly about sex, love, and anything else. He once told me that he was the only one of his elementary school friends who finished high school. So he grew up in the midst of lumpen elements (*dureyes*) but overcame all of that and finished college. He came from a family of educated people. Probably his father had some level of formal education. I was told that he spoke French fluently. Yohannes seemed to me then the most cultured and the most brilliant of the EPRP leaders I knew.

One day, Mezy, I, and Arabu were sitting together and talking about nonpolitical and family matters. Mezy bragged about her daughter and said she had the most beautiful child in the World. Yohannes responded, "I would not make that kind of statement before I saw mine if I were you." He was not married, but was dating, if I remember correctly. Mezy insisted that nobody can be like her daughter, to which he said it all depended on the seed and that she could see by looking at him. I intervened and told him that may be true, but I added, "Remember there is also mutation." He was taken by surprise and said, "You are like Birhanu; you bide your time and attack unexpectedly when you get a chance." That was true of me, but was not a correct observation about Birhanu. I was mostly quiet in front of them out of peasantlike deference to these individuals, who were better-educated, more confident, and smarter. Birhanu, while not of Arabu's caliber, however, had a very devastating wit and used it unsparingly.

I never imagined Arabu as a leader in the sense that I saw Gimachew to be. I never saw the kind of courage that I felt leaders have to display in Arabu. To me, he lacked the iron will, the steely calm that I felt leaders ought to have. He ate *khat* and drank much more frequently than I suspected. He did all his writing while chewing *khat*. He wrote very often and told me that he wrote something almost every week. Although he had never been outside, his English was better than many who spent years in America. More importantly, he wrote in an Amharic style that had tremendous appeal. I thought and think even now that Arabu's prose (I have read very little Amharic since) had no equal in Amharic political literature at that time.

Arabu was also somewhat loose disciplinewise. He was a freethinker (a Marxist freethinker, isn't that an oxymoron?), an intellectual who spoke his mind much more freely than anybody I knew. He was never an orthodox Marxist, and probably would never have been one. I suspected he despised Stalin and looked at Trotsky more charitably. Rumor had it that Tesfaye Debessai and Arabu got along very well and that the former had a great faith in the intellectual prowess of Arabu. That rumor was very surprising to me since Tesfaye's lifestyle and discipline was antithetical to that of Arabu. Arabu's lack of discipline got him arrested once for violating the curfew. He was taken to one of the local police stations. There was a big tension within the party that it was a matter of time before he was identified. Many of the people I knew were reprimanding him for this inexcusable transgression. I don't remember if he was caught with a pistol, which he carried. Many of them did at that time.

The party was tipped off the day he was going to be transferred from the police station. A squad of two EPRA fighters, I was told, was dispatched to rescue him. The unsuspecting guard had no choice but to oblige, and Arabu was freed. This was one of the few instances that EPRA units succeeded in freeing members from capture. The other time was the freeing of a wounded fighter from St. Paulos Hospital. Both of these freed men met their deaths later.

I had sufficient reason to believe that Arabu wrote most of the issues of *Democracia*, especially the earlier and the most famous ones. I knew his style. *Democracia*, in my view, was both the strength and weakness of EPRP. I loved *Democracia* and everyone that read it loved it, if I remember correctly. In retrospect the paper's analysis of the Ethiopian situation was in many ways flawed. Within this limitation, however, it never lacked depth, grace, and humor. When *Democracia* came out, people who read it felt very high. The youth, EPRP's backbone, was lifted by its defiant spirit, its exaggerated image of strength, its uncanny ability to ridicule the Derg, and make its members feel good about EPRP.

Democracia was the paper that fought the Derg and made EPRP seem stronger than it was in actuality. EPRP did not have the organizational strength that its opponents had. Nor did it have any urban army in the true sense of the term, but a few foolhardy individuals who could shoot and kill some *kebele* leaders. But it had *Democracia*, which won the hearts and minds of its readers, especially the Ethiopian youth. The others did not have anything remotely approaching the agitational power of *Democracia*. Some of the issues of the *Voice of the Masses* probably analyzed the Ethiopian situation more correctly than *Democracia* did. Nevertheless, it never gained the appeal, the readability, and the power of *Democracia*. Soon, however, its readers began to dwindle, its issues to be irregular, and its content to lack the analytical rigor it once displayed, and more importantly, it began to reach fewer and fewer readers as the party structure began to crumble by the Derg's systematic and repressive attacks.

After Arabu died, the style was never the same, the quality dwindled. Soon it became a dry publication and it required a great deal of patience to finish reading an issue.

One day in September 1976, after I returned from Dessie, *Goh's* company automobile, a Russian-made Lada that was driven by the company's chauffer, Teodros, who was also related to Mulu, was nowhere in sight. I asked Wolde Ab where Teodros had gone. Wolde Abe said, "Mafia [it is true the term was used by EPRP members] has gone to Sidamo to bring money that was liberated from a government treasury." This was a salary fund that was going to be paid to employees and apparently the payroll person who carried the fund had agreed to run away with the money and give it to EPRP. The indefatigable Birhanu (who seemed to be everywhere at the time), Teodros (a very courageous member that I used to call a declassed blue blood because of his feudal connections), and an unnamed lady had gone to bring the money and the government official. Using *Goh's* vehicle made sense to pass the checkpoints unsuspected.

That evening, Birhanu, the man responsible for the money, and Theodros made it safely to Addis. Wolde Ab told me they had a beautiful party member near the passenger side to deliberately distract the soldiers at the checkpoint near Addis. Looking like professionals returning from a vacation in Langano, they easily made it through the checkpoint with approximately 200,000 birr. When Birhanu made it home, he heard the even better news that the mission to kill Mengistu was successfully carried. "Mission accomplished," called the squad leader after the unit returned to their "bases," according to Mezy. They all drank to a successful operation that was to radically change the alignment of forces in the Derg.

Early in the morning, I, Wolde Ab, and Berhane, his roommate, were awakened by a knock on the door. This was one of the editors of the *Lab Ader* and was going to tell us what happened the night before. None of us had heard the shots or the news of the attempt on Mengistu's life. He said, "Mengistu is dead." We were all ecstatic. He said, "It happened last night. Automatic weapons and hand grenades were used. The squad followed

Mengistu's convoy all the way to the gate of the Fourth Division, where Mengistu slept. People who saw it expressed joy and happiness. Nothing happened to the attackers." I was very elated.

A little while later the official news was on. It said that "anarchists" had made an attempt on Comrade Mengistu's life last night. Mengistu received a slight wound on his rear end, which was not serious. In fact, his voice was heard on the radio that afternoon. The operation apparently was a total failure and the fighters who participated could not have known that he did not die. Apparently, they pursued him up to the gate, although they must have misfired. The euphoria turned into depression. We knew that EPRP should never have tried, and if it did, it should have made sure that it was professionally executed.

I felt it was a terrible mistake too. I never expressed any misgivings about the attempt on Mengistu's life, although later there were ideological differences as to the correctness of it all. I had come to believe that Mengistu was the most important person in the Derg; he had amassed enormous political power, and it was crucial to remove him. Somehow, it did not make sense that they missed, because we thought they were well trained urban fighters.

Later that day, at Wolde Abe's house, we discussed this with his friend named Gebre, who later garnered some reputation as one of the better commanders of EPRA in Tigray. I have heard very little to convince me that EPRA ever functioned as a fighting force before it was routed by TPLF. A friend of mine who was in Assimba had actually confirmed this to me. He said it conforms to what his colleagues who came to Gonder from Assimba told him. In fact, TPLF fighters were ridiculing them as an army that simply feeds on honey and goats but could not fight. At the time, TPLF was engaged in a series of battles with the Ehtiopian Democratic Union (EDU) and at times with government troops. It engaged government forces on a number of occasions.

Gebre used to travel back and forth. He told us that he knew all along that they would never be able to accomplish this. He also said that in a trial mission to kill a hen, this unit was a complete failure. He mocked their skills and experience. I did not know that fighters train with chickens and I was not sure where they did it, but I believed what he told me explained why the operation was bungled.

The attempt on Mengistu's life was in the planning for a long time. It was apparently aborted many times when the intelligence failed to show the direction he was following. Mengistu's security suspected there could be an attempt on his life and so his movements were carefully planned, but of course not as much as they were once this attempt failed. It looked like EPRP was tipped off about Mengistu's travel route and time of travel by someone inside the Derg, but all this invaluable intelligence came to naught when it was executed in an amateurish way.

Democracia had already announced before this attempt that the party would fight fire with fire. The war, which EPRP foolishly entered, was like that of David and Goliath, started in earnest. People who were considered to be on the government's side were killed. The earlier of these victims was Dr. Fikre Merid, a popular law school professor whose crime no one knew about. No one explained why he had to be assassinated. And later I came to realize that was one of the most meaningless murderous acts the party had undertaken. In these killings, the seeds of EPRP's destruction were sown. One day, there was a debate going on in another room where Wolde Ab and Berhane (not Birhanu) also lived. There were other people, including Jale Bia, in the other room and Wolde Ab was trying to manage the traffic so people would not see each other. The debate was about the assassination of Fikre Merid and apparently Jale Bia asked why. I told Wolde Ab that I wondered about that too. I could not see why individuals like Fikre Merid were assassinated. His only crime was his association with a Derg-formed group called the Political Organizing Committee. This organization was filled mostly with Meison members, but EPRP was also given two slots. Eshetu Chole and Yonnas Admassu were included because they were perceived to be EPRP members. The two left the organization. Eshetu Chole, the economist, left the country for Djibouti and unexpectedly returned back. Yonnas, on the other hand, appeared to have been sucked into EPRP and went underground. I know Yonnas was a good friend of Yohannes. Judging from the style of *Democracia* also, I suspected Yonnas had taken over the writing of *Democracia* after Yohannes died, although I have no proof of that.

When the armed struggle started, except probably for the attempt on Mengistu's life and maybe the assassination of Fikre Merid, it did not appear to be centrally controlled at a higher level. It seemed like every zone and subzone had its own fighting units, which were taking actions independently. Additionally, the youth wing, which was better armed and better motivated, was also taking actions at local levels on its own initiative. It was said that some units had fired on one another and members of the party have been killed in a friendly fire. Given the experience level and the trigger happiness that followed, this would not be surprising.

Also, when the party started the armed struggle, it was organizationally very weak. Birhanu, who was all for urban armed struggle, once asked a rhetorical question: "How could a party conduct an armed struggle without a strong organizational base?" I always thought this was the proper question to ask, but the individuals who could have answered that were the leaders like him. The party probably thought that it could organize and fight at the same time, or it just did not appreciate the gravity of its own actions.

Parties associated with Derg, such as Meison, Woz League, and other organizations, began to scream they were defenseless victims. They claimed that their enemies were armed to their teeth but supporters of the government were not. The government-controlled media echoed this propaganda, deliberately exaggerating the threat posed by EPRP to the revolution "led by the Derg with the cooperation of progressive forces." It was obvious that they did not take EPRP's threat lightly even though they were aware that it won't be able to get anywhere militarily. What they painted was a well-organized enemy that was out to destroy them. The military knew better than to underestimate its enemies. EPRP, on the other hand, began to believe its own strength based not on cold realistic calculation of the balance of forces, but on information its enemies were deliberately feeding it. It began to exaggerate its own strength, and slowly even to believe it.

Initially many members within the party believed that the party had some 500 fighters smuggled from Assimba under Berhane Meskel to wage an urban armed struggle. There was no effort to kill such rumors. There might even have been a deliberate effort at spreading such rumors. The problem was that few people knew that Berhane Meskel was losing power, or had lost power in the inner circle of the leadership that was responsible for waging the fight. Berhane Meskel and Getachew Maru had come squarely against use of armed struggle in urban areas.

This illusion of military power was also fed by a few successful military operations. The assassination of the leaders of the newly reorganized All Ethiopian Labor Union, which were now supporting the government, was one of these cases. This action was taken by individuals dressed as military personnel and driving military vehicles. The other was the raid on the bank in Merkato, which was said to have netted the party two million or more birr. Little did we know at that time that bank robbery was one of those relatively simple actions that urban guerilla forces had to be able to undertake at will.

Despite these successes, it was apparent the armed struggle was not going to get anywhere. But no one spoke against it. We never even discussed it. Our initial group was now in prison or in hiding, but I never remember any discussion pertaining to armed struggle. Whatever voice of dissent existed in the party was suppressed and never came out into the open until later. At the same time, EPRP's enemies were arming, mobilizing, and politicizing the so-called mass organizations for what they thought would be a decisive fight against EPRP. Rumor was rife that they would soon start a big search-and-destroy operations (*assessa*), the goal of which was to disarm the population and deprive EPRP of any source of weapons. They were also designed to flush out EPRP members from most neighborhoods and deprive it of any bases of operation. One had to be a complete fool not to see the implication of these searches, but EPRP, it seems, never saw that or knew how to deal with that.

I once asked Birhanu what the party's response would be to these impending *assessas*. He said, "Once we know where they are coming, we will have armed units stationed and waiting. The *kebele* leaders will be ambushed and killed." In theory this sounded good, and the party visualized that it would respond in kind and disrupt the *assessa*. It assumed that the *assessa* will be done piecemeal and at night. It was also assumed that once the participants had been fired on they would panic and disperse; after all, they were "bandas" and "bandas" by definition were cowards.

I don't think the party had an inkling or idea of how massive and systematic these *assessas* would be. They were done in stages, focusing probably on areas of weakness of the party and moving on to EPRP's strongholds and the more difficult places to conduct the operation. It was done at intervals, after intensive spying and information gathering was undertaken. The first phase was to clean the city of weapons. The next stages focused on detaining individuals and probably controlling operational houses. Each of these activities destroyed the already weak party structure. It deprived it of places to duplicate papers, and members, of places to hide. It made ordinary life for party members intolerable, let alone enabled them to conduct party business. It was increasingly difficult to hold any meetings with even the smallest party units. Many had to conduct this while walking in Merkato. I remember a zone committee meeting that I participated in while walking on the road. The four of us discussed party business while walking in groups of two. And then after a while a group of two would split and form another group of two, so all four of us had a chance to meet and discuss. We conducted the serious business of revolution like this.

At the same time, Meison and the others were amassing considerable strength in the newly formed mass organizations. Their members were becoming motivated, well-armed, and feeling invincible. They did not run when EPRP fired. They fought back. While EPRP was clearly a youth organization, its enemies were making inroads among city workers, teachers, poor people, and the unemployed. They were teaching the same Marxist ideology, but they were able to do it openly. So while the ideology, for whatever it is worth, ceased to be studied within EPRP cells because of the repression, the Derg, Meison, and Woz League members were reading it with more motivation and gusto. The organizing strength of the ideology was now skillfully employed by EPRP's enemies. Lenin is said to have remarked that Marxist ideology, when embraced by the working class, becomes a material force. Not EPRP, but its enemies were able to make Lenin's statements come true. They were able to deploy the organizing and oppressing capabilities of the ideology to its fullest potential. Unlike EPRP, its enemies felt most affinity with Stalin. It was the monstrous and repressive terror tactics of Stalin they grew very fond of. They called their tactic "Stalin's Stick," and brutally employed it to break EPRP's backbone.

When I was imprisoned early in 1978, I vividly saw how seriously the ideology had spread within the leaders and cadres of the *kebeles*. Measured by the Marxist material they read, it was clear that these individuals were far more advanced than the average EPRP member. More importantly, they knew the part of Marxism that was more relevant from the perspective of taking over or maintain political power. I don't think they read Karl Marx or Friedrich Engels or any of the philosophical materials that a balanced Marxist curriculum is supposed to contain. They knew what they needed to know. They were confident they knew it. They were convinced that they were better Marxists. And they were eager to put it to practical use. I felt that in the *kebele* prison very deeply. It was one of those realizations that strike you with the force of a tidal wave. You realize that Marxism means nothing if it is not an idea combined with good intentions that inspire individuals to great heights of sacrifice and dedication. Put it to practice, you meet a more monstrous reality than the original humane intention that had made decent and well-meaning people believe in it.

That must be what those Bolsheviks thought when they all, one by one, went to the gallows of the system they created. To say Stalinism is not Leninism is crazy. It is not Leninism gone awry. It is Leninism, pure and simple. I don't know if Leninism is the necessary outcome of Marxism, but Stalinism is the necessary product of Leninism. EPRP Marxists who went through the horrific experience of the *kebele* prisons and the red terror have never been the same. They saw Marxism in practice with their own eyes and it was repulsive.

After the attempt on Mengistu's life, the situation in Addis became very nerve-racking. *Goh* was still alive, but no issue could pass the censors. At the same time, there were efforts inside the Derg to reorganize the committees and wrestle some power away from Mengistu. These were spearheaded by so-called democrats who were thought to be sympathetic to EPRP. The party leadership began to pin its hopes for a favorable situation that would be conducive to its existence on the ascendancy of these "democrats" in the Derg.

In the fall, conditions on the ground were actually deteriorating when the university finally opened after a long closure, and many students began to enroll. There was going to be a crash program to allow students to go to the next level. I started contemplating that return to the university would be a viable option for me. I was not very sure if the plan would work for me, but I was thinking of doing it. While I was debating on returning or not returning to school and how I would be able to pull this off after my association with *Goh*, I heard that the party's entire interzone committee was captured while holding a meeting. The members were captured with documents and names of people, ostensible targets that were to be "eliminated." They attempted to get rid of documents, including by chewing and swallowing some of them, but it did not work. Some of them were armed with pistols. Birhanu later told me that he wanted to shoot and run, but the others were not as cooperative. They probably felt they were too mismatched to fight it out. Apparently they lost crucial moments while deciding what to do and what not to do. They were captured red-handed.

It was a terrible blow. It was considered the next worst thing to having the entire central committee captured. In fact, the central committee, I was told, was rather dormant and the interzone committee was the center of political, propaganda, and military activities.

The group was taken to the police station in Merkato. The same day or the next day at night, it was said EPRA "elite" units were sent to rescue them. According to the story, the unit's car was intercepted on the way to the police station and fighting erupted. Later, I heard all kinds of rumors about how the unit managed to fight their way out and escape without losing a soul. The stories made it seem like these were well-trained commando units. The truth may not be known, but they probably were no match to the well-trained government soldiers patrolling the streets of Addis. In any case, the effort was foiled and the party members were transferred to the much-feared security division.

Instinctively I knew the incident spelled disaster for me also. They normally torture captured people and force them to show where they lived and who they lived with. One of them, I later came to know, a very brave young student and friend of the poet Jale Bia brought the security people to his mother's house. He was pretty much messed up. The others were bringing the security people to different houses. But Birhanu, he later told me, decided to wait a few days longer to give the party time to clear the house. Finally, when his situation became unbearable, he came to the house in a security vehicle escorted by three security officers.

The night before Birhanu was to show the house, a bomb exploded in the cadre school, probably in revenge for the disaster that had befallen the party. The security officers mockingly told Birhanu it was his friends who threw the bomb at the building. When they came to the house, Mezy, who looked like a maid, and Melaku Markos, another EPRP leader and a longtime friend of Yohannes, were waiting in the house. For reasons unknown to anyone, the house was never cleared; there were weapons, cash, books, and materials.

Probably not anticipating any trouble, only three members of the security were dispatched to escort Birhanu to the house. When they arrived at the house, one was left at the gate to guard the compound; the other two entered the house. Mezy and Melaku were caught unprepared. When the security people barged in, Melaku, who was with Mezy, tried to run to the next room, but the security personnel aimed his pistol and stopped him in his tracks. Then they handcuffed him, his hands on his back. Because he had a small pistol tucked in his pants in the back, he moved his hands a little bit further from his body so the security officer would not feel the gun. Mezy was not handcuffed; she was taken for a maid. Next, one of the security personnel went to the bedroom. He was unprepared for what he found there: arms, bullets, books, documents, and money. Alarmed, he called his office and asked for reinforcements. While this was going on in the bedroom, in the living room Melaku signaled Mezy that he was going to shoot with one of his tied hands. Mezy saw what was coming and got ready. While the guard was looking in another direction, standing near Mezy, Melaku managed to fire his pistol. The officer dropped on the floor. Mezy quickly picked up the machine gun on the floor and shot the other officer. The one at the gate fired a round, which barely missed Mezy. She fired back and he ran for cover.

Mezy unlocked the handcuffs on Birhanu, who had been tortured and could hardly walk. Mezy and Melaku helped him jump through the fence of the house at the back, and all three escaped. I think they were able to unlock the handcuffs from both hands. Mezy and Birhanu took a taxi and went to Merkato to my second cousin's house that was also related to her. Melaku left for another place. As unbelievable as it sounded, all three managed to escape, just like in the movies.

While this was happening, I was at the university to register for a class and was on my way to Gob's office by bus. I heard automatic weapon fire in the direction of my house and suspected that it could be my house. When I reached the office, I heard Mezy had called the office and left a message for me to immediately leave the office. I took the elevator, went to the basement, and exited through the backdoor.

When I heard the story of what happened, I could not believe it. I knew they were lucky to have escaped; it was neither planned nor anticipated. It was only a matter of inertia and shock that the two had not vacated the premises. The story of the escape was later heard all over EPRP cells, and Mezy became an instant hero. Poet Jale Bia wrote a few lines about her. He declared that she was like smoke; the enemy could see her but not catch her.

When I met Mezy a day later, she did not seem like a hero. She was pretty shaken up. She was very happy that Birhanu survived. But I could see that she was still in a state of shock. I think she realized the gravity of her situation and instinctively felt it.

I now became a target of a security search, and was in a terrible danger. Up to this point I could really get out of EPRP if I decided or felt like doing it as I was not well known in the party. Enrollment in the university was the first step to doing that. Now there was no hope for me to survive except within EPRP, and I became a revolutionary against my will.

The party was hit with a series of tragedies at this time. Some members of its rural army were caught in Woldya, Wollo. The leader of the group was a European-educated revolutionary and was said to be known to Negede Gobezie and other leaders of Meison who were said to have interrogated them. It was not so obvious why this unit had to venture south so far away from the area of operation. It was incredulous they would do that, but nobody was in the mood to throw questions when attention was now focused on the gathering storm in Addis.

The government launched a convoluted propaganda campaign accusing EPRP of firing at poor peasants. "The revolutionary peasants captured hired assassins who were out to sabotage its revolution," declared the announcement on radio Ethiopia. It was also said that members of the interzone committee that were arrested were literally cannibalized in the torture. All these sent tremors through my system and I could not see how I could survive the disaster.

The first few days following this spectacular escape were the scariest and the most dangerous time for me. The tension in EPRP following the capture of the interzone and the EPRA group became immense. There was also a series of executions of EPRP members that terrorized people who were underground and in danger.

The party found me different houses to sleep in. Nights in houses that you don't know much about were terrifying. I was told that the security people had a very good description of me, my size, and my hair color. Luckily for me, I was not active in the university, so very few people knew who I was. It helped not to be suspected by members of other organizations who were now much more aggressive in their pursuit of EPRP leaders and members. At this time, these organizations never trusted the existing government apparatus except the ones they had infiltrated and controlled. It was claimed that the bureaucracy was in alliance with EPRP and EDU to disrupt and sabotage the revolution. In fact, they preferred what they called independent actions by the *kebele* leaders and militia, over which their control was growing. In that sense, my situation was preferable to that of Mezy, who had more exposure and was considered dangerous. The pictures of Mezy, Birhanu, and many other EPRP members were posted all over the country so the people could help expose them.

I received a pistol and armed myself. The idea was to use it to escape or commit suicide. I never for once felt comfortable with it, but carried it nonetheless. I imagined myself being stopped while I had the weapon, but never saw myself using it. When I look back at it now, it seems so crazy that I would do that knowing in my heart of hearts that I would never have been able to use it. Maybe I would have used it when I was under the influence of alcohol. Maybe I would have anyway. If I were crazy enough to carry it, who can tell what I would have been able to do with it?

To this day, I have never been able to clearly say why I did what I did. It was a life of deceit, but I was doing that to myself and not to anyone else. I must have had an inner urge to prove my courage and gain recognition, so much so that I was willing to engage in actions that were incredibly stupid. Maybe when you live in a situation like that—chewing *khat*, drinking alcohol, and balancing danger and party responsibility—you cannot think straight. For me the courageous thing to do would have been to say what I said after it was too late: "This party activity is not for me; I don't believe in it and it does not suit me. I am functioning at my worst level. My heart is not in it; my body is not in it; my soul is far from it." I should have screamed, "To hell with the Derg, to hell with EPRP, to hell with all these organizations who are brazen liars and murderers and power mongers!" To my friends, I should have been able to say, "I admire you guys. I know you are dedicated to the cause that you believe in, and that to me shows character and strength to some degree. But I am not like that. I don't want to be like that. I want to study, get a job, and help my family out, and help other people out if I could do it. I should have said that I am an aspiring petty bourgeois and I am not ashamed of it. I have no problem with what you do as long as you let me live my life the way I wanted it. I want my freedom." That was the courageous thing for me to do, and may have been the least risky if I had done it early enough before I went too far with underground activities.

Sometimes I wonder how many people found themselves in the same predicament that I was in. We would never know for sure. There were many people who lost faith in the party very early but went on with their membership for inexplicable reasons. When you talk with party members you know and are friends with, you notice a deep-seated skepticism about it all. To move from this skepticism to action that was contradictory to the party may not have been as bad as it seemed. But why people stayed on can only be explained by the psychosis of the situation we were in. Many people could only leave the party by going to the other side. That was treachery that very few would feel comfortable with. That meant betraying people you know and you are friends with. The enemy never made it easy to get out and stay independent. They want you to come and do what, to your mind, is most treasonous: expose your friends or the people you work with. You could not get out of the intolerable situation that you were in without doing something that you cannot live with for the rest of your life. Meison, Woz League, and the others raised betrayal to the level of revolutionary virtue. What I heard and saw about the pro-government organizations made them the worst the country had ever produced. I am sure they can say the same thing with justification about EPRP remembers. There was no honorable way of getting out, and so many just had to perish because the enemy did not provide any chance to exist with one's dignity and self-worth intact and without having to feel treacherous.

Many eventually did that. They were caught, and to save their lives they had to betray others with whom they worked. Blaming the party on the mass media was probably acceptable and may have been done out of the genuine feeling of disappointment. What must have been terribly difficult was probably the humiliation of betraying one's comrades, who may have refused to do the same thing. In the end, it is said that most of those who gave in were used, abused, and murdered. Such was the option that most of us were left with, we stayed with the party that gave us some support, cover, and hope, and maybe after all it might even be able to turn the tide around.

A very brilliant poem of defiance was composed by a poet that Jale Bia called the "greatest Amharic poet" in the country. The poem, entitled "*Tigel Menun Tigel Hone*" raised profound questions about what revolution means if it does not entail what was happening to the party then. In my view this was a magnificent work of poetry. Even when you have doubts that the party is not what is has been pumped up to be, you wonder where such words of inspiration came from except from an unflinching belief in the cause of the party by some of its members and youthful fighters. It was poetry of the spirit of the Ethiopian youth when it threw all it had to the cause of EPRP. It was the spirit that was soon to be completely crushed by the Red Terror. It may be telling of the story of the time the poet of defiance was later arrested and broken up by torture.

Coming back to my story, despite being faced with enormous danger, I began to slowly feel adjusted to my situation. It is hard to think that you will be captured every day, so the mind sort of develops a mechanism to avoid this uncomfortable reality and build hopes and expectations that have no realistic foundations. You cling to these because they make sense of an otherwise insane situation. Once a week or two passes, you feel the crucial period has passed and nothing may happen to you after all.

DEBRE ZEIT

One day, the poet Jale Bia told me that he had found me a place to stay in Debre Zeit through a good friend of his who was professional artist at the national theater. Jale was fond of a drawing by the artist that depicted a fierce cockfight between red and white roosters. This was a metaphor for the struggle between the red EPRP and white Derg. This artist knew two people who worked at the Debre Zeit Agricultural Station and lived outside the city by one of the lakes. They had told their friend that they were willing to accommodate me. Jale was genuinely concerned about my safety and my health, and had gone out of his way to find this on his own. Things were generally done like this and it really depended more on who you knew than on your position in the party structure. I decided to see it, and accompanied by the artist, who was legally working in his field at that time, left for Debre Zeit by bus.

The house was built near a beautiful lake outside the city limits and past the agricultural experiment station. There were other houses around, including a beautiful one with glass walls facing the lake, half a kilometer away from where I lived. It was owned by one of the former officials, but seemed unoccupied at that time, to my surprise. We could only see this from the lake. At the back, a little further from the house was a Christian mission, probably a Seventh-Day Adventist mission with a big compound and garden. Many white priests and their families lived here. There was also another house nearby, rented by a research scientist who had lived in the USA. My hosts were not EPRP members and were very apolitical but sympathized with the party very much. I was supposed to teach them and recruit them. They were very nice and caring individuals with whom I got along very well, but never really made any effort to recruit them.

Life for me at Debre Zeit at this time was a God-sent respite from the terrible tensions in Addis. I stayed inside the house during the day and read.

Near the lake were different kinds of plants, including *khat* trees. I would chew *khat* and read most of the time by myself. When I first came, there was a lady from the area who was cooking for my friends, but they got rid of her and brought another one from Addis. They must have done that to give me maximum security.

A few yards away was another house, where a young lady who studied botany in the United States and was working in the agricultural experiment station lived. She dated a guy with a PhD in horticulture from United States. Neither she nor he was interested in the politics of the times, but he claimed to know many people in other organizations. He was an easy-going, jovial individual with a good sense of humor. He told me about life in New York and America, to which I listened very intently and with envy.

The lake offered me a peaceful environment and a chance to relax by canoeing a boat. After I learned to canoe, although I did not know how to swim, I would often go on a boat for hours. It helped me meditate, think, and reflect about my life, which was now in shambles. I completely ignored my family, about whom I could not do anything. Avoidance was a way of dealing with an uncomfortable and painful reality. But canoeing was the most beautiful exercise I engaged in. It helped me to burn the fat on my stomach that my sedentary life had forced me accumulate. I loved the area, loved my hosts, who showed me around and got me an ID card from the agricultural station. I began to live a relatively secure and tremendously luxurious life, which included reading, canoeing, and chewing *khat*.

I read a number of books, including Stalin's book on the opposition, given to me because of my open dislike of Stalin and visible interest in Trotsky. I read an autobiography of Trotsky, who was to me the most readable of the Marxist authors, and completed his biography on Lenin and a book on socialist literature. Jale Bia and I thought Trotsky was the most brilliant Marxist, with the possible exception of Lenin, who became a historical giant, revolutionary icon in Trotsky's later writings. I read a book on Marxist economics by the French Marxist Earnest Mandel, considered to be a Trotskyite. I wrote some poetry.

My area of movement also expanded once I got the ID card. I walked around and canoed the boat to a house on the opposite side that was rented by a family and a friend of my hosts. The husband worked as an accountant in the agricultural station. I felt relatively safe here and enjoyed a luxury that I was not accustomed to. On weekends we would go out to Debre Zeit and I never had to worry about anything since I was carrying a very valid ID card.

One day I was standing on the small pier of the lake with a book entitled *Communist Morality* that Jale Bia had recommended I read. A priest who lived and worked in the adjacent mission not far from where I stayed was also paddling aimlessly and calmly. Many times he passed by where I stood and we exchanged glances. He said, "Good morning," and I returned the greeting likewise. He must have sensed that I was carrying a book or that I was eager to talk too. He asked me, "Are you familiar with this book?" waving a Bible in his hand. I responded in the affirmative. He told me that he was fasting and meditating that morning. He looked deeply religious. He said that he fasted most of the time, because abstinence and self-denial are healthy for the soul and the body.

We started talking about the Bible, and one thing led to another and we got into an argument. I regurgitated the regular Marxist litany: why the Bible is wrong and is used by oppressors to preserve their power. "The Bible supported the slave society and hence reflects the values of a slave-holding society, which to me is indefensible," I argued. He was very much engaged in our discussion and we talked for hours. The book I was carrying, *Communist Morality*, was an anthology of writings and speeches by leading communists, including Vladimir Lenin, Nadezha Krupskaya, Rosa Luxemburg, Felix Dzerzhinsky, and others on what is moral and what is not among Communists. It was full of statements that claimed what is moral or not depends on the class position. Additionally it had writings about what these Marxists said about love, parenthood, children, etc. Dzerzhinsky wrote very emotionally about his love for children and how it was tough for him to balance this emotion and his revolutionary spirit. After I told the priest what I was reading, he suggested that we exchange books and come back the next day and discuss. He asked me to read a few pages from the book of Mark, and he promised to read as much as he could from *Communist Morality*.

When we met the next day, he had, to my surprise, read the entire book and I had read only a few verses just to prove to him that the Bible was inherently contradictory and did not make much sense. He told me that he was impressed by what Dzerzhinsky has to say and his love of children, and he found him the most interesting. We discussed for a long time; I was feeling cocky about what I knew and he was most eager to tell me that I should try to save my soul. Even as I stood my ground very firmly, however, I said that this guy is not that stupid not to notice what I thought were contradictory ideas in the Bible. I suspected he must have looked at it differently than I did. But I never gave him any impression of any doubt about my hardline position.

At the end he invited me to come to the mission. He said I could watch movies and discuss with him. He told me that I should accept Jesus as I my savior. When he mentioned salvation, I told him that I won't do that, and after some exchanges I told him, "I will never accept Jesus Christ as my savior." He was terribly upset and almost in tears, and said, "Abebe, you should never say never, you should never say never." I was touched by his solemnity and kindness. Compared with the mechanical way I was discussing, I thought he seemed full of spirit and passion and cared about people. I have never ever forgotten the tone of his voice when he said, "Abebe, never say never."

Many times I thought of joining the mission and using it to escape out of the country. I often wondered what my life would be like if I could attend the mission and disguise myself as a member of the church. I had doubts that it would work for a long time without being exposed since that involved a great deal of cooperation from the members of the church, of which I could not be sure. While the religion was not my main motive for joining the mission, I reasoned that I could leave the country through their member churches in the border provinces like Wollega.

I never followed through on this idea, but it crossed my mind many times. I imagined what a relief it would be to get out of this terrible fix I was in and enjoy freedom, the freedom to walk and talk freely. Every time I passed by the mission for one of my meditative walks, I went through this idea in my mind, but I never even came close to acting on it.

One day I had a terrible dream. The house in Debre Zeit was surrounded by the military calling me to surrender and get out of the house with my hands up. I woke up in terror, drenched in cold sweat when in my dream the military stormed into the house. I was terribly scared. I wondered if this would ever come true. Prior to this experience, I had stopped having dreams altogether. However, as this dream occurred when my situation was relatively much improved, I dismissed it just as a bad dream and went on with my life.

I went back to Addis one weekend. I heard the story that there was a factional struggle within the leadership of the organization. Wolde Ab told me that two members called "Ha" and "Le" had formed a different faction. The "Ha" and "Le" were Getachew Maru and Berhane Meskel respectively. Getachew was a member of the politburo, and Berhane was a member of the central committee of EPRP. I did not understand the full significance of the factional strife. Wolde Ab told me that it did not make sense for the party to smooth over the problem and should instead openly discuss the rift between the two factions.

Apparently this big rift that had split the party into two warring blocks with regards to urban armed struggle and the mode of opposition to the government and other crucial questions of strategy was not widely known. I was a fellow traveler who was passive in the organization, but it seemed that even members who were more active were not aware of the division within the party. Sometime that week I met Birhanu and Mezy. They asked me what I thought about the factional movement in the party. "It is more appropriate to discuss it openly than cover it up," I said carelessly. I was repeating what Wolde Ab had said. Birhanu said that the security situation in the party was so tense now that it was not possible to call a party congress, as the faction was insisting, and discuss the issues. He added that most meetings are now held under the protection of military guard; there was no way a party congress could be held. I thought that made sense too since I was even surprised the party could function under the prevailing atmosphere. I did not care what happened one way or the other

Later, I heard that Berhane, the guy who lived with us in Addis and was a good friend of Wolde Ab and Jale Bia, was in the faction and that he had been stripped of his organizational responsibilities. He stayed with Wolde Ab and went out with us for drinks, but seemed lonely and depressed. Berhane knew Berhane Meskel. I was never sure if it was just personal friendship or organizational work, although I suspect it was the latter. Berhane Meskel was a household name with probably a highly exaggerated reputation. The average EPRP sympathizer thought he led the fighters in Tigray and now in the urban areas. The rumor that he had split up from the main party leadership was bound to hurt EPRP, I assumed.

Berhane Meskel, it seemed, had quite a following within the organization who espoused his line. When I began to understand the factional strife, it seemed bigger and deeper than was thought. I read a long paper that espoused the factional line, which argued against the urban armed struggle and expressed support for some kind of rapprochement with the Derg. It even said Mengistu initially wanted to work with EPRP but was rebuffed by the leadership.

It was also said that people that espoused the factional line were taking actions contrary to the main EPRP lines. Later, I heard that the party had the two leaders under detention but Berhane Meskel had actually managed to escape. This was surprising to me since that made him a fugitive among fugitives, a terrible position to be in at that time.

While this factional strife was going on within, luckily for the party the movement within the Derg to shrink Mengistu's amassed political power was gaining some momentum, and the party was buoyant about it. The atmosphere in Addis was relatively relaxed and EPRP members were very emboldened. Meisons and the others, on the contrary, were nervous about this surge of opposition within the Derg, which expressed opposition to the independent actions that the *kebele* were taking against suspected EPRP members. Many innocent people were being hurt as a result of these callous actions by their members who were determined to destroy as many people as was necessary if that would get them at EPRP.

One morning, early in 1977, this brave, somewhat naive democratic movement within the Derg, which was symbolically led by Gen. Tefferri Banti, was swiftly crushed by Mengistu, who personally led the assault on these members of the Derg. In the brief exchange of fire, Senai Leke, a PhD in chemistry and one of the boldest political figures on the side of Mengistu, was killed. Mengistu emerged as the unchallenged leader except that he still had to settle a score with the Derg's vice chairman, Col. Atnafu Abate.

I remember I was in the furniture store owned by Dil Nesa Negatu but actually served as a front for EPRP when this bad news was broadcast. Our hope was completely dashed by this sudden and negative turn of events. While nothing was officially said by the party, this was seen as the most dangerous turn of events by the leadership. There was a paralyzing shock. There was a realization that soon the full might of the state power would be unleashed against the minuscule power of the party.

The party began to prepare and defend itself from the first *assessa*. Nobody knew exactly when it would start but its start was a foregone conclusion. The party began to prepare by sending members who were the most exposed outside Addis, although no one was sure whether staying outside Addis Abeba would be safer or not. People had seen limited *assessas* before, but no one knew what a comprehensive *assessa* would be like. There was a generalized panic in EPRP.

When the *assessa* came in March 1977, I was in Addis sleeping in Wolde Ab's apartment. There were pistols and guns in this place and people took turns to guard the apartment. The plan was to run into the Ras Makonnen Bridge if the *kebeles* came at night. Wolde Ab, Berhane, and others took turns to stand sentry so others could sleep. The *kebeles* were expected to come at night. We spent terrible and sleepless nights in this building.

I am not sure if this was during the first *assessa* or the second *assessa*, Wolde Ab believed the apartment where they lived was safe. The *kebele* leaders in the area were either party sympathizers or they had become good friends with him. He still worked for *Goh*, which was not making any money in the publication business. However, *Goh* was doing some translation work for the Derg as a result of the connection that Mulu had with a senior Derg member. On the other hand, Sarah, the other owner, had already been arrested and sent to the main prison for her suspected connection to EPRP. Sarah languished in prison for many years before she was released. Wolde Ab's *Goh* connection was very good for him and gave him some legal cover. The room we slept in, I remember, was decorated with pictures of nude women from *Penthouse* and *Playboy*, ostensibly to distract the searchers.

We passed the first *assessa* on the streets of Addis. I was carrying an ID from the agricultural station in Debre Zeit, so I felt okay to walk. As it turned out, the *assessa* was not as costly in terms of human lives. Members of EPRP who were in Addis managed to get through it. The safest place was to be on the road, in a taxi, or walking. Many members of the armed forces who participated in the *assessa* believed this effort was just to disarm the city. Members of Meison and the others had other agendas and were more aggressively looking for individuals, typewriters, and other clandestine work paraphernalia. But the soldiers' target was weapons, so people who did not look suspicious winged these *assessas* rather easily.

It was a relief for most of us. The *assessa* was cashing in huge quantities of weapons. It looked like Addis Abebans were fairly well armed. Most people readily gave up what they had, but others hid weapons. Some weapons were dug out from the ground. On the whole, the first *assessa* seemed to have achieved what it was intended to. We were, however, naive enough to think that it failed because most of the party's weapons and members were untouched. According to the Ethiopian radio, one or two units of the party apparently resisted and were destroyed by the huge fire power of the government.

While the first *assessa* seemed rather benign contrary to what was expected, it also claimed the life of Tesfaye Debessai. I was playing table tennis in a bar with Berhane when the announcement came that Tesfaye Debessie had committed suicide by jumping from a high-rise building while resisting arrest. Berhane was shocked. Since I did not know him personally, my reaction was muted. I was rather surprised that he stayed in Addis in a very difficult period. Berhane told me that he was a member of the politburo, and his loss would be irreplaceable.

Soon another debacle took place. Arabu, Melaku Markos, Yonnas, and Nega Ayele tried to leave town in a Jeep through the regular checkpoint. Their driver was a professor of geology in the university and perhaps of US or British citizenship. They thought that he would be a good cover and they tried to leave Addis in the direction of Debre Zeit through the checkpoints. Apparently, the plan was for the three of them to walk around the checkpoint while the professor drove through the checkpoint with Nega Ayele. He was to wait for them past the checkpoint and pick them up. I don't know whether government was tipped off on this or not, but this ridiculous effort failed.

Arabu and Melaku were caught while walking. Yonnas apparently managed to evade and escape. The professor, when he saw what was happening, tried to run through the checkpoint and was shot and killed. It was not clear what happened next. The story goes Melaku killed Arabu and killed himself while they were in militia custody. Yonnas managed to survive this and the terrible Red Terror.

I met with the late Yonnas Admassu in Addis Abeba in 2012 and asked him to confirm this story. The story as I have written was initially shared to me by Wolde Ab right after it happened. Yonnas essentially said the same thing. However, the story also left me with more questions than answers. Yonnas said he was following Yohannes and Melaku from a distance when he saw a student at the university that had always carried a grudge against Yohannes. He knew this meant trouble and changed direction. As he was walking away from the scene, he could not see what really happened but heard two shots. He concluded that it was murder-suicide, and he knew Melaku would do something like this rather than give himself up to the enemy. That is how he concluded Melaku killed Yohannes and then turned the pistol on himself. One reason he concluded it was a murder-suicide was that Yohannes' face was so disfigured from the close-range shot that the cadres did not identify him. Now I realize there are so many gaps in this story that only an investigative writer with access to the government files could uncover.

I was shocked by what happened. I was especially sorry for Arabu, whom I had come to know and respect. I thought he was such a brilliant revolutionary writer that it would be impossible to replace him. The deaths of these individuals were announced on the Ethiopian radio.

What Arabu, Melaku, Yonnas, and Nega did was not the smart thing at all. Most of us were surprised that they would attempt to get out of the city that way, especially all four of them carrying weapons. That was a collective suicide. It seemed a desperate and reckless act. Apparently they were concerned that they would not make it through the checkpoint without being identified by the swarming government-supported cadres who participated at the checkpoints. However, with the proper identification, which I was sure they had, they should have been able to individually pass through the checkpoint had they taken a bus. In any case, their chances of escape individually were much better.

There was a palpable fear that the party would not survive the first *assessa*. Panic seemed to reign within the leadership; that was why Arabu and the others tried to get out of the city the way they did. Underground life is difficult and isolating. When one's security situation is so bad and one is confined to one or two places and rarely mixes with others, one's judgment is severely hampered. In talking to Arabu many times before, I had noticed that sometimes he did not seem like he was in touch with reality. He was fed false information, and whatever picture he had of the struggle was formed based on this lopsided and exaggerated information that was being fed to him.

Some people think the loss of Tesfaye Debessai and Yohannes was detrimental to the party struggle. From here on, the journey was a downward spiral to ultimate destruction. I doubt they would have been able to avert what the party faced subsequently. Maybe by then the party was irreversibly set on a course of a showdown with the Derg and it was not possible to make midcourse corrections. What could have possibly been done at this point was to cease all hostile activities and get as many people as possible out of Addis. In any case, with the death of the two at the hands of the government and the murder of Getachew Maru at the hands of the party, it seemed the major elements of the entire politburo were wiped out. Soon, according to the information we were getting, the party's central committee was fully depleted by arrests and killings. The party's center of activity was the zone committees, which coordinated their activities through the interzone committee.

After the first *assessa*, Birhanu was sent to Sidamo. At first I thought it was for security reasons, but then realized that he was to lead the party organization in Kibre Mengist, replacing Melaku, who in a valiant but desperate act undertaken with Mezy had managed to rescue him. Last-minute attempts were being made to start an armed struggle in the south. Actually there were guerilla fighters in the area whose political goals were vague and were receiving some form of support from the Somali regime. Part of the effort was to infiltrate these armed gangs and reorient their politics. Mezy, I came to realize later, was unhappy about this separation and Birhanu's new assignment. But the decision was not hers, and Birhanu may have even volunteered for it. After his near-death experience following the arrest of the interzone committee, he may have thought his chance of survival was better outside Addis. Birhanu replaced Melaku, who died trying to escape the *asesssa*.

Wolde Ab went fully underground following an attempt on his life in front of his parents' house. He was returning to his parents' house in a Volkswagen with his sisters when he found his parents' house surrounded by cadres. He managed to escape unharmed from the hell of bullet fire that rained on him. His sisters also escaped. That was it for him. From then on he went underground and served the party until he was killed in another major shootout.

I was now under pressure to come to Addis and assume party responsibility. I did not like that and began to stall. Then I was told that I could join the party committee in Debre Zeit and work from there. I agreed to do that. I was given a code and met a young guy who regularly commuted from Addis and was in charge of party activities in the area. He was also working in the surrounding rural areas and seemed very active.

This committee in Debre Zeit consisted of an individual who was in the air force, a teacher, the contact person, and me. There may have been another person, but I don't remember. The meetings took place in the house of the teacher. I remember the first meeting I had with the group. We stayed most of the night discussing what was going on in the area. At this point, party activity in Debre Zeit was not that great except for writing of graffiti by the youth. Debre Zeit had not experienced an *assessa*, which made things relatively easy. We were getting reports that some *kebele* leaders were pushing for *assessas*. The report also said that the party should take action against these leaders.

I soon came to realize that there was a so-called defense squad consisting of people in the air force and airborne that was willing to take action. These came up once or twice, and I could see there was a consensus developing for action. The squad was not only willing to take action, but it was also insisting that it should happen. I don't think I said much in these meetings. I instinctively felt that if we did that there would be vicious counterattacks on everybody and suspected that we would all be in danger.

Coming from my area of residence to these meetings was a very uncomfortable experience. Soon my hosts also began to worry about what I was doing. They knew that whatever happened to me could eventually affect them. In addition, I soon realized that the place we were meeting was not a safe place. Many times at night we had to stop what we were doing when we heard voices or noticed a car pass by. It was a scary thing and I wished I did not have to go through that. But I continued to meet them a few more times.

One day during the day I came to town to buy *khat*. I don't remember if I walked to Debre Zeit or someone gave me a ride. It took more than an hour to walk from where I lived to the town. After I bought the *khat*, I heard that there was an *assessa* underway. I decided to leave with my *khat*. I rented a cart (*gari*) and headed back to where I lived. Before I reached my area of residence, I noticed the key road leaving the town in the direction of the house was being guarded by two soldiers. When I saw the soldiers, I knew I was in trouble. I calmed myself and prepared to get checked. I got out of the cart and put my hands on my head as ordered. One of the soldiers untied the *khat* and looked. Then he asked, "What are you doing here at this time of the day?" I said, "I am on vacation and I had just gone to town to buy me some *khat*." I responded as calmly as I knew how. He asked me where I worked and I told him that I worked at the agricultural station. He took my ID card and glanced at it for a long time. I knew he was suspicious. I began to worry that he would ask me to stay until he confirmed my identity with the station. At this point, as if by divine intervention, the other soldier ordered his comrade to let me go. I was surprised and puzzled. I knew he intervened to save me the trouble. I was relieved. This was a close call. I kept thinking what would have happened if the other soldier had not deliberately intervened to save my life. I thought he was either a supporter or a sympathizer of the party.

My friends came for lunch. They told me that they saw soldiers and passed through a checkpoint. I told them that I had also managed to do that. They did not seem to understand what the consequences could have been had I been captured with a forged ID card from their station, or they preferred not to show it.

Following this close call, I avoided the next scheduled meeting of the committee. I was also afraid that most of the members had decided that an action would be taken against one or two *kebele* leaders, but I did not want to be part of the decision. I was, as usual, very reluctant at the earlier meeting but could not openly oppose this. That would make me a suspect or a member of the faction "anja." I was nervous that this would not help our situation. If anything, it would make it worse. It seemed the *kebeles* had never been deterred by what was happening to them. Even if they were scared, they had no way of resisting the pressure on them to undertake *assessa* without being labeled EPRP members. Now it was becoming increasingly clear that it was safer to be against EPRP than for it. The strength of Meison, Woz League, and the others who supported the regime in these organizations was getting stronger by the day.

Following the close call, I noticed my hosts began to be concerned about my presence in their midst. For a while I decided to go back to Addis and stay there. Deep down, I was also attempting to avoid meeting with this committee. A couple of weeks later, I came to Debre Zeit and rented a cart to their house. When I reached the house, I saw the biologist who was working in the station. She told me that a bomb was thrown the night before in a bar and two *kebele* leaders and the bartender were killed. I knew this bar and I knew the bartender. She had served us food there and I had chatted with her before. I felt very sad for her. I knew whoever did it did not worry about what happened to the innocent. They had thrown the grenade and escaped on foot by one of the lakes.

When I heard what happened, I returned immediately to Addis. I never went back to Debre Zeit. Right after this, one of my friends who worked at the agricultural station got a scholarship to Russia and left. He felt that he was coming under suspicion for sympathizing with the party. I knew he did it to save his life, and I wholeheartedly supported him.

I met the chair of the committee in Addis and asked him about what happened. He told me that the squad was able to escape, but in the *assessa* that followed many party members were arrested. It was obvious nothing tangible could be accomplished in Debre Zeit now. He told me that the prospect of doing organizational work outside the city, especially in the rural areas, was better and that he would keep on working at that level. This work with peasants always puzzled me. It is probably the riskiest thing to do then.

Soon the peasant areas were the most inhospitable, especially for someone who had no relative in the community. Many of the peasant youth uprisings in Wolkite (Showa) and other densely populated communities were violently suppressed. A series of lesser uprisings were also crushed in Keffa. We heard about these stories, admired the heroism of the individuals involved, but never raised questions as to whether these uprisings made any sense or not. These actions, I suspected, were mostly spearheaded by militant youth from these rural areas that have come under the influence of the party.

When we met in Addis, the chairman of the Debre Zeit committee also insisted that I give him my Seiko watch since the additional features in it would be helpful for his evening activities. I had a nice and somewhat expensive watch that I bought in Dessie with the help of a friend who defrayed part of the cost. My watch looked so technologically advanced that I used to tell people that I could communicate with the party on its radio.

This discussion put me in a very embarrassing situation. Actually, I saw my watch as an investment that one day, if in a real bind, I would sell and use the proceeds for an emergency. Though I was embarrassed, I wanted to tell him the truth. I said I planned to sell it and send the proceeds to my family. He was puzzled by my reasoning, which actually was true. But he insisted on it, so we finally agreed to swap his Seiko for mine.

Now I started to live in Addis. Wolde Ab and Jale Bia asked me if I would like to go to Assimba since my safety was not assured in Addis. I refused, saying that I was not revolutionary enough to do that. I did not think I would survive in rural Ethiopia. I knew I was not ready to carry arms and fight. I said to Wolde Ab, "I think I am a petty bourgeoisie. I am used to the easy life in town, to alcohol, *khat*, and everything else that I could not survive as a guerilla fighter." That was true. I also felt that once I went out there I would not be able to get out, whereas in Addis I harbored the wishful thinking that I could.

I began to seriously think about leaving for Djibouti. A second cousin of mine told me that people leave for Djibouti through Dire Dewa, and suggested I do the same. I considered this option for a long time and wrote my friend Gerry Jones in the United States if he would take me there if I were to make it to Djibouti. Gerry wrote back to me saying it was difficult to come to the States, but he would try to help me get out to another African country to pursue my studies. This was a good response, but at that time I found it discouraging and stopped pursuing the idea of going to Djibouti. I also was not sure if it could be done.

My information about Djibouti was wrong. I heard that my childhood friend, Mohamed Ahimed, had left earlier but was in big trouble in Djibouti after he fled the country. I also heard the same story about Aziz, who was active in campus politics but smartly avoided the terrible underground politics, was in dire circumstances in Djibouti. At that time going to Djibouti did not seem as easy and was fraught with dangers. I heard that people did get caught on the way and were never heard from again. In the end, though, I could have pursued that avenue better than just waiting in Addis until I got caught. I was discouraged. I did not know if I could go to Dessie and live peacefully until I left the country. I knew that staying in Dessie was next to impossible with my fugitive status since people knew Birhanu and I were friends. So I dropped the idea of leaving Addis and kept foolishly hanging on.

Once again the party came up with an assignment for me. I had informed them that I could be involved in a non-organizational activity or capacity, meaning something related to propaganda. Working with the so-called armed wing was out of the question. Both Mezy and Wolde Ab suggested that I should hold political classes to EPRA fighters, and I refused to do that. Mezy then told me that the party was opening a political (cadre) school for youth and the working-class members. I asked what these schools would look like. She told me it would be a class of at most ten or so people and would be held behind shops or stores. A political school, it did not seem plausible at that time, but I thought the party had another trick under its sleeves that I did not know much about. Using stores for classes made sense and I decided to give it a try after Mezy assured me that it would not be too risky.

The idea behind a political school was to combat the factional claim that members were now lacking serious knowledge and depth in the ideology. It was also to combat the factional line and teach members about the correct line of the struggle. The government and its associated organizations had a well-organized cadre school that was minting party ideologues and other cadres who would assume responsibility in the expanding mass and political organizations. That may be the idea behind EPRP's cadre school, which was not a school in any sense of the word but in name only.

My youth class was in a small room in the Tekle Haimanot region in Addis. There were about, at the most, five young people, who were very smart and knowledgeable, who attended. So much for party school, I said. This is like any study group. They all had finished high school. We went through philosophy, politics, and economics maybe for two or three sessions. I prepared good lectures and they all seemed to enjoy them. But I was very unhappy about continuing like that. One night, the guy who was my contact told me the house is now gone and that we won't be able to meet for a while. My other group, the working-class group, met maybe only once or twice, but neither they nor I were in a mood for Marxism under the prevailing atmosphere of terror. This was the "Cadre School of EPRP" and who knows

I may have been the only one to run it. I told Mezy and Wolde Ab that this school stuff would not work. They realized that there was no way a political class could be conducted at this point in Addis.

The only visible party activity that was being conducted at this time was the occasional assassinations meted against government cadres that were going on. Either because of increasing desperation or gaining more experience, there were more of these occurring even though the party's political work was pretty much paralyzed. *Democracia* was coming on and off irregularly and it was barely legible or readable. There were also regular intraparty killings. Additionally, most of the arrests and killings that the party was experiencing were now being attributed to massive defections caused by the faction that pitted a party member against another.

A case in point was a youth called Thomas who apparently left the party defense unit and became a notorious killer for the government. He became so successful that many of the areas in Merkato that gave perfect cover for party members now became dangerous for many young people. He would often come in a car to tearooms and summarily execute individuals he knew. This young man became a moving terror and a prolific killer. Eventually it was rumored that he was sent to Russia to study Marxism. No one had done more terrible damage to the youth organizations than Thomas.

From the mass media stories I heard, the EPRP-instigated assassinations continued unabated, although some of the media claims seemed dubious. Some of these were high-profile assassinations that were attributed to EPRP but probably were the settling of scores among the pro-government organizations themselves. It should be noted that soon after Meison also became a target of these killings by other pro-government cadres.

In the USA, while working in Tennessee I once met a woman named Haimanot Kassaye (now deceased from some kind of stomach cancer). Haimnot was a deeply religious woman who belonged to the Pentecostal Church in Nashville. She lived with her younger brother. In their apartment they had a big-sized picture of their father who was assassinated in Addis. Haimnot, it seemed, was traumatized by the death of her father. She used to tell me that she thought her father was still alive and could talk to her. She said, "I never think he is dead when I see his picture and talk to him." I sympathized with her plight and trauma. Her father, Col. Kassaye Mandefero, was a senior police officer and was also a governor of Keffa Province at one point. He had studied in the United States and seemed destined to rise through the ranks in the Ethiopian police force.

One day, while driving a car with his son on the passenger side, the colonel's car was stopped by a dump truck. After the car was stopped, people in military uniform got out and riddled the colonel's body with bullets. The son, on the passenger's side, was not touched. The assassins left. The government blamed EPRP and hastily buried the officer in a military ceremony that might have been attended by some Derg members.

Haimanot showed me an *Addis Zemen* article that featured her father. The paper talked about "Comrade Kassye," his contributions to the revolution, and how his life was cut short by "EPRP's hired assassins."

I always had some suspicion that the colonel was assassinated by EPRP, but when I read the newspaper article I was sure that EPRP had nothing to do with it. For one thing, EPRP's people could not have left the son untouched. This was clean professional work, not the messy EPRP assassinations that were usually undertaken by a lone young man with pistols. I told Haimanot that I did not believe EPRP killed her dad, and she said that she had heard rumors that this was an inside job, but it did not matter who did it as far as she was concerned. She said that they rushed the burial and the family did not get the details about what went on. Her mother might have had some ideas, but it appears the children did not. But it looked like such killings took place and were deliberately attributed to EPRP, but were clearly beyond EPRP's military capability. There were some months in the summer of 1976 when we read daily assassinations of what the official media called "revolutionary comrades." The thrust of the party's activity was now centered on these assassinations. It was amazing that these went on in spite of the terrible loss they were exacting on the members of the party itself. These assassinations were often followed by wholesale arrests of the youth in the areas where the killings took place. That usually meant some members of the party or sympathizers were inevitably arrested. Innocent people and bystanders were also affected. These actions now began to affect the morale of the youth, which supported the party with an unusual zealotry.

The government's effort at depicting these assassinations as the work of hired guns was beginning to be believed by the Ethiopian people as well. Many of the *kebele* leaders that were now being killed were heads of family households who would be survived by their wives and children. The propaganda machine depicted the killers as inhuman beasts who did not care for human lives. This propaganda, coming from the most murderous regime in the world after the Khmer Rouge, seemed meaningless, but it was beginning to have its effect on the morale of the people. People now doubted whether EPRP was what it purported to be. Some of these *kebele* leaders who fell victim were probably innocent individuals who had to do what they were ordered to do. They also helped abate the excess of the actions that the cadres wanted them to take. But they nevertheless fell victim, and these actions made EPRP look as bad as the government itself.

It was clear that this mini-war of terror and counterterror was a full-fledged civil war in Addis. Like any civil war, it separated family members from one another. There were brothers or sisters who fought for different sides. There were children of the *kebele* chairpersons who remained on EPRP's side while their parents had to do the dirty work of the government. This war really became so ugly, with brother killing brother and parents arresting their own children. All the seeds of a society in degeneration that we witnessed during the years of Derg's rule, I believe, were now being planted at this time.

To counter the successful propaganda of the Derg, EPRP units began to raid *tej bet* (liquor house) and movie theaters and to address the public. Units of EPRP, in groups of two or three, would take over a public place like this and tell the people what the party stood for and what the government stood for. This was most common in the Merkato areas. It is doubtful that this had any propaganda value whatsoever, other than stirring up an already intoxicated patron, but it seemed to inspire most EPRP members. We talked about these anecdotes when we chewed *khat*. After one of these "armed propaganda" sessions, one of the *tej bet* patrons is said to have remarked, "It is the first time in a long time I had *tej* made of pure honey." He was speaking in metaphor, an overvalued and overused style in Amharic language. Apparently he was satisfied with the propaganda. I was always impressed with the dedication of these young people who never ceased to take risky actions for the party.

This so-called armed propaganda took place many times in one *kebele* in Tekle Haimanot, an EPRP stronghold. This was the place where I used to meet Mezy and Birhanu. This was the place where most of the cash from the bank robbery made it. This was the place where some of EPRP's most successful units were stationed and operated from. Armed propaganda was conducted here many times. According to Birhanu, hooded armed youth would stand in the dark with a microphone and talk about the party. Other units would be stationed at key entry points to deter any effort by the government to enter the area. In retrospect, these never made sense except for identifying the area as the most dangerous area to the government. The government moved en force into these areas very late. When Tekle Haimanot, Adre Sefer, and some key areas in Merkato were successfully invaded by the government, all EPRP's armed activities ceased. It was the end of the game.

One day one of these propaganda units took over Cinema Ras, controlled the door, and spoke to the patrons. The person who addressed the audience was a young lady, who according to the person who heard it was fearless and impressive. For some reason, I thought it was Mezy who did that. I was not sure what she was doing then, but suspected she may be involved at some level in these party activities. When I next met her I mentioned the story of the armed propaganda and added, "You know, the person who spoke is a female." I tried to see how she reacted. She told me she had heard about it and was very buoyant about these activities. Then I said, "I think it is you who did that." Her response was the most surprising and the most honest I have heard from her. In a very frank and somber tone, she said, "I don't hate my life that much to do that." That was the most frank admission that she was having doubts about the activities of EPRP. I also noticed in her a strong instinct of self-preservation. She did not seem prepared to die needlessly. She and Birhanu had a daughter living with Mezy's parents in Dessie, who was very much in Mezy's mind. I noticed she wanted to survive, if not for anybody but for her daughter, who had never experienced the presence of her biological parents for any extended period. That was just like me. Neither of us was ready to die.

One morning I was sitting in a room behind the store that my second cousin owned, reading or just passing the time. Mezy sometimes used to come here and we would talk and have *khat*. It was in the morning and she looked extremely depressed. She now wore all sorts of shabby dresses and looked like a maid or a poor woman. With her youthful face and clever disguise, I never thought Mezy would ever be captured unless somebody told on her. She lived and slept in an old lady's small house somewhere in Merkato. She looked very pitiful and it always broke my heart to see her in that condition. After a long silence, I asked how she was doing. Then I asked if she had heard news from Birhanu or if he was coming to town. I knew he had been back many times, but has not returned for a long time now. She burst into tears and started crying softly for a long, long time. I suspected something was wrong. She said that she was told that Birhanu was killed in Sidamo. She may have said Birhanu was "martyred."

I realized she had been crying all night so that her eyes were swollen and her cheeks were inflamed. I deeply felt sorry for her. It was obvious that the tragedy had now hit home. Many people in leadership positions were now dying at frequent intervals and that death was everywhere. Arabu, with whom she was good friends, had died. But this was her husband and the man she had rescued from death. This was the father of her daughter, Martha. Tears were rolling down her cheeks. I did not cry. I tried to console her but decided otherwise. Nothing I could say would reach the depths of her heart and make it not painful. She was hurting inside and outside, and was in deep pain. I let her cry. I thought about how I had introduced these two lovers who from the start were star-crossed. I thought about how my life had been so unwillingly intertwined with theirs and that we all now seemed doomed. I thought a great deal while she quietly and profusely wept, sitting on a bed in front of me.

I asked her what was said about his death. She said, "I am getting conflicting stories about it. One story says that he was caught in Kibre Mengist while waiting to meet a comrade. When he realized that it was a trap and had no hope of getting out, he tried to run and was shot and killed from behind. The other story said that he was taken to prison. He died in prison from cyanide pills, an apparent suicide." She seemed doubtful about the veracity of either of the stories. She was angry that the party could not tell her what exactly happened. She was also angry that they would let him die like that in a hopeless situation. She said that the last time she talked to him on the phone, he had given up about the work he was doing in the area. It was unfortunate that he could not extricate himself away from it.

Mezy had a strong suspicion that his death was caused by the factional struggle in the party. At that time every mishap the party experienced was being attributed to the factional elements. We decided to meet at my second aunt's home the next day and split up.

At this time again started another round of rumors of a power struggle within the Derg, this time between Col. Atnafu Abate, the vice chairman in the Derg, and Mengistu, who was the chairman and the all-powerful dictator. Atanafu, it was said, was disgusted by the bloody turn of events and by the generalized atmosphere of fear in the country. He was opposed to the call for independent action by the *kebele* leaders and the newly reorganized trade union leaders. At the same time, people were talking about massive diggings at the outskirts of the city. Nobody knew what they were for, but people thought they may be used as grave sites for mass burials. Whatever it was, though, there were ominous signs of mass destruction that was going to be unleashed.

Meison and the other left groups aligned with the Derg spoke about the bureaucracy being in cahoots with the enemy. The bureaucracy category encompassed a large group that often included the opposition to the Derg, like Atnafu Abate and others who voiced some misgivings about the direction of the revolution at one time or another and some civil servants. The groups claimed that the bureaucracy was scheming to reverse the gains of the revolution by stifling the "revolutionary actions" of the masses. Among many things, they accused that the so-called bureaucracy was releasing prisoners. They called for the summary execution of prisoners lest the bureaucracy let them out into the streets to assassinate the "genuine revolutionaries."

Of all the things I remember about the Ethiopian revolution and the individuals that took part in it, none has disturbed me as much as this one.

Sometime after the first *assessa* there was a concerted propaganda campaign by the pro-government groups calling on the government to stop feeding prisoners. A series of newspaper articles and radio and TV commentaries spoke about why the government should not feed anarchists and other prisoners, and instead get rid of them. Every time I read such stories I felt enormously angry and hateful toward these people. What they were advocating at this time was a wholesale slaughter of all prisoners that were suspected of being EPRP members. It was not because they were actually costing the government money for food—their relatives fed them for the most part—it was because they wanted to see all these people, who were powerless to do anything in or out, dead.

I used to say that I wish the commentators argued for hard labor, for removing prisoners from the city, or some other harsher prison terms, but not call for the death of these young people. But what these pro-Derg groups wanted was the slaughter of young people who were incarcerated simply because they suspected that the bureaucracy would release them. I always remember reading this with my blood curdling and thinking where in the world these people came from. After EPRP became politically bankrupt, I thought the political line of Meison's made much more sense than EPRP's. I thought Meison's leadership was smarter in preserving its people, although in the end Meison made the same mistakes that EPRP did in prematurely confronting Mengistu. For this they tested the ruthless hands of Mengistu, whom they had supported in battling EPRP. But when it came to caring for human life, they behaved no less brutally than the worst of the Derg cadres.

It was often said that most of the leaders of EPRP, Meison, Woz League, etc. did their studies in the United States and Europe and knew each other very well. It was clear that the personality conflicts and the differences in the style of leadership emerged while they were outside. These differences, I thought, were benign enough not to cause irreparable damage to one another. But once these differences were imported to Ethiopia and manifested in different organizations, they became not only irreconcilable but also deadly. Now they were out to destroy one another, and in the process destroy anyone aligned with them. I have never been able to understand the ferocity of the hatred that these leaders displayed toward each other. This hatred was couched in the name of love for the Ethiopian people. All claimed to fight for the cause of the Ethiopian people, the poor, the oppressed. All claimed socialism and Marxism-Leninism as their ideology, but all were hell-bent on destroying one another in the name of the people.

Just recently I read a fine book about Meison's story by Andargachew Asseged. Andargachew makes a credible case against EPRP's leadership for initiating this homicidal behavior. He argues that EPRP was the one that started the murderous rampage with the assassination of Fikre Merid. When I came to America, I asked Andreas Eshete about Fikre Merid. He painted to me not only a capable intellectual, but also a decent human being. I don't know who did this and who was responsible for this decision, but EPRP's leadership can't extricate itself from this crime, and for this there would be question marks on their character, humanity; an albatross on their neck that they would not ever be able to get rid of. What makes it all the more incomprehensible was that it happened before EPRP came under any really serious threat. It happened when its leadership could sit down in relative peace and chart out the course of its actions. It happened before the full weight of the Red Terror. I am sure EPRP has its own explanations for this. One could even argue the killing of EPRP members preceded Fikre Merid's death. However, it will be extraordinarily difficult to establish Fikre Merid had anything to do with the murder of any EPRP member to justify his assassination by EPRP.

I have tried to imagine if some of what happened really was inevitable, or maybe if in any way even rationally, if not morally, explainable given the type of struggle that was waged. Clandestine armed and political activity reinforced misunderstandings between enemies and elevated them to mutual hatred. The conflict transformed itself into a fundamental issue of who lives and who dies since the existence of one group was seen as the negation of the other. But why one would want to destroy incarcerated political prisoners, I have never been able to understand.

THE BEGINNING
OF THE END

After I returned from Debre Zeit, I received another assignment from the party, as usual through the insistence of Wolde Ab. Wolde Ab, Jale Bia, Berhane, and I met most of the time in the house that Jale Bia was staying in. Berhane was now fully rehabilitated, thanks to Jale Bia and Wolde Abe, and was active in party activities. The house was in Adre Sefer. This was the place where we often met and rested in between party responsibilities. It provided relative security in the sense that we could see what was happening before danger came our way. We had escape routes at the back, and we had dug holes in the backyard to hide pistols and party documents. This place was untouched until the height of the Red Terror, sometime before which Jale Bia ostensibly left for a rural area in Shoa. I don't know if he left on his own or his departure was arranged by the party. I never thought that the poet, skinny and underweight as he was, would ever survive hardships. He was a very tiny human being whose facial bones protruded and looked every bit as famine stricken as a starving peasant's. He never survived rural Ethiopia. To this day, I don't know if he died a natural death or was killed by the government.

My newest responsibility was zone propaganda. I was a member of a zone committee of four individuals. One member chaired the zone organization and was our interface with the interzone committee. One member represented the armed unit. I don't know what the third person represented. I was responsible for secretarial responsibilities such as taking minutes, and also preparing agitation materials for this particular zone. Nobody mentioned what geographical areas our zone covered. Nor did I care to find out.

The chairman of the committee, an engineering student, was one of the ablest revolutionaries I ever met. He had a unique feature in that his front upper teeth protruded. He spoke Amharic with a Tigrigna accent, but he spoke it as well as anybody. He was also exceptionally fluent in English, and by all measures, seemed to be extremely bright and talented. I thought he was as intelligent as any person I have met in the party, although he was more serious minded and not given to any humor.

Our first meeting was in Senga Terra, somewhere near Wolde Ab's parents' house. This house probably belonged to a party member with a legal job who was allowing it to be used for such activities. But then, he may not even know this. While we were in session here, there was a knock at the door. We cleared the table and the chairperson opened the door. It was an employee of the Ethiopian Electric Company registering the meter reading. He did so and left. We all were nervous about what happened. Given the tension of the times, no one could have given an explanation for the presence of four young people in a one-room place other than for clandestine activities. And who knows who this guy could be. He could be a member of another organization. We completed the meeting that day, but agreed not to meet here another time. Later, I learned that the house was taken over by the *kebele* and the person who lived in it was arrested. We winged this one, but sadly a party member with a legal cover was put in serious jeopardy again.

Our next meeting took place in another one-room place across the engineering school. I have never been to a more exposed place before. We met here during the day and conducted party business a few times. This went on for a couple of months and I prepared a couple of monthly reports about our activities for the zone committee. The chair remarked that the report indicated that we have been more productive than he thought we were. He liked my report and I was very pleased.

However, the chair was very critical of my propaganda pieces. He said that it was full of hyperbole and needed to be made simpler. His criticism was on the mark and correct. No one had criticized my writing before to me. Although my ego was a little bruised, what he said made sense. He often radically edited what I wrote before it was printed. He also wrote some of the issues himself. I noticed what he wrote was more detailed, contained more relevant information, and was more analytical. He wrote in a matter-of-fact tone that was dry for a propaganda piece, but was always to the point. He seemed to do it effortlessly while I agonized over what word to use and how to make it appealing.

I told Wolde Ab, who knew this guy and probably worked with him at another level, how impressed I was. He was highly disciplined, did not drink or chew *khat*. He seemed also an indefatigable worker who had more meetings than anybody I knew. He was punctual and was very neat. On the other hand, the guy who was in the armed wing was very different. He often wore an army jacket, which itself betrayed his identity. I thought he wore the army coat to hide his gun, which I suspected he carried. I could tell he *chewed* khat, smoked heavily, and was the archetypal EPRP member.

The third guy was a middle-class type with a very peculiar voice, who probably was a student in the university. He was clean-shaven, wore nice suits, and wrote very well.

One day, the chairman and the armed-wing guy said that they had circumstantial evidence that made them suspect the third guy to be a member of the *anja* (faction). The chair said that the three of us needed to discuss that and confront him. He provided evidence that purported he had seen him many times in areas where the chair met other party members. There were also rumors of his associations with suspected members of the *anja*. Since these meetings were arranged by a code, seeing him in those places did not seem to him to be coincidental. He said once or twice was coincidental, but it was showing a pattern that made him uneasy. The guy in the armed wing also said he had his own suspicions and offered more circumstantial evidence. I was puzzled. I did not suspect he was, but then these things never interested me.

What the third member was suspected of was a serious crime in the party at that time and he could be killed for it. Many others had lost their lives because they were suspected of belonging to the *anja* even though they had not done anything harmful to the party. The party was now conducting war on its own members as well as on the government. Party units were taking drastic actions against suspects without examining the facts. Again, underground work would not allow the full examination of these allegations and taking only those measures commensurate with the crime. Instead, many resorted to killings. Even if one looks charitably at EPRP for the "justifiable self-defense" against *kebele* members and government-associated cadres, it was now clear that the party had begun to slowly degenerate to the level of its enemies, even by its own standards, in its callous disregard for human lives when people were considered to be internal enemies.

In our committee, I argued that what was said was very circumstantial and could not be used against him for any purpose. I said in the prevailing circumstances EPRP meetings were taking place in only a few areas that were considered safe, and people may be spending their leisure time in these areas too. We decided not to confront him but also not tell him sensitive party information. He stayed in the committee, but we agreed to keep an eye on him and not tell him anything other than what he needed to know for his responsibility.

What happened to *anja* suspects probably depended on the particular committee composition they were in and who they knew in the party. Probably *anja* suspects in the armed wing were much more harshly and summarily dealt with than in other units. Military activity may have required that level of decisiveness, but given the conditions that prevailed, such suspicion only led to one thing: summary executions of suspects. EPRP's armed units were not necessarily the most disciplined and the most ideologically or intellectually mature of the members. Many, especially in the youth wing, included lumpen elements with criminal tendencies. They were carrying weapons, including automatic weapons, without the appropriate training. This may account for a lot of the destructiveness and callousness displayed in the party, especially toward the end.

I became aware of these fundamental weaknesses in the armed wing toward the end of the game. Two incidents especially changed my attitude. One was the arrest of one of the most famous of EPRP fighters about whom I had come to learn a lot from others. This individual took part in a bank robbery, in the attempted assassination of Mengistu, and in a number of other operations. Mohamed Arabi, who used to stay in the same house, told me that this guy's units raided *kebele* for weapons and took action against some of the most feared *kebele* leaders. He was active almost every day and night and was a great inspiration to people like Mohammed Arabi.

When he was captured, he turned out to be one of the most destructive party members of EPRP. First, he exposed one of the most secure party houses in Tekle Haimanot. He also led to the arrest of many of his comrades, including a young woman who delivered food for him. He turned out to be more destructive than useful to the party. I took notes of this guy about whose courage I heard a lot in the beginning, and who after his arrest became the most treacherous person in the party. When I heard about this, I thanked myself for refusing the party's frequent request to become a political cadre to EPRA fighters.

The second incident that sort of amazed me came late in the Red Terror after I escaped from prison. There was a big shootout and one of EPRP's squad leaders was killed. The government declared that he was a notorious *magerat mechi* who terrorized the neighborhoods. I dismissed that as typical of the government's notorious lies. However, Mohamed's sister, who knew and admired him, told me what he used to be. He was a well-known *magerat mechi* before he was recruited by EPRP for urban guerilla warfare. He was notorious in the neighborhood for his ruthlessness against prostitutes. That was not to say he was not changed once he became a party member. I remember reading in *Fanshen: A Documentary of Revolution in a Chinese Village* about murderers who once they became Communist Party members turned out to be great Communists who "selflessly" served the people. This guy may have turned out to be a genuinely converted party member without a trace of his criminal past. But I was never convinced that was the case.

To his credit, though, he died resisting arrest and did not cause any further damage. But I was told that some women in the area celebrated his death when they heard it on the radio.

EPRP's armed activity, whether intended to resist terror of the government or to be the main form of the struggle, was ill-advised and wrong. It never had any chance against well-armed, well-organized mass groups that had now become the lever of power for the government. The party had the right instinct in fearing the first *assessa*. Its problem was in refusing to devise its political struggle reflecting these changed realities. The first *assessa* amply demonstrated what the government's intentions and its capabilities were.

Some people have given the decimation of its most experienced leaders as the reason for the party's persistence in this self-destructive route. It was clear that the *anjas* had the more realistic grasp of what the party faced. But the *anja* line was probably never discussed as an option. Instead, that line was equated with treason, and the members who advocated for it as treasonous.

Fighting the regime with force in Addis was now de facto the party's main form of struggle. There was no other political or economic form of struggle. The trade unions had been pretty much cleaned of the party sympathizers. The *kebele*, the chief locus of political control, had by now for the most party fallen under government control. A few EPRP members or sympathizers were left who still controlled some *kebele* leadership positions, though clandestinely. But the higher *kebeles* were now completely anti-EPRP, and these were the associations that were taking the initiative in plucking out EPRP people from every neighborhood in this big urban jungle. So the only thing the party felt it could do was challenge this monster with its minuscule armed power.

EPRP actions consisted for the most part of graffiti work and assassinations. Both of these actions were exacting a huge toll on members. Once graffiti was painted in a neighborhood the area became a target of the *kebeles*. It demonstrated defiance, but it became as useless as the armed propaganda effort in the beginning. It only marked the *kebele* for government suppression.

Following the Ethiopian New year in 1977, a massive effort to arrest the youth and destroy EPRP started. The government knew that the only active part of EPRP was now the youth, and if it could crush the youth, it could crush EPRP. The Red Terror was in full swing. The *kebeles* turned into huge concentration camps with torture chambers. Following the death of Lt. Colonel Atnafu Abate on November 13, 1977, "independent action" of the *kebeles* became the order of the day. The operative word now was "exposing" (*magalete*) with a massive number of youth exposing other youth of association with EPRP; mass arrests now became universal. Many of them were exposed for one crime or another and murdered. Their bodies were thrown on the streets.

Others managed to become new and converted cadres of the government. They became brazen zealots who would not spare anything to demonstrate their new loyalty. EPRP members appeared en masse on TV and began to tell its crimes to a believing public. Parents gave up their children in hope of lenient treatment. The Ethiopian youth, the backbone of EPRP, was now in the camp of the enemy. Others who refused to betray their friends or who could not make the right connections with powerful cadres simply perished.

The youth of EPRP became the torturer of EPRP. This was a spectacle. I think this probably explains the deep-seated animosity that people had developed toward the party since it was destroyed. Some former party members became unbelievable killers and torturers. Former party members exceeded one another in their cruelty to their former comrades. Toward the end of 1977, EPRP was fully suppressed. The youth, its mainstay, was spiritually crushed and became a spent force. Now the regime, for the first time, had the Ethiopian youth under its wing. EPRP was relegated to the dustbin of history.

While this was happening, I asked Mezy what the party was planning to do to combat this massive onslaught of terror. To my surprise, she said that the party structure was still intact. What was destroyed, she said, was the youth wing. She said the party was planning to attack the *kebele* on a "brigade" level. This higher form of military organization, from her explanation, meant using a number of squads on a single attack. I asked in amazement, "Can we do that?" She said this had been successfully attempted at one *kebele* in Merkato. I had heard of an unsuccessful attack on a *kebele* in Merkato. I wondered if that was at all possible and questioned how something like that could be pulled off in the prevailing atmosphere. I always wondered where these fighters go back to once the mission was "accomplished" or merely attempted. There were few houses left even to sleep in, let alone station armed people.

I do not believe now EPRP would have succeeded one way or another. The *anja* line would have preserved the party's human resources and caused less loss of life. If another political line could have succeeded, Meison should have. But as a group they were never meant to succeed as long as they challenged Mingestu for political power.

Ethiopia was heading to be a Marxist state once Mengistu realized the value of it for holding power. He learned a lot of what needed to be learned to establish a Marxist state power. What he could not learn for lack of time, he had others to help him with. There was no room for a second or a different brand of Marxism. There was no need for it. There was a Marxist school; there was a swarming of Marxist cadres; and there was the international Marxist connection. Those who failed to see that like EPRP and later Meison and others, have never understood the history of Marxism in the Soviet Union. Marxism is primarily a tool for maintaining state power effectively and ruthlessly. Mengistu instinctively knew that. The Meisons, who thought that they would be able to build this state machinery stealthily, working under the regime and then take it away from the regime, were setting themselves up for a rude awakening.

No one could ever have toppled Mengistu by saying Mengistu was not Marxist enough, or his was not a true socialist government. That people believed in this up to 1980 was foolish enough, but anyone who persisted in this after 1980 was insane. In the end, it was not the Marxists who overthrew him, but the so-called nationalists. It was the dogged persistence of the Eritrean nationalists aligned with TPLF who carefully and systematically undermined Mengistu's hold on power. With his huge army tied in Eritrea and his Marxist policy bankrupt inside the country, Mengistu's hold on power was successfully chipped away over many years. This internal erosion of power was given a powerful boost by the international debacle of the Soviet Union and its empire. With his external resources cut and his huge army bleeding over a large part of the north, the groups who were ethno-nationalists in their outlook and Marxists in their organizational structure assumed power as the old Stalinist order simply imploded.

One day, I was having lunch at my second cousin's house. The night before, there was a big gunfight that lasted for hours in Aboare Sefer. My aunt surmised the fight was in the palace, and she had never heard anything like it. I don't remember where I slept, but I had not heard the shootout. But it was one of the heaviest that the city had experienced. I had finished lunch and was getting ready to leave when the afternoon Amharic news came. In a short cryptic news article, it declared, "Four heavily armed and fortified anarchists have been destroyed after they refused to give up and opened fire." The announcer listed their names and said that one of them was called Wolde Ab according to his driver's license. I felt numb. I left my aunt's house abruptly and called Berhane on the phone. He said that house was suspected of being exposed and they should not have had any meeting there. Here, somebody I knew and respected had just died, and I could barely show any emotion. I don't even know how I felt. I did not internalize the news. I did not cry. I did not agonize. I showed no emotion. It was very strange how we were taking these loses of human lives without any expression of grief. People don't cry except when their loved ones or immediate relatives were affected.

It felt bizarre. We lived in a strange world, and our senses had gotten numb from these endless deaths of people we knew and cared about.

I was closer to Wolde Ab and Jale Bia than Mezy and Berhane at that time. We shared a lot of time, laughs, and tribulations together. We drank and gossiped. Both of these two were some of the nicest human beings I ever knew. They loved life, and they cared for human life. They both wanted me to leave Addis for my safety. I refused. Wolde Ab, on the other hand, wanted to leave Addis but was refused by the party. There was an attempt on his life. He was of Eritrean descent and was known by many people in Meison and other leftist groups. He was aware of his situation and wanted to leave Addis. I don't know who the guy responsible for this was, but his request was refused, and Wolde Ab, being an honest party member, obliged.

Three days later, when I saw his picture in the house we sometimes stayed in, in Adre Sefer, I cried. It was the first time I cried in a long time in Addis. This revolution had become a meaningless carnage. People were quietly dying when it was obvious the odds were overwhelmingly against the struggle we were waging. People smarter and more intelligent than I were dying for EPRP, and it did not make sense.

My ID was produced in the *kebele* that Wolde Abe and his comrades laid their lives at. Soon the entire *kebele* leadership was arrested and the area cleaned of EPRP members. Carrying that ID card was now dangerous and I was told to get another one.

The next time I met Mezy at the back of the store just before the end of 1977, she was preparing to go to Assimba. We talked about Wolde Ab and how he had disregarded the information about the house. I mentioned to her that if he had his way, he would have been in Assimba. Her plan was to go through Dessie, visit her daughter, and leave. She was spending what I felt was more money than appropriate buying clothes for her daughter, but I did not say anything. She also gave me the impression that her departure date was a little bit far off. We scheduled to meet at my second cousin's house and departed. The next time we met was in the United States in 1981.

I was puzzled by Mezy's abrupt departure. Unlike Wolde Ab, I was offered the opportunity to go to Assimba but I had refused. Assimba turned out to be a good escape route to America, but at that time nobody knew it. If I had known that the place was safe and that I would have had a better chance of survival there, I would have left months before. I did not know. What I knew was that it was the base of operation for EPRA, and as such would be the next target of the government. I expected a lot more bloodshed in Assimba than in Addis, although under a more favorable atmosphere for the party people. But from what I came to hear, it was safer until the fateful clash with TPLF. After my arrival in Djibouti, when I heard that EPRP was decisively beaten by TPLF, I could not believe what I heard. I had heard that elements of TPLF were harassing EPRP units and the conflict between the two was getting uglier and uglier. But we all thought TPLF was a minuscule army that was no match for our EPRA. But then we had no way of knowing what was happening in Assimba except the occasional news information in the EPRA newsletter, which proved to be grossly inaccurate.

Mohammed Arabi, on the other hand, opposed my going to Assimba. He jokingly made the statement that Assimba is not a refugee for people who want to run away from the real struggle. He believed the real struggle was taking place in Addis at that time. According to him, if one had to go to Assimba, it must be to fight and not to escape death in Addis. His was a more honest and consistent statement. The struggle in Addis had ceased to be a struggle at that time; it was suicide. It would have made sense for the party to get as many people as possible out. Most of them would have probably fought better in Tigray, or that not happening, they would have escaped the carnage in Addis, later in Gondar.

The chairman of our committee one morning failed to show up for one of our scheduled meetings. Days later the guy we suspected of membership in the *anja* told me that he had been arrested. I suspected it was in the house where we used to meet. I was sorry for this guy for whom I had developed enormous respect, both as an intellectual and as a revolutionary. After I knew him, I felt people like him in EPRP were not that many. He must have been irreplaceable. Now we got a new chair, a lady who I came to know went to school in the United States. We decided to have our first meeting on Churchill Road and discuss the party business while walking down to the Revolutionary Square, then known as Meskel Square. The four of us were to meet in groups of two and walk at some distance from each other. I was told to walk with her and switch to the "squad member," and then finally with the guy suspected of being in the *anja*.

When I met her, the new chair was extremely calm. She was covered from head to toe and dressed like an *Adere* woman. First we talked about my ID card situation. She asked me to give her my picture and that she would get me a different one from the *kebele* where she lived. The chairman of this *keble* representing Piassa area was apparently an EPRP member and she lived in the chairman's house. She was confident she would do it. Then we started to discuss propaganda and politics. She said that we needed to write about members who are now incarcerated and tortured but had not been broken down. She said that we must extol the spirit of these members so others could learn something from it. She was calm and businesslike. She was talking about these things when we did not have even a place to meet at all.

I have never forgotten this brief conversation I had with her. To begin with, walking with her at that time at the height of the Red Terror was one of the highest risks I have taken in my life. That outfit she wore was already identified as the preferred dress of "female anarchists." This woman who was in mortal danger for her life was talking about doing some propaganda work when the most we could do was meet on a roadside. I expected her to say that we stop these activities for now and preserve our human resources. After all, this was after Atnafu was killed and there was massive detention of young people all over the city, and EPRP was pretty much crushed. To me, it was obvious EPRP was permanently crippled. But this obviously smart, well-educated party leader either did not want to see that or refused to give in to the government's terror.

I was impressed by her courage. I kept thinking that these people were made from stuff different from mine. I could not believe how calmly resigned they were to their fate and to the fate of the party. I walked with her until the national bank and briefly switched with the "squad member." He was wearing his usual army jacket, and I was really scared to be seen anywhere near him. I don't know why he had to look so obvious and so different. Walking with him was extremely uncomfortable. Finally he said that he had another meeting to attend to and broke away from me. The lady went her own way and I and the *anja* suspect started to walk up Churchill Road on the opposite side we came from.

We walked leisurely. We both looked well-dressed and clean-shaven. Neither of us looked different from the usual crowd of office and government workers. We talked about the party, and I must have told him if it was not time to cease all these activities and just send people out to the EPRA base areas. Just when we reached Tewodros Adebaby, we heard machine-gun fire. I said this sounded like an assassination and was probably by EPRP. It came from the direction we had left fifteen minutes earlier. I said to myself maybe the guy who was walking with us was involved in this shooting. It was a wild guess. Maybe he left me for this assignment. We both agreed that it sounded like assassination. EPRP had almost ceased shooting. Could it be the beginning of another cycle? We made an appointment to meet and parted.

When we met the next time, he told me that the young woman who served as the chair of our committee was killed along with the *kebele* leaders the night I gave her my picture. I don't remember if he said she committed suicide or was killed in a shootout. That *kebele* was now destroyed. This was the same *kebele* in the vicinity of which I was later arrested. Since the *kebele* was deemed unreliable, another *kebele* was going to come and conduct the *assessa*. I felt sorry for this brave young woman who only a few days before was talking about the spirit of EPRP members under duress. She was very much like those people she described. I could have written about her and the many others who were now bravely facing death at the hands of a ruthless and better organized enemy. But what sense does it make? One is a hero only when one's cause has prevailed. She was now gone. I thought about my picture, but dismissed it as an irrelevant problem compared to what happened to the life of that woman.

Then my "comrade" who we suspected to be in the *anja* told me about the shootout we heard. He said that involved the squad leader who had walked with me briefly before he left for his appointment. According to the story he had, he was caught while walking by a squad of armed people driving in a van. They surprised him, so he was not able to react. They had him lean on the wall of the national bank with his face toward the wall. He was shot from behind with a machine gun in full view of the public. This was one of the few times time I ever heard of a killing of this kind. Normally what they do is take the captured person to *kebele* prison. It was after they had tortured the individual for more information, names of accomplices, that the killing took place. Sometimes, if the person resists, they kill him or her on the spot. This story was unique in that it did not fit the pattern. But then, anything was possible at that time.

There were now only two of us left in the committee. He said he would try to reestablish contact with the higher committees, get me a different ID card, and also get me some money. Now I thought only about getting my ID card straight and completely cease party activity. I now realized that the situation was hopeless. It was a matter of time before I died or got caught. I feared for my life.

While all this was happening to the committee members, it never occurred to me to suspect this guy of having something to do with what was happening. Long after I left the country, I wondered if it was just coincidental that all three of them were caught or killed. I never knew what happened to him. The night before I was scheduled to meet him, I was caught red-handed. Our meeting was to be in Addis Hotel in Merkato. I never made it there.

Every time I went to occasions in America where former EPRP members attended, I sought hard to find this guy, whose real name I don't know. The truth is I have also forgotten his underground name. But I remember his face, size, and specially his peculiar voice. I often wondered if he died or made it to Assimba. Sometimes I also wondered if he really betrayed the party and exposed the three of them, since I was convinced he had no hand in what happened to me. Who knows what happened. Who would ever know? But I sure want to talk to him one day if perchance he is still alive and I get the opportunity to meet.

Watching the movie *Anzio* after I came to America, I heard a quote of Napoleon, who said, "A general who worries too much about his men is doomed to failure." Whether EPRP leadership heard of this or not, it lived up to this military maxim to a fault. Any consideration of what happens to the security of the members seemed foreign to them. Birhanu used to tell me, "Mafia (EPRP) never worried about human life." He said if the Vietnamese did a cost benefit analysis of the amount of space they liberated over the number of people they had to sacrifice, they would never have won over America. Some military objectives are so crucial that a consideration of the loss of human lives cannot be factored in the decision to take them. Vietnam was, of course, the party's fighting model. Even the party's fighting song, which would have been its national anthem, had a Vietnamese tune. No wonder it was so difficult to memorize and sing. Only the most dedicated members with some level of education learned to sing it.

Some of the words were:

For ages I have lived in the abyss of an oppressive system
Chained in cruelty
But now, to establish my right and crush the oppressor
I have revolted and risen up in arms.
I am the champion of the masses
I am the soldier of the working class
I have taken up arms,
I am determined to fight
The enemy shall run in terror
The opportunist shall be crushed.

We learned this one night after I and my friends became party members. We sang it in unison again and again until we had the words and the tune committed to memory.

With a leadership determined to win at any cost, the loss of human lives was staggering. But the party lived by this Napoleonic maxim. There was no tradition in the party for preserving the life of individuals. However, to their credit, the first group of leaders also never tried to preserve its own life. In that sense the party leadership that perished in the urban jungle of Addis had enormous integrity. One can criticize their judgment and leadership qualities, but most never run for their lives while leaving their army in battle.

I think the party has a lot to answer for the way it handled the factional strife within. It was in this area the party probably degenerated to the level of its enemies. Maybe it is easier for me to say that I was never a committed party member. However, there is no denying the fact that people were killed in the party because of circumstantial evidence of antiparty activity. Many of these people perished without a place to stay and home to live in. And many may have just given up to the government to salvage their lives.

Could the party have treated the *anjas* differently than it did? Every time I answer this question, I realize that I am not the best person to judge that. For a long time now I have said that EPRP was the wrong organization for me and the wrong political organization for the country too. I have often wondered if it was any different from Meison, Woz League, or the others. And my answer to this has been that it was not to a very meaningful degree.

The way I have chosen to deal with EPRP is to separate the organization from the individuals, which in effect meant from the individuals I knew. I have said the organization was a lot less than the sum of its constituent parts, its membership. This argument probably does not take me too far. This may be somewhat of a heroic attempt to exonerate me and the people I knew from the crimes of the party. I don't know if I or anyone can do that.

After I left Ethiopia, I often felt that I had come out of my past connections with EPRP relatively guiltless. I had never recruited anyone to join the party; I have never caused the death of anyone. Most importantly, when I was arrested I did not cause the arrest of anyone associated with the party. I felt very happy about that. Of course, I was lucky in that I was never put to extreme test through torture. I could not say what I would have done under such circumstances. In fact, nobody could. So my story had a good ending for me and my family in that I did not lose my life. I thank God for being alive and able to tell these stories.

Nevertheless, I had gone a little bit too far in distancing myself from the crimes of the party. I had forgotten my guilt, if nothing else, by association. I worked briefly with a party committee in Debre Zeit. Later this group decided to take action against the *kebele* leaders, in which lives were lost, although I was not in attendance when the decision was made. I could never forget that a poor, innocent woman, not to mention *kebele* leaders whose crime I could not corroborate, was murdered through no fault of hers. I could not have stopped it, but that does not make me clean of the action. But still, my conscience was unjustifiably clear on my past association with the party until a friend in America straightened me up one day. He said, "You may have come out relatively clean, but there is no way you should think better of yourself than the others." He said, "I am lucky I spent those years outside the country (in another African country). There was no telling what I could have done if I were in Addis and had to fulfill my party responsibility." It is like saying but for the grace of God it could have been me who killed *kebele* leaders, *anjas*, or whatever. Who could tell what could have happened if I were a more fervent believer in the cause of EPRP? Who could have said what I would have done if they had threatened me with castration, burned my anus, or subjected me to the most inhuman treatment that many others had undergone through torture?

Through it all, I never fully gave up on my life. I always wanted to live and thought I would live. In the end, when it came to a choice between trying to live and dying for the party, I chose to live while four of the people who were with me chose to die for their party. In the end, I was willing and ready to denounce the party in the mass media to save my life, although luckily for me it never came to that.

People may rightfully admire the integrity of my friends who died for what they believed in more than my story. Theirs may be the more compelling story. It probably is. Passing judgment on my friends is not the goal of my biography. Telling what I did when I did it and why I did it is my modest aim. If in the process I have succeeded in showing these people, for all their weaknesses, were decent people, some of them even great human beings, I can say I have accomplished my objective in writing this story. The reader is free to judge me on my record, although judgment is better left to posterity.

The *anja* story is something I know very little about. It was true that I was instinctively opposed to the way the EPRP dealt with the *anja* problem. I was especially disgusted to hear of the death of fourteen fighters suspected of being members of the *anja*, who were incarcerated in Assimba by EPRA, a story that I hope some other *wore negari* would one day give an honest account of so future generations will learn from our mistakes. Fourteen deaths is a higher causality rate than what EPRA lost fighting TPLF. Whoever passed judgment on that must also give a full accounting of what really took place. To me, as little informed as I am about it, that seemed murder, pure and simple. I have asked many people if there was any military danger that necessitated that action. I have asked if there was any logistical problem that made it difficult to sustain them. All the answers I have gotten were that this was a cold-blooded murder of a group of people, who like everyone else were in Assimba to fight the regime. What makes these murders so unacceptable is the fact these people were killed when the army was preparing to leave for Eritrea and subsequently to Gondar through Eritrea before disbanding within two years. What leader would waste the lives of fourteen young members under these circumstances? Who would want to leave these people dead when the rest of the army was preparing to save its life? There are many details of this murder that I don't know very much about, but nothing indicates a compelling reason for doing it. Vengeance? Maybe.

Some years later in Washington, D.C., the leader of the remaining EPRA that was operating in Gojjam was asked about this. His answer was chilling. He said that they were given due process of a hearing and found guilty and punished accordingly. He said the party would not apologize for this. I was stunned to hear that. I thought he would say that mistakes had been made in the past that the party was not proud of, and this was one of them. There was no tone of regret, no remorse whatsoever. He, in effect, said that they deserved it. He said it to an audience that was intimately linked with the party but was mostly dissociating itself from it. I could not stay in the room after that. I left.

I think the case of *anja* in the urban struggle was much more complicated than it was in Assimba. In Assimba, the case could have been given a better opportunity for a hearing, and dealt with more democratically or humanely. In Addis, while EPRP should never be exonerated for what happened, a compelling argument could perhaps be made for what the party did on the grounds of necessity and security. It is like what Americans call the "fog of war" that claims friendly lives. But to this day, EPRP has never admitted that innocent lives were indeed lost in the factional infighting.

I think the situation in Addis was terribly complicated. Given the party's emphasis on armed struggle to wrest power from the government, one could perhaps argue that the *anja* case would not have received either a democratic or humane treatment. The party, I surmise, saw the group as detrimental to its existence and treated it accordingly. The leadership may have made the calculation either the *anja* existed or the party existed, with no choice in between. This was true in the eyes of many party members who were passionately engaged in this factional warfare.

As I said a number of times, my own experience with *anja* is limited. The only person I knew who was in the *anja* was successfully rehabilitated. Of course, one wonders what would have happened to him if he had not been a friend of Wolde Ab and Jale Bia. A different type of person could have seen him as a high risk that had to be dealt with one way or another. But his friends wanted to rehabilitate him, and not get rid of him. He probably took actions to prove his worthiness to the party. He had worked with Berhane Meskel and was his admirer. But he was beginning to denounce his authoritarian leadership style and his ego toward the end.

Berhane stayed in Addis until almost the end, and left for Assimba after I escaped from *kebele* prison. Before Berhane was rehabilitated, Jale Bia one day asked me in almost total desperation what he should do about Berhane. He was angry with him about something that I don't remember. I told Jale Bia, jokingly of course, "I think he should be eliminated." Jale was taken aback and shocked. He said, "You don't mean that, do you? You don't mean that, do you?" He could not believe his ears. I was not serious of course and said that facetiously, unless it was a Freudian slip. Jale Bia, whom I always saw as one of the most humane individuals that I knew, could not possibly want to see something like that done to his friend. But could he?

One day, when I came to the house where Jale lived. I found him extremely agitated and nervous. He was restless and pacing all over. He asked me if I had money and could buy him beer. I told him I could and we went to a bar in Merkato and talked. We rambled about this or that issue, and his effort, which was now fizzling, to form what he called a close-knit community of writers who were in the party. At this point, he was trying to write a poem about what he called "Fascism on trial" and Yohannes, as the articulate voice of EPRP whom he also highly admired. His first project was not going well, but his poem about Yohannes was beginning to shape up. He read me a few lines that I still remember:

> The eagle soars high in the sky
> The warrior falls in the battlefield
> And revolution has its voice
> that emanates from the spirit of a fighter (Yohannes).

Jale told me that he had a secret that he would like to share with me. He asked me to promise that I would never tell anyone about it. I did. Then he said that he would like to read me a poem he completed that afternoon. So we went back home and he read it to me. It was about baptism by fire. It spoke of how he had been baptized in fire. It went on to say, "for my party, EPRP, for its victory and triumph, I have shot my first bullet, and I have killed an enemy."

This was serious stuff, and I knew he had done something terrible. He told me the *anja* person has been impossible and had been doing a series of actions damaging the party. The *anja* was his friend and the other one saw him as his friend too. At this time, the preferred and clever way of eliminating people in *anja* was to use their friends to lure them into a place where they then would be killed by others waiting there in hiding. I suspect this was what happened in this case too. The unsuspecting guy came to the tearoom to have coffee with his friend. Then EPRP units shot him, probably from behind, and left. This was a betrayal of trust. Jale knew that, but he had to do it for his party—a higher imperative, in his view. The party probably insisted that he do that. They probably built a very convincing case against this guy, saying that he was becoming detrimental to the lives of many party members.

What does a true believer in the party do when faced with these facts? What does one do when the party tells you that this person you know has to be destroyed or else the party will be destroyed? Probably by doing what he did. If one is ready to lay down one's life for a cause, is it not a contradiction to refrain from killing another who is destroying your cause? The prevailing atmosphere was that of war and pervasive war psychosis. What he did made sense in his moral construct of right and wrong. Who would accuse him of lacking integrity? Who would cast the first stone against him?

How did I deal with this? I did not pass any judgment on Jale. I knew whatever he did was enormously troubling to him. I just asked myself if I would be willing to do that. The answer was, "No, I wouldn't do that." I would never have allowed this to happen, which only goes to say I never believed in the cause of the party to be so imperative for me as to harm somebody I call my friend. The friendship imperative weighed more for me at that time. I said that I could not do this, but by just staying with the party all the way to the end and pretending like I was a true party member I was doing violence to my psyche and conscience.

Even then I saw the moral ambiguity of the story Jale Bia told me. To me, nothing is always that clear. The world was not divided into political enemies and friends, right and wrong, black and white. I knew that kind of thinking has no business in the party that was now engaged in mortal battle with its enemies. Jale Bia was a true party member; I was not. What he did made sense for him, although it must have been extremely painful for him to do it. It is one of those moments that I really hated myself for staying with the party that I did not belong in.

I have agonized over and over again whether I should tell this story of trust to other people. This is one of the most compelling stories of EPRP I have ever heard or experienced. Jale Bia was no average individual. He was a great poet, a passionate human being. To me he was the greatest of friends, who did everything he could to keep me alive in a difficult period. He wrote the poem on the Wollo famine, a testament of the depth of his humanity. He was in love with a girl about whom he wrote some of the most captivating Amharic sonnets I ever remember reading. In fact, his political poems do not at all compare to the poem he wrote to his girlfriend and lover. Jale was a great human being and a great poet. No one who knew him could deny that.

I am violating his trust by telling this incredible story of a man who was deeply torn by the action he took. Maybe in this story we could learn the great paradox of revolutionary morality. Maybe this could help us reexamine our past and help us come to terms with it. Most of us who survived have a great story to tell for posterity. I know people whose involvement with EPRP makes a much more compelling and fascinating story than what is told here.

Maybe this book will help them write so all of us will learn about our past and teach future generations some lessons for the better. I think that is a very healthy thing to do.

I wonder what Jale Bia would have said if he were alive. He once told me that when the party came to power, he would like to be an ambassador to China. He had a very ambivalent attitude toward China. He was impressed with the extraordinary accomplishment of the revolution, but he thought the legacy of the Cultural Revolution that made people read only the *Red Book*, a collection of quotations from Mao Tse Tung, was wrong. I was a more partisan supporter of China's Cultural Revolution than he was, and was not as vehemently opposed to the *Red Book*. He thought that was dogmatic thinking. North Korea was the one country he could not believe should be considered a socialist nation. It was only after I came to America and read *Life and Death in Shanghai* by Nien Cheng that I realized the horrors of the Cultural Revolution. I was truly embarrassed by how gullible I was and failed to critically see what the Cultural Revolution did to the Chinese society, particularly intellectuals and artists. After reading that book, I got a clear picture of the enormity of the havoc brought on by this phenomenon. For me the important thing was China was making tremendous progress and was slowly able to feed its hungry population. What it did in the process of these changes, the collateral damage, did not concern me as much during those early times. It is only after I came to America that I was able to see that in every revolution, even the ones considered successful, there were the seeds of human cruelty to other human beings, all done in the name of the betterment of humanity or achieving higher ideals. Now I am convinced that one should not, in good conscience, accept the human cost that these changes would bring. People who were branded enemies were dealt with in the most inhuman and egregious ways. A change brought about with utter disregard for human lives, even that of enemies, is fraught with inhumanity and is bound to turn against its own adherents eventually. We have seen this time and again, and I think we can now conclude this is inevitable.

PART III

Prison, Escape and Freedom

My Turn

The months of November 1977 to February 1978 were the darkest in the party's history. The Addis Abeba branch of the party, and by far its most formidable organization, faced its ultimate extinction. Party members and sympathizers, even those who had the remotest association with it, lived in absolute terror of the random search-and-destroy operations. Only the roaming bands of armed men, mostly thugs, otherwise known as revolutionary squads, slept safely in their homes.

The *assessa* took place when people were asleep, mainly between 1:00 and 3:00 in the morning. A knock at the door by the revolutionary squads evoked terror. These mostly indiscriminate arrests were so successful in destroying the party's network, no meaningful party activity occurred. Most of the party cells were either destroyed or isolated and had lost their more militant and active members. Members that were lucky enough to have survived the mass terror campaign were either trying to leave the town to the so-called EPRP base areas in Tigray and Gondar, or were going to provincial towns to stay with relatives. Because this exodus was not well organized, many who went to Gondar and Tigray were captured en route and taken prisoner. Thousands of others were either rounded up or willingly exposed themselves in hopes of clemency or lenient treatment.

Personally I felt relatively safe during the day. It was easy to mingle with the human wave of shoppers in Merkato who come from all over the country and aimlessly wander all day long. Sometimes I would spend hours in a teahouse or a bar, most of which were now becoming targets of random *assessa*. But it was usually easy to escape this as long as one had a valid ID card and was not identified by one of the individuals who conduct the searches. But the nights never gave us many options. You only hoped that the house you stayed in had not been targeted. To me the onset of the evening always brought gloom and doom, and having to think about where to spend the night became simply a terrifying experience.

I don't have a clear recollection of what I did the morning before my arrest. Probably I was nursing a hangover from the previous night. That afternoon, as was usually the case, I, Mohamed, and Tekalegne had *kha*t at Mohamed's sister's house. Mohamed's sister was a passive partner in her brother's dangerous activities, quietly allowing her brother to use the house as he saw fit. Many relatives allowed this, not knowing what to do. She worried more about the safety of her reckless brother than what might happen to her husband, sister, and two boys, both of whom were under the age of ten.

Mohamed, of Muslim Eritrean heritage, had already been arrested, and released because of the intervention of an uncle who worked for the government. In fact, his mother told me she owed it to St. Gabriel of Kulebe, whom she believed helped to get her son released. Right after he was released, he became very active again. He was a brave individual who had little to no fear for his personal safety. He grew up in Awassa, Sidamo, and was a student at Ecole Normal. He left the school and joined EPRP and did everything he was asked to do. As far as I remember, he was not in the armed wing, but he always undertook the most dangerous political work or liaison, transporting money and weapons between party cells, with no regard for his life.

Tikalegne, a former university student and one of the original members of the Crocodile Group, was probably one of the few surviving members of the EPRP leadership at this time. He had come from Hararghe, where I suspected he was leading the party's effort to organize an armed struggle or link up with rebel groups in the area. Where in Hararghe he lived I did not know, but suspected that it was close to Harrar. With Tikalegne in Hararghe was also Kassye, one of the original members of our study group. Kassaye, who was from Wollega and spoke Afan Oromo, was sent there because of his facility with the language. I had suspicions they were both trying to organize armed struggle in Hararghe. Efforts to do the same thing in Sidamo had failed, and Birhanu, who was responsible for that, had died previously as discussed earlier. The party was making a last-minute rush to find areas to operate in and take off the pressure from Addis. Otherwise, party activity in Addis seemed to have come to a standstill. What was happening outside Addis was too little and too late; many of these efforts were simply overwhelmed by the massive power of the government.

Tikalegne, I was told, had brought fifteen to twenty AK-47s from Hararghe. I was surprised at how successfully he managed to smuggle that at an exceedingly difficult time. I was truly amazed that this guy, who grew up in Addis, was well known among university students, and was sought by the government security, could risk his life to come to Addis in the first place at this time. But not only did he come, apparently he had also brought weapons with him. This was during the Somali-Ethiopian war, and weapons in the Hararghe area were very much available to buy. But to import them to Addis and in such quantity, that was a different story.

That I would hear about these weapons and where they were hidden (not the exact place) was telling of the level of discipline in the party. There was no need for me to hear that, but either Mohamed or Tikalegne must have told me to impress me that the party was still capable of performing extraordinarily heroic acts. At that time, something like this was daring enough for the truly faithful, but in actuality, EPRP was about to become history, at least in Addis.

Around 6:00 or 7:00 p.m., we left Amina's house and took a taxi to Merkato. From Merkato, we started to walk on foot to Banko DiRoma near where we had planned to sleep that night. Walking to Banko DiRoma took us to the main road, adjacent to Somali Terra where Tikalegne grew up. This was, in retrospect, an insane act. This was within eyesight of his neighborhood, and it did not occur to any of us that what we were doing was dangerous and foolish.

I remember Tikalegne and I talked about the Red Terror as we casually strode to Piassa. As we walked up the hill to Petros Monument, we saw Addis Abebans sitting in the bar and drinking. Music played from both sides of the road. In a very pessimistic mood made worse by the wearing out of the effect of the *khat*, I made this statement, "The government is destroying us. This time, they are catching the very people that are important in the party and effectively destroying them." I have seen that happen with my eyes time and again. I know this was true, and in my heart of hearts I felt that the party was pretty much finished in Addis.

Tikalegne, in a defiant statement that I have never forgotten, responded, "You shall wait and see." In a blind statement reflective of the self-delusion that had characterized the party leadership all along, He added, "When we hit these people, we hit them where it hurts most and we are going to do that." I remember vividly where we were at when he made this statement. We had just passed the Habtegeorgis Bridge at the cross section of the road that goes to Somali Terra, and were passing by one of these roadside bars on our way to Piassa. At that time, I could not be sure whether he was sincere or bluffing. We were less than half a kilometer from a house in Somali Terra where he grew up and lived all his life, a real danger zone for him and for us. I have never forgotten this defiant statement.

I suspected the weapons were in his parents' place at that time, waiting to be transferred to the party cells. I did not ask for an explanation as to what was holding this transfer. It was obvious there was no functioning party or fighting units to receive these weapons. Actually, for some time now the party had not shot a bullet, and what the government called the "White Terror" was completely smothered by the "Red Terror."

As the night approached, I began to worry about where to sleep. The night before I had slept in a small motel near Ras Makonnen Bridge. The revolutionary squads came after midnight after I was sound asleep. When I heard the knock, I opened the door, wearing only my underwear. They asked me what I was doing in a different neighborhood. I replied as honestly and as calmly as I could why I was there. I figured if I was blunt with the truth it would disorient them.

I did not look like the stereotypical EPRP member: skinny, youthful, and disheveled. I was heavyweight, and from my appearance looked like a small businessman. My main fear was my identification card, which indicated that I lived in Abouare, where all the *kebele* leaders were arrested or killed on the grounds of EPRP connection some weeks earlier. The arrests of the *kebele* leaders followed a big shootout in which Wolde Abe, a personal friend and a party leader, and three other members of EPRP were killed after they refused to give up their hands and opened fire, according to the government announcement. So what I was carrying for ID was grounds for further questioning, but the individuals who saw that must not have been aware of this to make the connection. I do not remember what they said, but they left. It was a piece of good luck. I did not sleep the rest of the night.

That is why that day again I had to worry about a place to sleep. This was a big concern for all of us, although the others did not dwell on it as much as I did. We ate our dinner in one of the little neighborhood restaurants and were joined by two more members. We went to a bar to drink in the same block of neighborhood. We all had quite a bit to drink. In the bar, I remember seeing a man I knew from high school in Dessie. He was completely drunk and singing. He was singing a new song, the lyrics of which goes like this:

> *Aybaba aybaba whodesh*
> *Aybaba aybaba whodesh*
> *Borkenan man bashageregne*
> *Dessie lie gudaye neberegne*

Translation:

> Don't feel sorry (for me)
> Don't feel sorry (for me)
> I wish someone would help me cross Borkena River
> I have a date in Dessie

As was customary at this time, we did not exchange greetings and pretended like we did not know each other. I contrasted my life with his and felt deeply sorry. His was probably a life that had not much to be envied, but compared to mine, which was now teetering on the edge of the abyss, it seemed incredibly happy, free, and safe. I thought of what I would do to be like that at that time.

I had given up on EPRP for a while now. I was confused as to what to do and how to get out. Some months before, I had really thought about leaving the party and fleeing to Djibouti, but somehow let that pass. Now, I had reached a point where I was living from day to day with the real possibility of being caught and did not have any idea what to do. I was totally immobilized, maybe by fear or deluded that I would not be caught or God knows what.

Just before the onset of the midnight curfew, we went to sleep at a nearby furniture store. We used to sleep here before and it was considered one of the safest places at that time. Some party members and sympathizers worked at the store, and it was considered a safe haven for many of us for a long time. But that had changed. A few weeks before, one of the individuals who worked there or used to come to this store was arrested. I was not sure if the party had any money in this one, but another furniture store that may have been partly owned by the party was closed and the owner arrested some months before. As I said earlier, Dula managed this store and paid a heavy price for his suspected association with EPRP after he was arrested. That was our daily and most important hideout, and its closure had really hurt us badly. In addition, there was palpable fear that Dula, under torture, would tell about us—where we lived and slept—and that we would all be finished. But Dula withstood a tremendous amount of pressure and brutal torture to hide the truth about the store and the people who frequented the place.

There were five of us now, having been joined by two more members at the dinner place. One was Kadri, who lived underground but used to work in a textile plant. The other one was a young carpenter who worked at the furniture store and had the key to the place.

I must have been the only one who was extremely uncomfortable about sleeping in the furniture store. We were faced with two equally unattractive options in terms of finding a place to sleep. We could split and find a motel to sleep in, which had its risks, or take our chance at the store, which we had reason to fear was exposed. Had we calmly weighed the pros and cons of the two options, we would have definitely decided to split up and find a place to sleep, each on his own. We were not trained to think like that. Many of the people that were being captured were often risking this kind of information. I had often criticized others who were caught for being foolhardy enough to go to places that were prime targets of the *kebele* security squads. Little did I know that I was going to repeat the same incredible mistake myself.

Mohamed reiterated that we had no other choice but to sleep at the store, and all went along. I did not strenuously object. I did not have any money to sleep out. In any case, the night was late, I was inebriated enough to disregard the risk, and so we all went.

Before we slept, we briefly discussed emergency procedures in case the house was to be searched. Mohamed carried a hand grenade, and Tikalegne was armed with a pistol. I had stopped carrying a pistol once I knew that I was not ready to use it, and that was one of the most sensible things I had done. There were a couple of loaded rifles in the ceiling and Mohamed knew where they were hidden.

We discussed that we would run downstairs through the backdoor and try to get to the street in case we faced danger that night. Mohamed said he would go to the ceiling, get hold of the guns, and give us cover while we tried to escape.

The front of the furniture store was on a road that joined Churchill Road at Banko DiRoma. The furniture store was adjacent to a row house. The corner of house right by Churchill Road was a teahouse. The teahouse was across from Banko Di Roma. On one side of the furniture store there was an empty space where an elderly man had a small shoe repair store. After this empty space was another corner store facing a street that goes to Theodros Adebabay. Behind the furniture store was a fence, and behind the fence was the backyards of hotels, apartments, houses, bars, all the way to the Tewodros Adebabay. The backyard had some outlets to Churchill Road.

So if we went out through the backdoor, we could run through the backyards of houses and bars all the way down to Tewodros Adebabay, which is on Churchill Road, or exit through one of the outlets to Churchill Road. The whole area where the store was located could be seen as a triangular block, with Churchill Road (north-south) on one side, another road going east-west and intersecting Churchill Road, and a third from northwest to southeast and intersecting with Churchill Road at Tewodros Adebabay. Militarily, this triangular block was easy to completely cordon off, and that was what happened that night since none of us managed to escape.

After this broad and brief discussion of emergency procedures, we slept on the floor, as usual, with our clothes on. I could not fall asleep. The alcohol quickly wore off and I had this premonition that something terrible was going to happen. I heard sounds of cars passing by and human voices, which were those of the *kebele* guards since no one was allowed to walk or drive at that time. Then at around 2:00 or 3:00 in the morning there was a knock at the door, followed by a command to open the door.

All of us stood up in terror. For a few minutes as the banging persisted we did not know what to do. No one mentioned our plan. I suggested we give up our hands. No one responded, but it seemed that was not considered an option by anyone of them. There was no talk of anything. When the knock persisted, we stepped down the stairs to the door, opened it, and began to slowly walk. While we were rushing outside to the backyard, the dogs started to bark. The light from the bank was flickering, so I thought that was the light from the security people trained on us. We all stopped right at the back of the store and regrouped. Then we approached the fence that was near Churchill Road. We heard footsteps of the *kebele* guards as they approached the fence from Churchill Road behind the tearoom. They were methodically advancing to where we were standing, all five of us. As they began to climb the fences, Mohamed signaled Tikalegne if he should throw the grenade. Tikalegne gave his okay with a nod of his head, and Mohamed threw the grenade. There was an explosion, followed by a loud scream. I thought I heard a voice say, "They massacred us." After that we ran, each in his own way, through the backyards of the block, the dogs barking and gunshots roaring. When I reached the fence near the Tewodros Adebabay, I stopped. Tikalegne and the carpenter had already tried to exit to Churchill Road. I suspected they were hit because of the amount of firepower released. Mohamed felt that he could not escape and came back to where I was.

I don't remember if Mohamed ran with me all the way down or tried to exit, and when he saw that the *kebele* guards were everywhere, firing, returned. But he came to me and we tried to escape together. At this point we were on the compound of the bar we were at that night before we went to bed. Kadri was there too. He said that a splinter of the bomb had hit him in the stomach and he was bleeding. He was obviously in mortal pain, but we did not know, nor was that really a particular concern. He knocked at the bar, which had motel rooms, and begged to be let in. But they refused. Finally he lay down and covered himself with what looked like a straw carpet that was lying outside. He was shivering. I went to him and lay near him. He told me that he was bleeding hard and that he was dying.

I was terribly scared and in a daze. Briefly, the intense realization of what a fool I had been hit me like a thunderbolt. I realized the end was coming and panicked. I said if only I could get out of this mess, I will never ever get involved in politics of any sort. I realized that I had let down my family—my mother would never survive my death and I had completely bungled up my family's future.

I started to pray. I had never done that for a long time, but I started to pray to Allah. I was not sure whether I had the right prayer or not, but I was saying words in Arabic that I knew from my childhood, the meaning of which I never understood. Mohamed came to me and asked me what I wanted to do. I told him that I did not want to die. I do not remember if I asked him to pray or not. Mohamed said that we should all fall together.

I was not ready to die and told him in agony that I wanted to live. He suggested that we climb a tree and hide there. I thought the idea was to stay there, hidden by the branches, hoping that they won't find out in the morning. It did not make sense to me and told him so. Mohamed climbed the tree. At this point, I started moving back and forth to find a sewer that I might use as an exit. I returned to the place where Mohamed had thrown the grenade, looking for some hole or sewer that I could hide in and escape. I knew the block was completely surrounded and there was no way of escaping on the surface. After maybe half an hour, I heard a machine gun fire from the direction that Mohamed was at and I knew it was directed at him. They had spotted him on the tree and asked him to get down. When he refused, they sprayed machine-gun fire and killed him.

Having given up my search, I found an open garage or a service room that looked like a servant's room. I went in and sat there for what seemed to be an eternity, my mind frantically thinking to escape once the morning sets in. When the sun came up and people started getting out of their house, I went to one of the open doors and asked them to say that I am one of them and take me out with them. They said the *kebele*s knew them and they won't be able to do that. Then I asked them for water to wash my face and comb my hair. I washed my face, combed my hair, straightened my shirt, and tried to leave like someone from the neighborhood. When I started to walk to Churchill Road, I noticed the area had been cordoned off and blocked to traffic, and there were a lot of people watching the spectacle. One of the guards shouted that no one from the neighborhood was allowed to leave and that I must return to my house or risk being shot at. I shouted, "I have to go to work," but was told to return and did so. I went to that empty room and sat there thinking of what I must do next.

I heard footsteps as the guards approached the service room. They came through the gate and I met them inside. I told them that I had slept here last night because I was drunk. They knew that I was one of the people they were looking for and started beating me on my head with their rifle butts. I received blow after blow on my head, but never fell. They searched me all over, handcuffed me, and took me to a van parked on Churchill Road. Near the van was Kadri, lying down, and it looked like he was dying. He had already told them how many of us were together that night and they were aware that I was the only one unaccounted for. They asked him if I was one of them and he positively identified me. With Kadri there was another man that they caught when they were sweeping the area. I used to see him

170

at Addis Abeba University. They asked me if he was with us; I told them that he was not. They put me in the van and drove to the furniture store, where they suddenly stopped. I do not remember why they stopped, but Kadri was not with us. I heard them debating whether or not to take Kadri with us. They said that it was not worth their while to carry him. Then there was a burst of machine-gun fire. A prisoner later told me that he took more than twenty bullets before he fell. Being inside the van, I don't remember if I saw what was happening or had blocked out what must have been the most traumatic scene of my life. But I still seem to remember seeing him fall. Whether that was a picture I had constructed from what I later heard or was what I actually saw, I could not truly say.

They drove me around the Tewodros Adebaby. Near me was the student from Addis Abeba University, who sat there calmly while I was in a state of panic. Looking at my ID, they said I belonged to the feudal class and was facilitating the sale of arms. They accused me of being a member of the Ethiopian Democratic Union (from my weight and bulging stomach, I suspected). They were very happy with what they had accomplished that morning. They asked me in jest who we were conspiring to murder that night and roared with laughter at what must have seemed to them our incredulous stupidity.

On the way to the *kebele* office, I saw myself in the van's rear window mirror and noticed a neurotic smile plastered on my face. I could not believe what I saw. I thought I had lost my mind. In some sense, just reeling from the massive blows on my head, which I had absorbed while my body was still in a state of shock, I must not have realized the full impact of my situation. I looked dazed, mildly crazy, and on the verge of a breakdown. I had never discounted that I would be arrested, but never had I imagined that I would be caught in a situation like this, which was totally hopeless.

They said to each other that the grenade had killed only one person. Some were wounded, but this person must have absorbed the full impact of the explosion. I received a slight wound from it near my eyes, but it could have easily been me who was hit by the splinter since I was near Kadri. I was, oddly enough, slightly relieved to hear that no more people had died on their side. I thought that would make them spare my life.

Prison, Interrogation, and Escape

The drive to the *kebele* was short. I was taken out of the van, given some more blows on my head, and thrown into the prison room, where there were about twenty others. It was a small room, enough to allow each one of us to sleep. During the day, it was easier to sit, because some of the prisoners were allowed to get out and walk inside or mix with prisoners from a larger room. The prisoners in the other room were considered less dangerous. They were receiving political education. A few among them were allowed to go out with the cadres and come back. They visited their parents and even socialized. Among these was a young student whose mother's restaurant we used to frequent in the neighborhood. Rumor had it that she was dating Haji, the *kebele* leader.

Haji's notoriety as a killer was legendary among *kebele* leaders. He is said to have started killing people and leaving their bodies with the picture of Emperor Haile Selassie. He was a prolific killer who was among the most feared by parents and prisoners. He was said to have been a guerilla leader in Hararghe, from where he joined one of the left organizations (I don't remember exactly which one) and was executing the government's call on the *kebele* leaders to take independent action on antirevolutionaries to a fault. After I left Ethiopia, I was told Haji was arrested following the fallout between the Derg and its civilian supporters and was badly beaten and tortured. This story was probably true, as some of the mass murderers were finally considered expendable in the government's effort to ease the terror and win popular support once EPRP was completely wiped out from Addis.

Nothing happened to me that day. It was the longest day of my life. I was completely shook up. I was terror stricken. I remember some of the prisoners saying I must not be a leader in the organization since I was so scared. And scared I was. I felt like I was going to die a meaningless death for something I had truly never believed in. Human life had become so cheap and mine was going to be one of the most worthless ones.

They had arrested a number of people from the neighborhood that night: shopkeepers, former employees of the furniture store, students, and all sorts of people, some of whom knew me. I ran into an EPRP member who was also active in the trade union movement and was a good friend of Mohamed. He was taken the night they combed the area. We pretended we did not know each other. A few days later, we talked like we just met in prison. I told him to try to save his life. It made no sense for him to die such a death. I am sure he probably would have done that, but I wanted to reassure him there was nothing wrong in trying to save his life. Life had become so precious for me that I did not want him to risk his life in any way. He was taken to the textile factory, where he was handed the next day to the textile workers to deal with him. The last I heard of him, he was given political education and his life was spared. Also taken from the prison, although I never heard the full story, was the student that was from the university and was in the same van with me.

I do not remember if anything happened the next day either. I believe it was on the third day that I was brought to Haji for interrogation. By this time, I had sort of, over and over again, gone over what I was supposed to say at the interrogation. I had prayed that they would not interrogate me the first day. I was in such a state of shock that I was not sure what I would say. So the three days have been a God-sent interval that I used to regain my composure.

There was a giant man holding a club or some kind of torturing object made of hippopotamus skin. I don't remember his face, but may have just looked at him once. The three of us sat together; the man ominously holding his club simply watched and waited for Haji's order. Haji warned me to tell the truth and expose everything I know or else face severe punishment. He looked in the direction of the torturer.

It is hard to remember the exact details of what I said to him. He called me a hired assassin, and I told him with a firmness that to this day surprises me that I was not. I added that I had never harmed anyone in my life. I was a member of the party. I had always served mainly in the agitation-propaganda section, including as a writer for *Goh*, which was a legal paper until it was banned, I repeated. I told him my level of exposure was so high when I was writing for *Goh*, the party never assigned me sensitive positions. I was recruited by another *Goh* writer, Mezy, who by that time had left for Tigray. I was there that night because I had no place to sleep. I had asked them to give up their hands, but they did not want to. I must have repeated that again and again.

I must have also told him that I knew only one of them, but which one I do not remember. It must have been Mohamed that I said I knew, although in retrospect I do not know why I was not asked more in that direction. I also remember telling him that one of them, from what I heard the night before our arrest, was from out of town, possibly from Hararghe. Shimaglew's brother, I was told later by one of the prisoners who was released, was actually a cadre in the same *kebele*. I suspected that he had seen the body of his brother, although he may not have admitted it.

Haji was in a very happy frame of mind from the start, and I remember him listening to my story intently. He interrupted me a few times to ask questions, but on the whole he seemed genuinely interested in what I had to say, although I did not know why. I told him that most of the people I knew were arrested or had left the city. Most of the houses I worked at have been taken by other *kebele*s. I said, "I am willing to officially condemn the party, learn from my political mistake. I am willing to cooperate, but I do not know who to expose because most people have left town or have died."

I knew the crucial part of interrogation is where they expect you to expose your associates or tell them where weapons are hidden. I was sort of tempted to tell them that there may be weapons in the ceilings, but I felt if there were any they would find them; if there were not, there was no point tipping them, because then they would ask for more. I had learned this even before I was arrested. To the extent possible, it is better not to volunteer important information or they would ask for more. Regarding people, I told him I know places that EPRP members frequent but there was nobody I could point to.

That must have been one of the luckiest days in my life. Nothing happened to me. I was not tortured. I was sent back to the room, to the astonishment of the inmates, who expected me to come messed up like most of those in the room. I have not figured this out to this day. It was a miracle, a divine intervention that I was spared torture. I was at that time probably the most important prisoner in the *kebele*, caught red-handed in the exchange of fire. Haji did not order for me to be tortured.

Some days later, I was called to the office of the vice chairman of the *kebele*, who I was told was from Wollayta. By this time I had sort of relaxed into my predicament and was hoping that my life may be spared. It was rumored in the prison that Haji and this other guy belonged to different groups like Woz League and Malerid. I never saw them speak together. When he called me to his office, I thought of exploiting this possibility. His first question was whether I knew the worker that was detained in the prison. I said that I did not know him. Then I added very firmly that I had told everything to Haji and that he could ask for the transcript of my statement. He seemed puzzled and did not want to ask me further. I returned to my cell.

The situation in prison, if you had not been beaten and are not nursing wounds as many were, was tolerable. There were some merchants who were detained from the same area that I was caught. Many of them felt sorry for me. They had plenty of food, which they shared generously with other prisoners. Many of the inmates were young people whose parents brought food to prison. So I was well fed, and I remember eating all the time.

One of the inmates was a young student who was accused of trying to blow up the telecommunication center in Senga Terra. He was a nice, well-behaved child who came from probably a rich, merchant Muslim family. At the time he was in good terms with every leader in the *kebele*. It was rumored that it was only a matter of time before he was released because his relatives had intervened to Haji. He confided to me that he would leave the country when he was let out. I trusted him and we became friends. After maybe a week, I gave him the name of my relatives and told him to tell them where I was at. A few days later, my second cousin came to visit me and gave me twenty birr. My friend, who was fourteen or fifteen and was mature for his age, was said to have migrated to America but I am not sure where.

On the whole I became quite reconciled to my fate. I began to sleep well. When I was asleep at night, I was told the revolutionary guards would come from one of the late-night *kebele* sweeps and ask where I was. They often called me a hired assassin and pointed fingers at me before they left. I do not remember them waking me up. So I got used to life in prison, although I never came to terms with the possibility of dying.

I had decided to try to escape if the opportunity offered itself. But I had also advised myself not to do something foolhardy that would definitely get me killed. I thought about going through the small window in the bathroom, but felt that was too small and near the office of the cadres, so they would hear the noise from anyone trying to escape. I had heard that someone was once caught trying to escape and beaten almost to death.

My relationship with the inmates and some of the guards also improved dramatically. One night, we were all outside talking and telling stories. I told them one of my favorite stories that I had read in an English class in ninth or tenth grade. The story is about a commoner who was arrested because he was in love with the daughter of a king. According to the tradition of this fictional kingdom, punishment was administered in a coliseum in full view of spectators. The punishment was for the prisoner to open one of two doors facing the tribune in a coliseum. Behind one of the doors would be a hungry tiger, and behind the other, a beautiful lady. The princess for whose love the prisoner was now paying the price was in the tribune section of the stadium watching her lover. When he faced the tribune, before opening the door she gave him a signal. Apparently she knew what was in it, and he

175

opened the door that she wanted him to open. So the question was whether she wanted to see him die or live married to another person. The choice had always seemed to have tragic qualities, intertwined with love, passion, and death, and had intrigued me when I was young. Sure enough, my listeners were enthralled. They argued and debated and wanted me to tell them what happened. I did not tell them. They were enormously agitated and excited, which was a good thing to happen in such a place filled with melancholy. So slowly I was becoming a likeable guy with whom many sympathized.

People told jokes in prison all the time. One of the prisoners was especially good at telling jokes. They also spoke about torture, courage, and cowardice. They joked about one another: who was going to die and who was going to live. They seemed to be very cavalier about their situation, which looked to me to be hopelessly sad. I did not like their jokes dealing with death and sex. I thought both subjects were depressing and irrelevant in that environment. As for me, although I managed to tell them one story, I remember I had difficulty focusing on any one thing. I had difficulty expressing my thoughts. I spoke haltingly and with a lot of effort, but they listened, and it seemed most, and this included one or two of the guards, showed some understanding toward my situation.

Two very young students were added to our room after I came. They were very young and were caught carrying arms. They did not seem particularly scared, but some of the inmates tried to jokingly terrorize them about their fate. I intervened and told them it would be okay. To some of the inmates, life had ceased to be valuable. They had given up on their life and seemed undisturbed by the fate that was awaiting them. They all knew about Haji and how ruthless he could be. They had seen people taken out, murdered, and left on the street. Still they joked about the Red Terror and life and death. It was very bizarre to me.

One of the most painful memories I have of the *kebele* prison was the revolutionary songs that the inmates in the other prison room were taught to sing. These were mostly love songs where only the lyrics were changed to express anti-EPRP and anti-EDU denunciations. It was not the fact they were anti-EPRP that troubled me, it was the spirit with which the children sang the songs. It was somber and sad. You could hear in their voices that these children were morally crushed, have lost all their spirit, and had become mechanical about everything.

Some of the words were:

> *Eihappa Ediu, tegentayoch hule*
> *Bekeye shibrachin yimeneteralu*

"EPRP, EDU, and all the secessionist forces will be completely exposed (uprooted) by our Red Terror."

Many of these children were actually singing about their own death. What was interesting was the actual song had become one of the most popular songs in this time of blood, death, and terror.

One morning, while we were sitting outside, Haji came and sat with us. He was talking with other inmates and seemed relaxed. The subject was prisoners who would face the Red Terror. It was amazing how such serious subjects about life and death were discussed so casually. It was telling of the spirit of the time and how much human life had lost its value. I brought my case up and asked Haji what would happen to me. He said as casually as if he was talking about drinking beer or playing soccer that I would face the Red Terror. His words sent chills through my spine, but I did not respond. Somehow I realized that I was slated to be killed and I must do everything I could to escape.

While I was in the *kebele* prison, nobody was taken out and killed. The rumor was that because of international outcry against these brutal murders, the *kebele*s were told to take it easy for a while. This was also following the visit of Sen. Ted Kennedy, who was said to have seen bodies of young people lying on the street. I believed these stories. I also believed that because the party is fully crushed, the killings would probably stop.

I thought about my family a lot while I was in prison. I never dwelled long on that since I felt it might break me down. Thinking about it was terrible, so I made every effort to avoid it. For some reason, though, the picture of my youngest sister would always come to me. When this happened, I became extremely depressed. I blotted out the thought of my mother. I said, "If I die I would never know what would happen to her, I would never feel it." The difficult part was now when I was aware of what could happen. I had these feeling that she would go crazy. She would tear her clothes and become lunatic. So I blotted out the thought of her. I said, "Thank God I would not know about her situation after I died."

When I thought about my sister, though, I would see her sitting on my mother's lap and wiping my mother's tears. Before I was arrested, I heard that she had done that and assured my mother nothing would happen to me. This image of Rukeya on my mother's lap was the most difficult thought in prison that I could never get rid of. It probably gave me the strength to try to escape. I always said if I got out safely from prison, my family would be my first priority in life.

One night I had a dream. I was trying to climb a small slippery hill and was getting frustrated. Then a beautiful woman, whom I could not place anywhere, offered me her hand to pull me up. I caught her hand and was beginning to feel confident that I was going to get out when I woke up. I never experienced such a pang of mental pain and anguish as I felt at that time. What a contrast with my dream, which was unbelievably delicious and happy! I hit the abyss. After the agony subsided, I said maybe this dream meant something. I interpreted the dream to mean that I will escape prison. I really believed that is what the dream was about and kept it to myself.

I became very wise in a matter of weeks. What I always took for granted in life now began to assume a special significance to me. Every time I saw people walk outside the prison, I envied them. "If only I could be free, be able to walk and do what others do, how different my life would be?" I asked myself a million times. But nothing seemed to have more significance than walking for some reason. It symbolized the full meaning of freedom. I wanted to walk in front of the *kebele* prison. My heart ached every time I saw young people my age pass by. This has remained one of my most indelible memories of prison life. To this day I could retrieve the sensation of my feeling about freedom when I see people walk. Nothing seems to match the intensity of human experience when faced with one's own mortality.

Bathroom overflow was a big problem in prison. These prisons were never made to handle these many people at one time. These were nationalized houses. The *kebeles* had taken the best of these houses and converted them into offices. These houses had to be used as prisons for thousands of mostly young people. They were overcrowded, and bathroom overflow was a constant problem. Cleaning the mess was the responsibility of the inmates in our room. I don't remember how many times I had to clean this stench, but I did it more than others. The one time I cleaned it, the entire floor was covered. When I finished, I smelled like stench. The guards laughed at me. They thought this would break me. That was one of my least concerns.

To relieve this regular overflow, which was bothersome to the cadres who worked nearby, prisoners were often taken out, watched by guards, so they could relieve themselves. It was a sign of the changed attitude of the guards toward me that I began to be allowed to get out of the *kebele* prison to relieve myself. The first time I went out, I thought of escaping. But it seemed like all the guards were looking at me. So I felt the timing was wrong and decided to wait for another chance.

It was nearly two weeks now. That day, I was sitting outside, most of the time looking at the cadres and other *kebele* leaders who came in and out. All these people who come to the *kebele* were armed with automatic weapons, looked very intimidating, and seemed very busy. One could also see that they now felt fully victorious, confident that the EPRP threat—which was never that serious, although they deliberately made it seem to be—was over. As I was watching this spectacle, I was in an upbeat mood. I borrowed a comb from one of the inmates and started to comb my Afro, which had become long and shabby. I did this in the full view of every inmate. An inmate who was there at that time and now lives in America told me that everyone noticed what I was doing. I thought that if a chance occurred I should always be prepared to take it.

It must have been around four in the afternoon. They lined the inmates to take them out of the prison to relieve themselves. I joined the line and signaled one of the inmates in my room to come and join. He did not feel like it. There must have been about ten to fifteen of us in this line and we were guarded by one person with a long rifle. While leaving the door, I sensed that he was slightly drunk. We got out, walked by the street that goes to the old post office, and after maybe a hundred meters we made a right turn as if we were going to the back of the *kebele* prison. This alley was a dead-end as it ran into a big stone wall. Behind this wall, I learned, was some merchant's storage, which was also probably a residential place. Escaping by climbing over the wall was a formidable thing. It was also easy for the guard to see since they looked in that direction all the time.

I went near the wall and squatted, pretending like I was relieving myself. I was not. I was actually watching what the guard was doing and planning the best way to escape. When I looked at the guard, he was surrounded by a bunch of prisoners and was showing them how the gun operates. I knew he was partially covered but could see in my direction. I decided to go toward him, if the situation allowed, and go past him like I was returning to the prison. I did that and noticed that he was not paying attention. I walked back and reached the main street, pretending to make a left to prison. I looked back at the guard and the kids. His sight in my direction was still covered. In that instant, I decided to go the opposite direction. The risk at this point was from the other guards that stood at the gate of the *kebele*. I was in their full view if anyone was looking in that direction. I decided not to run so as not to arouse the people's curiosity. I walked to the end of the block and made a right turn. This road goes all the way to Taklahymanot. Within minutes I saw a taxi flying in my direction, stopped it, and got in. I calmly said that I was going to Cinema Ras. This was truly my day because the taxi was actually heading in that direction. I got out at the corner of Cinema Ras and went to the shop where my second cousin worked. I went through the shop to a small room at the back where the shopkeepers slept. They were all shocked and looked in amazement. They did not know what to say. I had some illegal documents stashed in this room, but found they were removed. There was a fire accident nearby and the room was completely cleaned. I was very angry at myself for what I did and risking the lives of these individuals who knew nothing about it. However, I was not sure that they noticed.

I washed myself, changed my clothes, and went to a barber. One of the shopkeepers gave me a decent jacket. My hair was cut short, which made me look different. I bought a hat and looked like a normal person.

Then I went to my cousin's house. When I went in, my uncle, who had come from Wollo, was there. They told me that they had just been to the *kebele* prison and delivered food for me. I became extremely anxious. I thought they had been followed and that the *kebele* people may be around the corner. In the house was my cousin's brother in-law, a private who had served in Eritrea and was discharged because of a bullet in his head that had not been removed. He and I had arguments about Eritrea and Eritrea's right to self-determination. We had violent arguments. I knew he was not just a soldier who served his country. But from what he had told me, he was a ruthless murderer with a lot of innocent lives in his hands; he spoke openly about his brutal exploits in Eritrea that I was ashamed to hear. When he found out that I had escaped, I noticed he was not happy. After a few minutes he left. I suspected he might tell one of the *kebele* people about me. My uncle and cousin had the same premonition. So I left immediately.

LIFE IN ADDIS AFTER PRISON

That night I wanted to stay in a motel. I had been told that the motels were refusing to accommodate anyone who would not show ID cards. I also knew that the *kebele* had now made it a habit to routinely raid these motels and arrest suspected individuals. Since I had no ID card, staying in a hotel was out of the question. Actually, living in Addis Abeba at this point without an ID card was simply impossible. You were casually stopped and checked for ID, and if you couldn't produce one, that was proof that you are a counter-revolutionary with no place to stay. Even if you say you lost it, you had to prove your area of residency, which was impossible to do unless a *kebele* leader would vouch for you. You can't leave town because of the many checkpoints where they ask for ID cards. Not having an ID card was simply a hopeless situation at this time. And thus my nightmare life in Addis, the most dangerous place in the world at this time, began to unfold.

I went to a bar and got myself completely drunk. I decided to sleep there even though the *kebele*s were also checking on these local bars. I did not sleep very well. Around three, I heard automatic fire nearby. This was one of the nightly killings that took place. A week later, I was told these were eleven of the people that were in the same room with me in the *kebele* prison. A year later in Djibouti, I was told that Haji did that in retaliation for my escape. On the other hand, I had also been told that was the night Haji had planned to kill me and others. So my escape had nothing to do with the killings.

In the morning, I went to a house in Adre Sefer that used to be one of EPRP's strongholds. There was a house here where I had some months before buried an ID card for emergency cases. The *kebele* looked quiet, almost haunted, with no youth insight. I was scared but decided to take the risk. This was the house where EPRP's most famous poet, Jale Bia, used to

---

181

live and write many of his poems. I knocked at the door, and the door was opened by a twelve-year-old boy who used to live nearby. He told me that the *kebele* had been fully cleaned; that he was arrested and let go after sometime. He said the *kebele* had checked the house many times and that he doubted there was anything in there. I looked underneath the wooden tile where I had buried the ID card, but could not find it. While I was searching for my hidden ID, we heard noises outside and he went out to check and came back to tell me the *kebele* are making *assessa* (searches) and were about to come to the house. I knew the ins and outs of this house and the entire escape route. I went to the back, jumped over the fence to the backyard of a well-known Muslim restaurant, and went to my aunt's house. This was a different *kebele*, so they were not looking particularly for me. They were making their usual searches or somebody had tipped them that someone who was not from the same *kebele* was spotted in the area. I never went back to the house.

My memory is vague from this point on. I must have met my uncle in the morning outside before I left to look for my ID card and received some money from him. My mother had sent some money through my uncle, who was visiting his daughter from rural Wollo. My mother had not heard I was arrested but suspected that I was in deep trouble.

I do not remember if it was the same day or the next day, I called Berhane, who I knew was in a responsible position and knew me closely. We had lived underground in the same apartment together. I went to where he was staying near Entoto. I don't remember if I got him there or not, but I met two girls, one of whom I knew he was dating. I must have waited for him there. On the way back I took a bus, which I realized after I boarded, passed through the front of the *kebele* where I was arrested and even made stops right in front of it. I got off at Menilik Adebabay and waited to take a taxi. It took me some time to get into one, which was a frightening moment for me. Finally I got a taxi, which added another person who was going in the Haji *kebele* direction. I told the taxi to drop me, and got off by the old post office that was within eyesight of the *kebele*. I went back to Churchill Road and took a taxi to the national theater.

I must have met Berhane once or twice. I remember meeting him in Full Wuha clearly. I told him what had happened to me. I asked him for money and an ID card so I could go to Dessie. I told him that I was not interested in going to Assimba and had given up on the party. All I wanted was an ID card to help me through the checkpoints. I will try to stay in rural Wollo and save my life.

Berhane said that he would arrange for me to meet someone with a code. The other person will provide me with an ID card and money. He told me to meet the person in front of a *tej bet* (liquor house) in Gojjam Berenda.

I believed him and did so. The guy never came. I went again the next day but did not meet the said guy. Berhane had told me that he was preparing to leave for Assimba, so I called the place where he was staying. They must have told me he no longer lived there or I must have gone and checked. But I knew I had been had by this individual for whom I did not have any respect. I was mad. I was fuming with anger. At that point, all EPRP seemed to me like Berhane—worthless, honorless, and cruel.

When I first met Berhane in America, he apologized for leaving me in Addis. In a candid statement, he remarked what he did was tantamount to a death sentence on me. In his view, I was a high risk for the party and it was better to leave me than try to help me out in any way. I was supposed to be a casualty of the war. It was just a matter of luck that it did not happen that way.

Not all EPRP people were like that, of course. Many EPRP members were the finest individuals one can find anywhere. They were brave and selfless. Many of these never left Addis. They died for an inglorious cause and gullible organization. In fact, the organization was much less than the many individuals who were members in it. EPRP at its peak had the finest members of the Ethiopian youth, who paid dearly for the poor leadership of the organization.

I came to know one of these individuals, named Abdella, who used to live with his mother near my cousin's house. He was living in his sister's house, and I somehow managed to contact him. His younger brother, one of the most daring EPRP youth that I knew, was slain a few months before in Merkato, and his mother was doing her best to save the older one. Once I was able to get in touch with him, my security position slightly improved. He was assisted by a network of family members who counterspied on the *kebele*; told us where to stay, which areas were safe, and other things.

It must be sometimes in the first two weeks I went to my aunt's (she is an aunt twice removed) house to eat lunch. A nephew of hers and a second cousin to me lived with her, along with her four daughters. My second cousin was detained in the *kebele* prison like tens of thousands of young people who were being mass arrested. While I was sitting there, my second cousin was brought back to the house by the *kebele* revolutionary guards. After they came into the house, one of them stood at the door, and pointing his pistol toward everybody in the house, ordered us not to move. I had seen this guard before as he used to come to the *kebele* where I was arrested. Then my second cousin led the other guards into the bedroom, and they started checking for bags, clothes, and jewelry. They came up with jewelry and passports. The daughters were half-Yemeni and were preparing to leave the country for Yemen, where their father lived. The guards seemed surprised and said, "You are thinking of leaving the country before you are exposed for your counter-revolutionary activity." Abdu Said, my second cousin, told the guards that only the two daughter in the middle knew what he was doing and may have collaborated with him in distributing leaflets, painting graffiti on walls, and other crimes. I realized why he did that. He knew the two were too young, naïve, and childish to be suspected of doing anything. He thought if he said the same thing about the older sister that may turn out to be more serious. I knew his reasoning. However, I was not too sure that he would not expose me. But he did not say anything about me either, although he had seen me carrying a pistol and burning EPRP documents at the back of the store.

It looked very hopeless for me. I suspected that sooner or later they were going to ask me for my ID card and that was going to be the end of it. I thought about running through the backdoor. I was sitting on a chair by the wall and looking at the floor so the guard would not identify me. Then he said, "Who is this guy sitting here bowing his head?" I calmed myself as much as I can and told him that I am from the neighborhood and was there for lunch. He did not ask any more questions and sort of got distracted by some jewelry and the passports that his comrades were looking into. Then things quieted down and they took Abdu and the two daughters and left. I left the house and never returned. I was told that my aunt did not want me to come back again either. Actually I never got angry about that. It could have been a terrible disaster for them if I had been arrested in the house and the guard identified me. I thanked God. And I thanked Abdu for keeping my secret.

After this incident, I went to the store of my aunt's son and told him what happened, which alarmed him. From his store, I called Mohamed Arabi's sister and told her who I was. I asked her if I could come to her house. I could have called Mohamed's sister within days after I escaped from prison and told her what happened. For some reason, I decided not to. Because she was not sure of what happened and whether or not her brother was dead, she would go out every morning to every *kebele* where bodies were thrown for display and look for her brother. She had done that for weeks. Had I contacted her as soon as I escaped, she would have known about his death and would not have gone through the agony of looking through human bodies every morning. I very much regretted that. I blamed myself for this, especially after she took extra care to help me, kept me safe for days in those dark hours of my life.

On the phone I asked Amina if it was safe for me to come. She said Seti, Mohamed's younger sister, will check the area and will wait for me by the road. I took a taxi and went to the neighborhood. The neighborhood looked deserted by young people like most neighborhoods at this time. Many of the youth were in the *kebele* prisons. The ones that were not exposed stayed at home. They avoided idle walks on the streets, which justified the

184

revolutionary guards in arresting them. When I got out of the taxi to the small alley, I saw a slogan on the wall: *Demo be Dimotphere* (For EPRP, a DMT-4 bullet). *Demo*, an abbreviation for *Democracia*, was used in place of EPRP. It must have been there even before but had not struck me as much as when I saw it at that time. Seti and I quietly walked and reached the house.

I told the family the full story of what happened. It was particularly difficult for the family to believe that Mohamed had died since I did not see his body. I told them that I had seen him climb the tree. I said, in the morning I heard the revolutionary guards say that he refused to climb down and was shot. They were saying how light-skinned he was. I told her that I knew it was definitely him. They did not want to believe that, but it slowly began to sink in.

This was a remarkable family. Seti broke down and started to cry, but Amina restrained her. The family, including the mother, finally came and started to mourn their dead. The next day other relatives came and joined the mourning. It was no longer a restrained affair, although they never mentioned his name for fear of retaliation by the *kebele*. His mother's words expressed anguish for all the young who were now being decimated by the Red Terror. But on the whole, it was a restrained effort. I do not remember spending the night in the house, but I spent many afternoons in the house and they took special care of me as if I were their brother. It would have been extremely difficult for me to survive this period without the support of people like Amina. She was a mother of two, whose education, it was obvious, was interrupted by her marriage. She was very bright and beautiful. Her husband, a very quiet, religious man who was probably related to her, worked in a hardware store and treated Mohamed just like a brother.

Seti, who was young and angry, told me of her strong desire to fight and kill her brother's murderers. Every time I told her that the fight in Addis was over, I could see she disliked my pessimism and lack of will to fight. To appease her so that she would not do anything foolish, I told her the only way to go now was to continue the struggle from rural areas. At that time, EPRP's sympathizers were saying that the organization was succeeding in the rural areas of Gondar and Tigray.

*   *   *

Sometimes right after I escaped, I thought about giving myself up to someone who was on the government side and who would be able to spare my life. I knew that my situation without the ID card was hopeless, and it was only a matter of time before I got caught. Finally, I decided to contact an old distant friend from Woizero Siheen High School who was working for the National Bank of Ethiopia. He had been sent to Russia for a year of training earlier in the Derg's period. When he came back, he became a senior bureaucrat at the national bank, and I thought that he might be somewhat associated with one of the political organizations that were on the side of the Derg. I found his number and called him. I had not talked to him for years, so he was surprised to get my call. I told him that I wanted to see him about a private matter and would like to meet him at a place of his choosing. He was very apprehensive, but agreed to meet me at the café in Full Wuha.

I knew he was suspicious and was probably even worried that I might do some harm to him. So I went there early and sat in a place where he could see me. He was around the area, observing, and when he saw me he came.

We talked about old friends. He asked me about Birhanu Ejigu, a classmate of his and one of EPRP's leaders. I told him that he had died and his wife had left for Assimba. I asked him about his job. Then I told him that I was involved, as he probably knew, with EPRP. I admitted what I did was childish, but now I felt it was time to get out of that if I could be assured of my safety. I confessed that I was in a bad situation, and had run out of *kebele* detention. He seemed genuinely concerned and expressed interest to help. He said that he was not associated with any of the organizations, but knew of a coworker who dated a senior person in the government. He trusted her and would ask her how best to go about doing it.

I met Kifle three or four times. In the end, I told him the full details of what happened to me. I said my case would not be a straightforward one. It had a lot of risks because lives were lost on both sides and I had escaped from prison. He realized that, and in his usual businesslike manner told me that my life cannot be guaranteed. His advice for me was to give myself up rather than risk being caught again. He gave me a name that the lady had given him and told me that the man had said that he would send a car that would pick me up from wherever I was. Kifle then said that it was not good for him to be meeting with me any longer and that I should take it from there. I took the name and number of the person and we parted. After I came to the United States, I heard Kifle was briefly arrested. I always wondered how he saw the fact that I had refused to give my hands up. I worried if this important humanitarian involvement to help me out had not in any way hurt him. The people who were on the government's side at this time were vicious and vengeful. You can never tell who they would turn against. Kifle's story had a happy ending. He actually came to the United States and confirmed for me that his arrest was not related to my case.

One day, while walking in Merkato I ran into a guy named Thomas, who I knew was a party member or a sympathizer. I used to see him in a neighborhood with a youth group of EPRP. He told me that he had also escaped from prison and was trying to relocate some people. I told him that I saw Abdella regularly. He said if he could meet Abdella he knew how to get hold of other people that could help us find ID cards. I helped Thomas meet Abdella, and Thomas was able to relocate people who were issuing ID cards and facilitating the evacuation of party members to Gondar and Tigray. With Thomas and Abdella, there were about five or six of us who were now regularly meeting and spending the night in different bars and houses. The others were waiting for somebody to give them a code to go to Wollo and meet EPRP guys who would then guide them to Assimba. It was amazing how many of these people went with these codes. It is difficult to know how many made it to Assimba and how many were caught en route. It was said that many of these young people were actually going into government traps and getting caught.

I had not told anyone that my idea was to go as far as Dessie and remain there. I had learned my lesson from Berhane. After Thomas met his people, we were promised an ID card. I was surprised there were EPRP people who were still active and doing that. This was around March 1978, and there was no tangible activity by the party at this point. I met one of the individuals who had made it his duty to help people out. His name, I just recently learned from Thomas, was Sirak Teferra. He was a student in Addis Abeba University whom I used to meet outside the proper channels in Abdella's house. His younger brother also came to this neighborhood. He came from a family with military connections in the emperor's government. I remember he brought interesting military information when the Derg first came to power. A general he knew or was related to was in an important command position in the old army. When I first saw him after I ran from the *kebele* prison, he told me that he was caught one day but the *kebele* people let him go because they could not find anything incriminating against him and no one knew who he was. This was in Nefas Silk. He told me that his sister worked in a government office and would be able to issue a work ID card for me. I could see he was determined to do that to as many people as was needed. He seemed to have taken the responsibility on his own to do this. Sirak repeatedly told me that his position was risky; he knew many members of the pro-government organization who would have him killed. I know Dawit, his younger brother, was sought by the government and had left for Assimba. It was obvious he was not the kind of man that should stay in Addis at all, and was aware of it, but was doing it to help EPRP members get out of Addis.

Sirak was like a quiet hero about whom no one would ever know. The day he said he would come with the ID, his sister was caught and my picture probably fell in the *kebele* hands again. He told me that he would use other sources and find us the document. He was cheerful, very calm, and looked like he believed that nothing would happen. One day he never came to our lunch meeting and I suspected that something had happened to him. Later Abdella told me that he was captured and nobody knew where he was. Very few EPRP members had impressed me as much as Sirak had, about whom I knew very little. This was an extraordinary individual. He could have left the city anytime. He could have saved his life. Sirak was running a one-man EPRP shop for the sole purpose of helping people out. This was the kind of people EPRP wasted. Somehow, I have never been able to erase him out of my memory. To me he was a hero, an unsung hero.

The ID card came but I don't remember how. It looked crude and primitive and was obviously forged. I thought it was good enough to cheat an illiterate revolutionary guard only. We also got some money. I don't remember how much, probably in the order of twenty to fifty birr. One morning, we went to a bus station and saw off one of them. I decided to go the next day.

Before I got the ID card, I would daily agonize over whether to give my hands up or not. At night, under the influence of alcohol, I would make my mind up to do it in the morning. When the morning came, I could not gain the courage to do it. I did not have the slightest trust that my life would be spared. When I thought about it, it was difficult to contemplate detention again. I could never reconcile myself to life in prison with so much uncertainty. I could not imagine how I could get out of that. Intellectually, it seemed the better thing to do than stay in Addis and risk capture. I was emotionally torn. I was unable to decide.

I called the number that Kifle gave me and asked to speak to Yusuf. I do not know whether that was his real name or not. The voice on the other end was authoritative, very firm, and very cold. He said he would send me a car if I chose to give up. Otherwise, I was risking my life. This talk was not encouraging. The guy was ice cold. I told him I would discuss it with my family and would call him back Monday. In English, he said, "The sooner you do it, the better," and hung up.

It is amazing how I was never caught during this time. I was moving from place to place constantly. Twice I saw Haji and his van in Merkato. I had changed my appearance. I was probably getting heavier every day. From the look of me, I looked like someone who had a comfortable life. Moneywise, I was doing fine. I would call the store of my second cousin and he would send some money through another cousin. He would give me enough for food, to pay for my lodging, which invariably was in bars or motels. I somehow managed to find a place that was not being checked every night. I frequented some places, but mostly changed places. The people never seemed to suspect that I was a fugitive. Sometimes all five of us or six of us stayed in the same block. We were lucky for the most part, because the *kebele*s had now realized the remnants of EPRP were hiding out in these slum houses at night and were checking them with deadly frequency. But the area of Merkato is probably the world's worst slum area, with countless places to sleep at. It was difficult to cover most of these areas at night. They often did a random search and left some places, the ones that seemed too shabby and poor to be bothered with.

One night, Abdella and I were drinking *tella* in this area. We sat in a small room within a grain storage that was rented by one his relatives. It was very safe since the *kebele* saw it as storage only. While we were waiting in this area, the radio announced that Jijiga had been liberated from the invading Somali army. This news was welcomed with enormous uproar in the neighborhood. The announcement made the usual connection between external and internal enemies and how all of them were now being crushed by the revolution. The applause was spontaneous; people felt genuinely proud of the accomplishment of the Ethiopian army, which supported by a strong Cuban armored division had ousted the invader. The Somalis were completely routed. When I saw and heard the reaction, I felt once again how out of touch we in the EPRP were with the people. I felt once again that we were doomed right from day one. There was no way we could have defeated such a state power that could mobilize hundreds of thousands of troops and had the support of the Soviet Union and Cuba.

The situation in Addis Abeba at this time was indescribably strange. The government was winning the war in the east against the Somali invasion. Every night there were announcements of victory after victory; people were very happy about it and applauding the announcements. The government's propaganda said that both the internal and external enemies of the country were being crushed. The propaganda also made it look like the victory against the invasion was directly tied to success against EPRP's "hired assassins" in the country. To support the war on the front, the people of Addis Abeba were being mobilized through the *kebele*s and asked to contribute money.

The most prevalent way of fundraising for the war was organizing festivities and selling food and drink for cash. Each *kebele* tried to outdo what the other had done by organizing these festivities where food, *tej*, and *tella* were sold to the people. People would go to these places, dine, and drink. This was going on all over Addis at the same time people were quietly mourning tens of thousands of their dead. The country seemed intoxicated with alcohol and blood. The *kebele*s were slaughtering thousands of oxen for these festivities, so much so that at one point there was a warning about losing this important workhorse of the country's farming system.

Blood was flowing in Addis and all over the country, and the country seemed to be celebrating. The country was in a strange mood, very strange to describe. Death of human beings and death of young people and death of animals and a celebration of the victory with a huge party all over town. There was terror in Addis among parents whose children were arrested and killed daily, their bodies were thrown on the streets. The same parents were also being forced to participate in these festivities or risk being accused of being sympathizers of EPRP. I had never wanted to leave this country more. It was blood and gore all over. It was like one gruesome horror movie on a grand scale.

Many nights I came close to being caught by the *kebele* revolutionary guards. They often came close to the places I used to sleep and miraculously stopped their search. These were close encounters that I survived from.

On the eve of my departure to Dessie, I drank more profusely than before. Because of my ID card, I chose to sleep in a motel. I was very emotional and chatty. I told a stranger I was going to see my parents the next day, whom I had not seen for a long time, and how happy they would be to see me. With so much alcohol in my system, I was sure that I was going to make it, although that was not a sure bet, especially given my suspect ID card. I also had serious misgivings, because I had told Haji where I was born. He could put people in one of the checkpoints near Addis to catch me.

The trip to Dessie was very smooth. I passed the first and most crucial checkpoint without any problem. The soldier did not even bother to look at the ID card; he just looked at the letter with *kebele* stamps that I was carrying. I did not look suspicious. Halfway between Addis and Dessie, I bought fruits and sugarcane and carried them in a basket just like people do when they visit their relatives. After I departed in Dessie, I walked from the bus station to my parents' house. Later I was told that some people did identify me while walking home. When I reached home, my brother Jemal was playing outside. I smiled when I saw him, but he instinctively knew not to make a scene and come to meet me. My mother and her aunt were outside, intensely talking about me. My mother recognized me from afar. Everyone kept quiet and looked in awe as I quietly walked into our one-bedroom, very tiny house.

My mother was elated and nervous. She did not know what to do. She thought about sending me that night to her parents' place outside Dessie. The crucial problem was keeping my presence secret, especially from the *kebele*s who might search that night. My mother felt that she had to tell some neighborhood people as they would find out anyway. Some came and talked to me. In the morning, my sister brought my uncle from a rural area about fifteen kilometers from Dessie. We rented a horsecart halfway and walked the remaining part of the trip. There was a little bit of rain in the country after a long dry season, and my uncle thought it was a good omen.

LIFE IN GRAGN MEDA

My stay in my grandparents' house ran into a big problem. They knew right away that I was too much risk for them to handle. My uncle's wife said that people had seen me come and they would sooner or later tell the rural farm association leaders who I was and why I was staying. Intense negotiations were going on without my knowledge between my mother and her parents. My mother felt she was let down and was crying every day. She was making the trip on foot very frequently and negotiating. I was more understanding of the situation. My uncle could never fathom the foolish thing I had done. He told me that his respect for educated people had hit rock bottom and could not understand why I brought this on me and my family. I had also come to realize what I had done was unpardonable and was blaming myself for my mistakes. I knew I had let down my family when I was their only hope out of poverty. My father's business in grain dealing had come to a complete halt and the family's survival was hanging on the balance. I was deeply hurt. Every time I saw my mother cry, it was very difficult to restrain my tears. I was terribly saddened for destroying my brothers' and sister's hope and letting them down.

This arrangement was to be a short one until I adjusted to rural life. A day after I arrived, my uncle shaved my hair and I put on peasant clothes. For the next fifteen days, I would leave the house every day and stay secluded in a wooded area, aimlessly wandering around or sitting and reflecting. I tried to write some poems, but I was too unfocused and dispirited. My mother came very often and visited, but I really did not like to see her. It created so much emotion and made me feel even more depressed. Some fifteen days later, my uncles on my father's side agreed to take me, and I went through Dessie to Gragn Meda, a rural area on the road to Worreillu. I rode a cart to Segno Gebaya and was met by my father and uncle, who brought a mule.

My father accompanied me to Gragn Meda. My father, who could not make the walk to the area because of his asthma and poor health, rode the mule. I was offered to ride with him but refused and took the long walk.

In Gragn Meda, I lived in a hamlet on top of a hill where seven of my uncles lived. Practically everyone who was living here was in some way related to me. I felt unbelievably safe. I could not imagine anyone betraying me.

The living arrangement was such that I was to sleep in the oldest uncle's house. He had an only child, a son, my age and was the richest of them all. He owned a pair of oxen and had a big house covered with a tin roof as opposed to straw—a symbol of wealth in rural Ethiopia. I was to eat lunch with another uncle, who was also considered well-off and had some business dealings with the older one. The arrangement was practical and allowed for some burden sharing. My other uncles were either very poor as the youngest one was, or had too big families for them to support me. But they all invited me to their houses and fed me every time they got a chance. I really loved them and was touched by their kindness and warmth.

Relations between my uncles were very friendly and generally warm. The oldest one was highly respected and acted as a father figure to them all. He mediated disputes, provided assistance when other families were in distress and provided leadership for the kinship. He was very smart, spoke his mind bluntly, and was considered very fair. As the titular head of the village, he had nominal but effective authority to arbiter disputes and counsel wisdom.

My father was the only one of the eight brothers who was not living in the rural area. Two of my aunts lived in different places, having been married off and moved to where their husbands lived. Before the revolution, my uncles tilled their ancestral land together and never redistributed their holdings. It was a communal ownership, although each also acquired properties through marriage and purchases. I was told that the arrangement worked well and there were no disputes that threatened to split up the land until the change in the landholding system brought about by the Land Proclamation Act.

My father was entitled to the land. He could have initiated for the land to be redistributed. I remember my mother used to pressure him to do so. But he refused and was happy to receive whatever grain they were able to give him when the harvest was good. I found out that my father was well liked by my uncles. He was a middle child and was the only one who had traditional Islamic education. So he read a little in Arabic, mainly the Koran, and was called *Shih*, a title that was given to men with basic Islamic education. Nothing came out of his Islamic studies, but my father taught himself arithmetic and was able to use that in his grain retail business. My father was exceptionally good in arithmetic (*hisab*); he always caught me making computational errors even in high school. He was especially good at mentally calculating large numbers, whereas I always had to resort to paper and pencil before I attempted to calculate them.

My father's very warm relationship with his brothers made my life in Gragn Meda very bearable. None of my immediate uncles were in the position of responsibility in the new farmers associations that were now mushrooming all over the country. But others they were related to by blood were chairmen and leaders in the newly formed revolutionary guards. For example, the chairman of the revolutionary squad was my father's cousin and lived in an adjacent village. The chairman of the association was related to them, but was also said to be my oldest uncle's rival and somewhat of a risk factor to me.

The relationship in the kinship was not always that friendly. In fact, there were serious enmities between their spouses that affected the sons and daughters and eventually my uncles. Some of these cousins were in competition with one another and would probably not hesitate to harm each other. Relations between my oldest uncle's wife and one of the others were particular hateful, with each accusing the other of scheming to poison or hurt her. The intensity of these hatreds was surprising to me. They would tell me stories to show how evil the other one was. Some of these allegations were so scary that it was difficult to imagine how long these conflicts could be subdued without one day breaking the kinship apart.

I brought a shortwave radio that I gave my family some years before when I joined the university and listened to BBC, Radio Germany, and Voice of America in English. I could not find a book to read, and my mother refused to send me any reading material for fear that I would be exposed. But the radio was my best friend and I listened to it a lot. I also herded the cattle, worked on the farm, and did a lot of manual work that I really enjoyed. My effort at learning farming was so awkward, my cousin refused to spend time to teach me. But I helped pluck weeds from farms, transported stuff, and provided some valuable service. I also began to teach my cousins how to read and write. Some of them learned very fast and some did not and consequently competition added to the conflict and tensions among them.

The rivalry was especially intense between my two cousins whose mothers hated each other the most. My oldest uncle's son was very smart, articulate, business savvy, and very cocky with unbelievable self-confidence. He was successful in his business dealings and was making money. However, for some reason he was slow in learning how to read and write. His rival, my other cousin, was not as successful in his business but very much excelled over the business-savvy in learning how to read and write. The former could not accept that and I could see he was becoming nasty about his weakness in literacy.

Nothing worthwhile that I can now remember came out of my literacy effort, but these young farmers impressed me with their intelligence and common sense. The only thing I had that they did not was some formal education, but they proved to me in many ways they would have been academically more successful than I had been if only they had the opportunity to attend. Many of these young men were especially good in arithmetic or what they called *hisab*. Knowing *hisab* helped with business. Being able to compute mentally helped one figure out whether or not a transaction would make or lose money. They had to do this fast in their mind and they had to be sure they got it right. Because of the intrusion of their daily lives, which kept these young men busy, I could not pursue the literacy effort to fruition in the six months that I lived in Gragn Meda.

My life in rural Ethiopia was quiet, busy, and safe. I felt really safe and began to think that I would be able to survive this ordeal. I was not sure how I was going to get out of the situation and join society as a free man. I did not think the situation would stay like that indefinitely. One day I knew that someone was bound to tell the authorities that my uncles were sheltering a fugitive. Sooner or later I would be asked to expose myself to the authorities and ask for forgiveness, for what I could never be sure.

*　*　*

The government's war with the Eritrean Liberation Front (ELF) and Eritrean People's Liberation Front (EPLF) was going very well in 1978. From Gragn Meda, about thirty kilometers away from Dessie, we could hear the rumbling of convoys taking troops, heavy weapons, and supplies to Eritrea. This massive transportation of goods, tanks, and weapons had scared Wollo into complete submission, although there was no resistance to the government to begin with. People talked about it and could not believe what they saw or heard. The government was all powerful, and they thought that one had to be completely out of his mind to try to rebel against it.

Soon the mass media was bragging about successes in Eritrea. ELF, which had taken more cities and areas all the way from the Sudan border to Tigray, was quickly thrown back by a two-pronged attack from the south through Tigray and the west through Gondar. Every night the government was claiming successes, and it appeared like ELF was finished. EPLF put up more impressive resistance around Keren. Five or six of the government's attempts to take Keren were frustrated. From Gragn Meda, I sympathized with what seemed to be EPLF's heroic effort. And every time the BBC spoke of about these engagements, I was fascinated by the determined resistance. Keren symbolized something to me, but I was not sure what. Some days I was ambivalent and hoped the war would be over. Maybe the government would relax and we all could return to society, I hoped. By this time I had completely given up on politics and had made a decision to stay out of leftist politics once and for all.

I never discussed politics with my uncles. To them EPRP and EDU were the same thing. They asked me if it was true the crown prince was pushing from Sudan into Ethiopia supported by Queen Elizabeth. I was shocked to hear that they knew nothing of EPRP. This convinced me again that EPRP was an urban youth phenomenon that the average person had very little in common with. Our language was alien, our songs foreign, and our slogans indistinguishable from the Derg. I thought we had really bungled it up with this revolutionary effort at the cost of tens of thousands of lives.

One day my uncle brought a student named Said from another neighborhood, who was living as a fugitive with his parents. He had gone to Woizero Siheen High School, was involved with EPRP, and was hiding here away from the authorities. We talked, quickly opened up to one another, and discussed politics. He sounded like he had faith in EPRP and expected it to win victories from its bases in Tigray. I was amazed at this illusion in the face of realities. I must have told him that EPRP was history now and that he should try to reconstruct his life and start afresh if he could.

Said became a very good friend to me. Having grown in rural areas, he knew the culture more than I did. He told me what to do and what not to do, some of which taken from chapters of Mao Tse Tung books on guerilla warfare. He advised me to stay out of trouble by counseling me against the one indiscretion that a youth of my age was liable to indulge in even at the risk of being exposed. He also invited me to his house. His father slaughtered a sheep to entertain me. I stayed there a few days and came back. We regularly visited one another.

I do not remember a bad time I had living in rural area. I was mentally getting out of the depression and the paranoia of life in Addis. I lost my excess fat and looked sturdy and fit. Except probably for my accent, I now fitted in the society and looked like any other rural young man. I spent the days either in the farm or herding cattle on the hills. There was no drought at this time in Gragn Meda; the farms looked bountiful. The streams were flowing and the hills were covered with green vegetation. These seemed like the rural Wollo I knew when I was a child and before the deadly famine of 1972. I wrote some poems and a short story about my life and rural Ethiopia, which was beginning to fascinate me. One of my short poems was entitled

"The Sea Coast." Although I had never seen an ocean before, I wrote about being stranded in the middle of the sea with the coast getting further and further away from me. It was about my yearning for freedom, which seemed as far off as I ever thought it would be.

*   *   *

The revolution had made few inroads into this area at this time. I did not try to learn the land-tenure system, or how the distribution of land was executed. I was not even sure if my uncles' ancestral land was divided up, although if it was it seemed like it was done without lasting conflict. However, there were two things that occupied the discussion of the peasants at this time. One was the talk of the establishment of cooperative farms, which everyone, poor or rich, was intensely worried about. I never heard anyone say anything good about it even among my uncles, who had worked on their father's land together for so long. There was a deep sense of uneasiness about this plan that I noticed my uncles were deeply troubled by it. Since I was also a believer in the superiority of the socialist agricultural system—although I also believed the Derg, lacking proper socialist credentials, would not be able to do it—I was astonished by the people's animosity toward it. I was convinced that they would never accept it unless it was imposed. I realized it was fundamentally wrong to do it when there was so much fear and hatred of cooperative farms. This fear was across the board. Even the poor thought this was a stupid idea that should never be implemented. I had never seen people who were more individualistic than the peasants of this area. The other thing that worried them most was the draft. While the draft was not as massive as it later became, people, specially the ones who could not afford the bribes and had more than one son, were scared their son would be taken off to Tateke Military Camp where the government was training soldiers. These two issues occupied every family's mind and were the topics of subdued discussions over coffee and food.

In one sense, I was elevated by the sense of temporary freedom I acquired moving to the countryside. This was the sort of freedom that I took for granted before but was now able to appreciate deeply. Roaming the hills of Gragn Meda lifted my spirits and energized my life and made me more optimistic of the possibility of one day becoming a free man.

My mother and I began to work on a plan for me to go to Djibouti, a country that shared a border with Ethiopia. My mother contacted my friend Mahmoud, a store owner whose wife knew people who lived in Asaita, a city near the Danakil Depression and close to Djibouti. Nomads and caravans moved back and forth between Asaita and Djibouti. Many young people had made their escapes to Djibouti, although some had also perished in the desert. My friend was apprehensive about the plan and told my mother that it was very risky for him to be seen with her since some people in the neighborhood knew who she was. His wife, on the other hand, was braver and told my mother that she would try to make contact with people she knew in Asaita. While we were planning this, my mother brought the news that Mohamed Ahimed, a friend that I grew up with, had made it to America through Djibouti and Greece. He was not involved with EPRP and had left for Djibouti before the Ethiopian revolution really turned bloody. I had heard he was in Djibouti and faced a hard time, but was surprised that he had made it the US and was even able to send money to his mother.

Finally the contact was made and a day sometime in September was arranged for me to go up to Asaita. My cousin got me a security clearance from Dessie under his name, and I was able to get a letter and ID card from a chairman of a peasant association who was related to one of my uncles by marriage. All of these went smoothly and I set foot for a town named Kombolcha, a town south of Dessie, from which I was to take the bus to Assaita.

I was accompanied by the youngest of my uncles since I did not know the foot trail to Kombolcha. When we reached Kombolcha, we saw a huge convoy of military supplies going to the north. We stood by the roadside and counted over a hundred huge trucks passing by. My mother and my younger brother Jemal met us there and we went to sleep in her cousin's house. Unbeknown to us, my mother's cousin's son was a youth cadre working for the *kebele* association. It had not occurred to me or my mother to check on who was who in the family. I could see my mother was terrified to see this young man who was boldly talking about the destruction of EPRP and other enemies of the people. Luckily my mother had not told them who would come to sleep that night, but had just told her cousin that she, my mother, and this *sheikh* (me) were going on a pilgrimage to a famous grave site in Getta, east of Kombolcha. A lot of Muslims go to this grave site and offer money for the fulfillment of their wishes and pray every year. That night, this young man chillingly talked about his exploits and how his organization was able to get rid of EPRP elements from the town while I listened.

My mother and I agreed to keep my identity secret since this relative did not seem dependable. My mother's cousin asked about Mezy and about me. My mother told her that Mezy was out of the country but I was living in Addis and was safe for the time being. My instinct told me she knew who I was although she would not say it. I kept my mouth shut, which by itself probably made me suspect to my relative. There was no incident, and in the morning I prepared to take the minibus that would take me to Asaita.

My father convinced my mother that he should go with me to Asaita instead of her. She reluctantly agreed. The night before, my mother gave me about 500 hundred birr, of which 150 came from the sale of my Seiko watch. I had kept this watch for a rainy day, and I was happy my friend was able to fetch a good price for it. The remaining money came also from him. Although he did not want to be personally involved in my escape plan, he was willing to fund it. I left about a 150 birr with my mother. I knew they needed it for food. The economic situation in my family had deteriorated so much that I felt my family faced starvation. My mother had started buying fifty or sixty kilograms of grain and selling them at small quantities to consumers who can only afford to buy what they can for each day. She probably could make a bir or two more if she sold the entire amount. I could see the tension—the frequent trips to my hideout and her heroic effort to feed the family—was taking its toll on her. She complained of ailments in her body, of headaches and heartaches, and was looking thinner and thinner. My worst fear was that I would not be able to make it in time to give her some support. The thought that my family could perish from famine (or even if they did not), could be completely disrupted, was sending me into feats of melancholy.

My father and I sat separately in the bus. The bus stopped at every town and dropped off or picked up passengers. I sat next to a lady who was chewing *khat*. She offered me some and I chewed what she gave me and felt a little bit euphoric. We passed Bati and reached the major checkpoint before we got to Asaita. We all went out of the bus and returned one person at a time, with a soldier standing by the door of the minibus, checking people's documents. These soldiers spent all day looking at these papers and were often visibly bored. I guessed they checked more seriously the ones that they suspect and let others off with just a glance at the documents. I was not scared about these checkpoints. Someone had to have told them about me to suspect who I was. I went in first and looked outside at my father, who was visibly shaking. I gave the soldier a folded document from the farmers' association in Anto Ena Abuto near Gragn Meda. The solider casually unfolded it and looked at it briefly and gave it back. My father was very happy.

We made it to Asaita late. We found a lady that my father knew and slept in a bed outside without a roof. I gazed at the blue sky and the stars and contemplated freedom. I knew the biggest hurdle was in front of me, but hoped I would be able to make it.

In the morning, my father and I went to a shop where I was supposed to meet my contact, who would connect me with the people that would take me to Djibouti. He lived three to four hours from Asaita by the Awash River in the middle of the desert. The owner of the store told us he had not been there and won't be there for another week. She told us that she had been told to give us shelter and food by my friend's wife. She was very hospitable and made us coffee and asked my father to make the *fatiha*, Islamic prayer.

My father stayed another day and left early in the morning. I told him I will be okay and wait for the person to come. He prayed and said that he was not sure that he would be able to see me again, but wished me good luck and kissed me goodbye. A sick man suffering from chronic and acute asthma, my father was not sure that he would live long enough to see me. I told him that my plan was to go to Saudi Arabia once I made it to Djibouti and try to find work. I was hoping that I would be able to find a job and come to the support of my family in the darkest hours of their life. My father died in 1988. I never made a special effort to bring him to the US and see him since I was focused on getting my brothers out.

ESCAPE TO FREEDOM

The wait in Asaita was tough and difficult. My safety was in jeopardy. I stayed and slept in the backyard of a shop owner with one of her servants. In the morning, I walked by Awash River and saw the daily laborers. These were mostly peasants who come here seasonally to make some money for taxes, and supplement their farm income. Life was harsh for most of these people and the environment was inhospitable. Many came with malaria and other diseases. I wandered aimlessly by the riverbanks with other people. I saw the Afars swim across the river, carrying their clothes on their head, to the other side and marveled at their swimming skills. One day, the lady told me that my guide will come the next day and would take me out of the town.

The night before I did one of most reckless things that I have always regretted. I went out to one of these local drinking places that I saw during the day. I went in and ordered *tej* or *tella*. Muslims in Wollo drink alcohol in public, but I was not sure if they did it in this area of the desert; the Afars were far stricter Muslims. I was not sure if doing that would not raise the suspicion of people. The place was not a big one where many people drink together. While I sat there and was drinking, I noticed there were two men flirting with a woman. I could see these were not locals, and from their looks, appeared to be every bit the feared cadres. I knew I had made a terrible mistake. I ordered a drink quietly with a big effort to sound like a peasant from Wollo. One of the men started a conversation, although I was praying they would not talk to me. He asked me where I was from. I told him that I was from Anto Ena Abuto, the village from where the farmers' association issued my ID card. He went on to ask more questions and I could see his curiosity was increasing. I now could talk with a peasant accent, although I was not sure how good it was. In fact, I had made it a habit of speaking that way so no one would ever suspect me. I could see this conversation developing to a very uncomfortable level and was looking for an opportune moment to barge out. The moment came. One of men left unexpectedly, probably to relieve himself. A few minutes later the other retreated to the next room. I felt that something was wrong. I knew how much the drinks cost, so I put the exact change where the lady could see it and left in a hurry. I went to the riverbank so they could not trace my way, and went back to my sleeping place. I knew I had blundered and was worried that they would do an all-out search specially the next day.

Luckily for me, my guide came the next day. I followed my guide to a bridge, the main crossing point for cars, animals, and humans out of Asaita to the surrounding areas. This was a crucial checkpoint, but we passed it without rousing any suspicion. Then we walked through the desert, probably about four or five hours, where no one who is not a native Afar or a government official lived. We walked through countless palm trees and manmade canals connected to Awash River and made it to a small village.

The Afars are a nomad people. The government had succeeded in settling only a small fraction of the people by the Awash River. The others roamed through this desolate area, a part of which is among the hottest areas in the world. I noticed they had a different way of life from the peasants I knew. They carried weapons and a big saber and looked very intimidating. Their social organization is based on clans who fight among one another for grazing land and water. They are probably like the Bedouins of Arabia.

My guide, who spoke fluent Amharic, told me that the caravan I was supposed to leave with had left a day earlier. According to him, there are two ways to get to Djibouti. The longer one takes fifteen or more days and does not pass through a government checkpoint. The short one goes through Affambo, a strategic hill where a brigade-size Ethiopian army was stationed. The caravan that passes through Affambo must go through a checkpoint. I would not be able to pass through without being able to speak the language. It was obvious that I would be easily identified as a highlander and captured. He then pointed out there are guides who could take me around at night so I will not have to pass through the checkpoint. He would let me know when he found out the next group of travelers.

I stayed here for another fifteen days. I learned to eat a special kind of cornbread and camel's milk. I traveled around with him from one neighborhood to another. I especially enjoyed walking by the riverbank to kill the day. There were some other men who were related to him. I don't remember them speaking to me. We ate *khat* in the afternoon and prayed. The women showed up to bring food, but I never even looked at them. However, from the few glances I was able to steal, I was surprised to find that they looked like Arab women. Life here was empty. I saw corn growing in their backyards, but farming was not a way of life. My hosts seemed reasonably affluent, with more than enough to eat and a place to sleep. Water is the common problem here. They drank the water from Awash. Because of the heavy commercial use of the river, the water contained all sorts of chemicals and fertilizers that wash into it from the commercial farms. Many people and animals are said to have died. But the Afars that I was with did not seem to care. They carried this water in a bucket made of animal skin. This kept the water cool, which only meant the water was not boiling hot. The taste was horrible.

My departure came unexpectedly. I was to leave with a caravan that goes through Afambo. I was told that the guide would take me around the hill where the soldiers were stationed at night and meet the caravan past Afambo. My guide had done this before and saved the lives of many people. I was told that this would cost me a hundred birr. My host charged me another hundred birr for the food and accommodation, which I gladly paid. I felt very lucky that I was charged only a hundred by the guide

We set out in the morning. In the caravan, there was a young lady and her son riding on a camel. There were about six or seven of us. We walked for many hours and we rested and we started walking again. We reached an open space with a camel route. At the distance was a hill. I heard them say that was Afambo. Halfway to Afambo, my guide signaled me to follow him, and we broke away from the main group. We went into a bush. Here, by the caravan route, was the place where Awash River disappeared. There were plenty of vegetation for miles and miles away and this was as thick as can be. We started walking through the bush, and after travelling for some time, my guide stopped me and signaled with his hand for me to look at the top of the hill. There, within my eyesight, were two soldiers with binoculars scanning the route the caravan was traveling. I froze where I stood. I was 100 percent sure they had seen us break away from the group. I saw the end coming. I felt my luck had finally deserted me. I was angry at this guide, who was intensely looking toward the hill. I said to myself, "What a fool I am to entrust my life to a man who is stupid enough not to wait until dark and bring me here." For what seemed like an eternity while we squatted in the bush and waited, I thought about returning. I had told myself not to take any chance on my life again and here I was taking a terrible risk. I debated with myself. I was mad at this guy, who did not know a word of Amharic and with whom I was communicating in signs. I signaled to him to tell him that soldiers had seen us. He did not get it. Finally, realizing that I had come too far to return and having no other way of getting out of the country anyway, I decided to take the risk and follow this man.

When darkness fell and the soldiers left, we started walking. Things were barely visible now. After walking for an hour or so, we started climbing the hill. At this point I was imagining that the solders would wait ahead, ambush and catch us. I was trying to think of stories that I should tell in case I got caught. There was nothing I could tell them that would get me out of trouble. It looked like we kept on climbing forever. He seemed to know where he was going. Many times I pushed on stones that rolled down with such noise I was sure that whoever was waiting would know where we were. At one point, he stopped and pointed in the direction we were going. I saw two bushes that looked like they were humans and froze. I was getting ready to put my hands up so they won't shoot at us, when I realized they were not soldiers. He smiled. I could not tell whether he was scared or not. He looked intent on getting the job done. This climbing took forever, but we might have just walked for a couple of hours. When we reached the top, the area began to brighten up because of the emerging moonlight. He signaled me toward one direction and I saw a flicker of light in the distance. I thought these were the soldiers' hamlets. We started walking down and in different directions. Now I began to calm down and began to think that they might not have seen us after all. As soon as we began to climb down, a spectacular full moon emerged in the horizon. I will never forget this scenery that emerged in the desolate horizon of the desert. It was a beautiful and heartwarming sight, and it could not have appeared at a better time.

The fire was that of the caravan that had settled down for the night. When we approached their place, my guide made a noise to let them know it was us. We stayed there a few more hours and started the trek. My guide returned from there. This time, he would take the direct route back. I was touched by what he did for me, but did not know how to thank him. That day we crossed the Ethiopian border to the Republic of Djibouti. I was very happy but very restrained, since some more days of traveling through a dangerous and desolate desert waited. I was optimistic but not sure that my trouble was over.

If traveling through the desert was difficult, I did not show it. I was not tired. I was no thirstier than they were. I was in good condition from trekking in the highlands of Gragn Meda. I slept well wherever we stopped. They had rugs and cloths to sleep on. I slept in the clothes I was wearing. I provided labor when they were loading and unloading the camels and never sat before all of them did. The Afars often laughed at my misunderstanding of their signals. During many of these stops for water at the oasis, we were met by armed Afar men. They came, talked to the people in their language, ate, and left. They all looked at me but never seemed particularly unfriendly, although they must have recognized I was not Afari. They looked intimidating with their weapons, and the very sight of them was often a cause for concern. I remember wondering what in the world they were doing in this terrible land and in that heat. These young men looked so pensive and unhappy in this isolated existence.

We slept a few nights in areas where some communities lived. We were fed camel meat and milk. Many times I joined in prayers. I saw a few of these communities with thousands of goats and cattle grazing in the open space. Otherwise the vast spans of this desolate land seemed empty and completely inhospitable.

Four or five days later, around 6:00 p.m. we saw Dehil from very far. This is a border city about five or six hours from the port city of Djibouti. I could see that the Dehil had electricity. My spirits soared. Finally It looked like I was approaching civilization, and with good luck, freedom. I kneeled down and kissed the sand. I began to talk to the kid who was going to attend school in Djibouti. I asked him what grade he was in and if he spoke French. Using the few French words I knew, I said, "How do you do?" which delightfully surprised him. They did not know who I was but may have suspected that I had some schooling. Now they all looked surprised at my sudden transformation from a quiet, somber young man to a buoyant traveler.

I started singing "Quanta La Mera," a Spanish song that I had always loved. I had always loved this song ever since I heard Sahle sing it in Jimma. In my mind, it had some association with Che Guevara. It was the song that came to mind. I sang it loud for all of them to hear. It was like briefly I became insane with excitement, like someone who just regained his speech. My eyes were filled with tears. It was one of the most beautiful feelings I ever experienced.

After we stayed the night in Dehil, I was told that I needed some document to get to Djibouti. I saw other refugees who were waiting for these documents. Some of these refugees said it was common for refugees to be arrested. I was told that some had actually disappeared and some have been taken back and left in the Ethiopian border. This troubled me a great deal but did not think it would actually happen to me.

I got some of my Ethiopian birr changed to the Djibouti frank and bought my friends Coca-Cola. I found that Coca-Cola cost a lot of money and the cost of living in Djibouti was so high that the cash I had left would not last me but a few days. But I decided to indulge anyway, and I thought my friends appreciated my treat. The next day, they talked to a minibus driver, who promised that he would get me to Djibouti without having to wait for a document. I decided to go. Just before we reached Djibouti, we were stopped and checked. I saw the driver talk to one of the policemen at the checkpoint. I was not asked anything, passed the place, and went to a place where it was arranged for me to stay until I found other refugees.

The people where I went to spend the night were very warm and friendly. They treated us to a delicious dinner of roasted lamb and rice, Middle Eastern style. After dinner, khat was served. I was really overwhelmed with joy and very emotional. I felt like opening up and telling them what had happened to me over the last ten months. Many times I was tempted to tell them about my life, the mistakes I have made that had nearly cost my life. Once again, this devout Muslim family reminded me of what I had given up in life when I gave up Islam and became half agnostic. Here was a Muslim family in all of their simplicity, generosity, and kindness. I was deeply touched. I felt like telling them that Allah helped me out from the terrible quagmire I was in. This was as close to a conversion experience as I had come in life.

Finally I had made it to freedom. For now, what awaited me ahead and all the other things did not matter. I was free, and I was experiencing it with all my being.

In the morning, my host told me where Ethiopian refugees hang out and how to get there. I went to a neighborhood called Carte Du, adjacent to the nicer portion of the town where the French used to live when this port city was a French colony. Near Carte Du, I met two gentlemen in a small place who made a living by repairing shoes. I told them where I came from and one of them told me that he used to be an official in Woreillu before the revolution. We talked about the revolution and what was going on in Ethiopia. I told them that the Derg was now fully in control in the country and there was no hope of going back. I noticed they had some illusions that EDU, which they supported and had a brief ascendancy in the early days of the revolution, would be able to overthrow the regime and restore them to their former status.

They told me where many of the Ethiopian refugees lived and how they lived. Many of them passed by their store and they would introduce me when they came. While I was sitting with them, a refugee named Sellesshi, a graduate of Yared Music School, came by. They called him and told him that I had just arrived from Ethiopia and that I was looking for a lady named Zebiba. Zebiba was the name I brought from Ethiopia so she could help me until I got settled. I told Seleshi that Zebiba was related to me. He said that he knew who she was and where she lived, and would be happy to take me there. I followed him. He was wearing a clean white shirt and shorts appropriate for the climate and looked well-kept and comfortable, different from the image of a refugee that I had in mind. He took me to a palace owned by a very successful and prosperous businesswoman. She owned bars and restaurants and other businesses in Djibouti. She was said to be a supporter of EDU and was providing food and shelter to a selected number of refugees, who I was told could prove family connections to the Ethiopian gentry.

I joined these refugees, both women and men, for lunch. These individuals were well dressed and seemed every bit as happy as if they were at home. They were well dressed, clean, and comfortable. The food was obviously very expensive and of high quality, the kind only the rich could afford. I was puzzled since I had expected the refugees to be ill fed and living in squalor. I looked very much out of place in the way I was dressed.

Seleshi took me to the apartment where Zebiba lived and returned from the door. Later I learned that he was not in good terms with the people in the apartment. Seleshi made money by recording songs and selling them among refugees. When I first came to Djibouti, he was the most listened to musician among refugees. His songs of love, country, and the plight of refugees were very popular among refugees and other Ethiopians who lived in Djibouti. His records sold very well.

Zebiba was not there at that time. Instead, I was received by another refugee from Woizero Siheen, Elizabeth Asfaha, who lived with Zebiba. She was warm and friendly and put me at ease. Elizabeth was popular among the people in the apartment who took care of her. She said, "I remember seeing you in Dessie, but you look completely different, and I could not recognize you." Without my Afro, I was a very changed person. Finally, Zebiba came and we all had very nice dinner of *tibse*. We chatted about Wollo and my travel through the desert. We knew many people in common. I was surprised by how excellent, clean, and well-kept the apartment looked. This was something that I was not used to even when I was working. Their life seemed qualitatively different and more affluent. Zebiba went to sleep in her boyfriend's house, an officer in the French army, and left the bed for me.

I could not sleep that night. It seemed like everything was going very well for me that day. The bed was so comfortable and clean it bothered me sleep on it. I was also worried that I might still have some lice that I brought from the Ethiopian highlands. The lice had not survived the last three weeks of desert life, but I was concerned that some or the eggs might still be left. I tried to read but could not concentrate. I rewound my story and went over and over the past. I thought how far I had come from Gragn Meda to Djibouti. I arrived in Djibouti a free man. I felt a mixture of happiness and sadness. What seemed practically impossible about seven or eight months ago, I had now accomplished through good luck, planning, and the help of friends. I had made it out of a bloody country. When I was in Ethiopia, I had promised myself I would work as a coolie in India in freedom rather than live in terror in Ethiopia. No feeling compared to the one I was feeling at that time. I was overwhelmed with joy, intermixed with some sadness, a sadness that had slowly crept into my system from the tragedy that visited my life. I thought how my mother would be delighted to hear that I had finally made it. The next day Zebiba called her parents in Dessie and told them I had made it.

Three days later, I met Mohamed Mussa, a young man from my neighborhood to whom I never spoke in Dessie. He knew Zebiba too and heard about me. He said he had seen me in Addis after I escaped from prison many times. He suggested that I live with him and four others who were now living in a Catholic mission. The arrangement was such that the refugees cleaned the mission in return for food and a place to sleep. We slept outside in the mission compound, which was by the ocean front. Trees provided adequate shelter from the blazing sun during the day. We never had to worry about rain.

I loved the mission enormously. I loved the shade of the trees and the quiet environment. To me this was the kind of place I needed at this time to sort out my life. The other refugees complained about the hard work and the quality of the food, which consisted of bread and tea in the morning and rice for lunch. Sometimes the rice had a little meat in it, sometimes it did not. An old heavy-set, emotional French nun, who never ceased to complain about us, supervised the work of the refugees. The main administrator we called Ma Meir was a sturdy, very cold French nun who kept a tight rein on this mission and was feared like God by everyone. The mission was impeccably clean. I never complained about the work, which consisted of raking leaves, wiping windows, and sometimes cleaning the hospital. Soon I began to notice that there were other refugees, including four senior members of Meison. The four of them stayed separate from us. There was little communication. However, I remember playing chess with one of them. All in all, there were about ten of us, including my friends, but many began to shirk their responsibilities; a few of us had to cover up for them.

A week after I arrived, I decided to spend what was left of my money and treat my friends to drinks. I had close to one hundred birr left, which was only sufficient for a booth for one night. We went to a place where the drinks were cheaper. The bars were too expensive. While we were drinking I saw a man I knew in Ethiopia who had become a businessman and traveled between Addis and Djibouti. Under the influence of the alcohol, I became extremely emotional and had to struggle to restrain my tears. I told this person to kiss Addis Abeba for me. "I would never see Addis again, and I don't want to see Addis again," I said, choking with tears.

For someone who had no responsibility, life in Djibouti was as a good as it gets. Many others in the town did not enjoy the same quality of life as we did. We had plenty to eat and money for alcohol (often taken from our food expense) and *khat*, which was prohibitively expensive. Food for me and my friends was never a problem. We rarely ate at the mission except for breakfast. Oftentimes we would go to Zebiba's place and eat. Zebiba and her friends, who all worked in the bars in Djibouti, served us food, khat, and alcohol. They were very nice people to us.

In Djibouti, I kept having recurrent dreams. This dream even followed me here to the United States. It is almost the same theme with a different format. Usually, I dream of being surrounded by soldiers, *kebele* militia, or even

Mengistu Haile Mariam himself. When I find myself in this situation, I start pedaling as if I were riding a unicycle. Often I manage to pedal and take off the ground and escape out of the encirclement. Sometimes, either I would have a hard time pedaling or I will not be able to lift off, and would wake up sweating when my imaginary captors are closing on me. For a long time after I escaped from the *kebele* detention center, in Djibouti and in the United States, this dream would haunt me. While the intensity and the frequency have decreased, I still have this dream even now, especially if I have signs of stress.

The healthiest thing I found in Djibouti was reading and swimming. Once I learned to swim, I would always go to the Red Sea in the afternoon to escape the heat and swim. I found that very relaxing.

One of my friends at the mission was Germew, another student from Woizero Siheen. He was a resourceful young man who made a tireless effort to improve our life in Djibouti. Germew found a Protestant mission that was willing to provide us with our own apartment and money for food. When he found the mission, it was headed by a French pastor with a colonial mentality. He was an officer in the French army. He took a liking to Germew and decided to help us. However, he was unexpectedly transferred and in his place came a Swiss theologian and scholar named Pastor Basset, who spoke, French, German, and English fluently. After I came to America, Pastor Basset was admitted to Harvard Divinity for his doctorate.

The mission rented us a room in Carte Du through the efforts of Germew. The arrangement was for us to study the Bible and participate in mission activities.

At first I refused to leave the Catholic mission because of its proximity to the sea and the quiet environment, which I needed. This strained my relationship with Germew. Finally, when I felt lonely and saw that living in Carte Du was not as bad as I feared it would be, I joined my friends. There were six of us, including Germew, Mohamed Mussa, and Abraham living in a one-room apartment. Adam Mohammed, who fled Ethiopia, later joined the group. We slept outside, as was customary in this area. No one was concerned about privacy.

The mission paid for the rent. It gave us money for food in addition to providing us with canned food and milk. They provided us books and subscribed to *Newsweek* and *Time* for us. The mission opened a French class in which we all enrolled. Pastor Basset also organized a Bible study class and started us with the Book of John or Mark.

Germew had told them that all of us were Christians. I told Germew that we did not need to say we are Christians for them to help us, but he was not convinced. I had to pretend like I was. I had no problem with the Bible class, and studied it very well. I was interested in religion now and tried to make sure that I understood what was taught. My only problem was with the Eucharist. I always felt uncomfortable about that.

Pastor Basset was not only scholarly and well-read, but his understanding of the bible was also expansive. I never got the impression that he understood the Bible literally. He was very respectful of Islam too, and from what I could see, was trying to understand the Muslims in Djibouti. He never made any denigrating remarks about another religion. He told me one day that contrary to what is believed in the West, "Islam is very tolerant of other religions. The history of Christians in Muslim countries was not one of religious persecution. Unlike the West, Islam never persecuted Jews." He prayed for everybody. I enjoyed his preaching and studying the Bible under him. His wife, who taught us French, was also a very warm and beautiful human being that we all very much loved.

I spent my days between studying the Bible formally, taking some French classes, swimming, and eating *khat*. We ate *khat* almost every day. Three days a week, we ate *khat* with Zebiba and her friends. Some days we ate *khat* at our apartment and played cards. I regularly read *Newsweek* from beginning to end. That was how I came to respect George Will. We drank Johnny Walker to kill the effect of *khat*, or beer whenever we could afford it. I don't remember having that much difficulty finding money for *khat* and drinks.

Life was going well for me at this time except that I knew I could not live like that forever. I had to worry about my family and about finding a job to help them. Very few refugees found jobs in Djibouti, and those were the ones that had come earlier. I started to try to go to the United States or Saudi Arabia, whichever would come first.

Mohamed Mussa and another of our friends managed to find a document to travel to Saudi Arabia. While working with Mohamed's help to go to Saudi Arabia, I also started pushing my friend and teacher, G.R. Jones in America to help me get out of the Djibouti. Gerry's initial response was very cautious. I wanted to come on a student visa, which looked like the easier way to get out of Djibouti. Gerry was not sure. The American Embassy in Djibouti was also reluctant about letting people out on a student visa since it was feared they would not return to Djibouti.

There was no resettlement program of any significance in America for refugees in Djibouti at this time. Most refugees left for France, Europe, and Egypt. Some left for Greece and Italy, which provided transit visas for refugees to immigrate to the United States. I wrote Gerry to find me a school and an I-20 from an American academic institution and send me an affidavit of support. My plan and its potential cost was obviously a concern for Gerry, who lived in New York and did not make much money to pay for tuition for me. But he managed to get an I-20 for me to enroll in an intensive English language program in Queens College in New York.

Mr. Cohen, the ambassador at that time, refused my first request for an F-1 visa. Then Pastor Basset had an appointment with him and talked the matter over. He agreed to see me again. He asked me if I would return back after I finished my studies. I told him I would come back to Djibouti or any other place that would take me once I am through with my studies. I don't know if he believed that or not, but he relented, and my visa to come to the United States was issued on August 14, 1979. I was ecstatic.

On August 29, flying on a Pan Am Airlines and wearing a warm winter jacket that was given to me by the church, I flew to New York through Paris. We spent a night in Paris and I arrived in New York the next day and was welcomed by Gerry Jones, whom I had not seen for many years. I was drenched in sweat. Gerry told me to take off my jacket. Wearing a winter jacket with a furry collar must have looked weird to most people, but I did not know any better. This ignorance of the summer weather in America was a metaphor for everything else I was to face once I stepped foot in New York City. With it started my life of freedom and struggle and frustration and pain. Just arriving in New York itself was for some reason intimidating and scary. Djibouti was peaceful, charming, and beautiful. In America, with all the freedom and opportunities came an enormous amount of frustration. I wondered if I would ever be able to cope with life here. I wondered if it was not too late for me to make something out of myself. Even my English, the only thing that I had any semblance of confidence in, let me down. I could not coherently make a simple sentence that people would understand, nor was I able to understand them as I thought I would. In my eagerness to make friends, I struck an awkward conversation with a group of black teenagers, who took pleasure in humiliating me. I did not understand a word of what they said. I felt there and then that I was a nobody—a dreadful and scary feeling of emptiness that very few would understand unless they had been through it all.

The End

POSTSCRIPT

In August 1979, I came on a student visa to New York and resided with Gerry Jones, who lived in a studio apartment in Manhattan. It was obvious the place was not big enough to accommodate the two of us. A week after I came to the United States, I took the train to Philadelphia to visit Mohamed Ahimed, who was living in West Philadelphia, near the University of Pennsylvania, with his wife, Yemeserach, and Birhanu Abegaz, then a doctoral student at University of Pennsylvania. Once again, Mohamed came to my rescue and offered for me to live with him in Philadelphia, much to the delight of Gerry Jones, who was terribly concerned about the living arrangement in Manhattan. I was happy, and Mohamed, Yemesrach, and Birhanu gave me the much needed space, support, and time to adjust to life in the USA.

I started my education at Temple University, taking English as a second language for a semester. Then Mohamed suggested that I talk to West Chester University (then College) to see if it would offer me a tuition waiver to attend. I took the bus to West Chester one afternoon and talked to the admissions officer, who without much haggling agreed to admit me to the college free of tuition. Gerry agreed to pay for off-campus housing, books, and other fees. I also found a job as a dishwasher in Stadium Hilton in Philadelphia and commuted for a year on weekends to work at the hotel.

After a year and half in West Chester, I transferred to University of Pennsylvania, Philadelphia. It was at Gerry's suggestion that I decided to transfer since he thought I would benefit from attending a big-name university. I was admitted not because I was a stellar student—there were many other African students with better grades and academic background—but because I seemed to offer a unique background that would add to the diversity of the student body and contribute to the learning environment. Penn offered me significant tuition assistance, but I still had to borrow money to finance my education. At Penn, I met professor Andreas Eshete

211

and took two classes with him. One was "Concepts of the Self," an abstract philosophical discourse on theories of the individual. I also audited his most popular class on moral philosophy offered to graduate students. I had never met a more impressive intellectual than Andreas as an undergraduate student at Penn.

I graduated from Penn with a degree in economics and political science. I was unsure as to where to go for graduate school. I decided to apply to public policy schools and was admitted to the LBJ School of Public Policy at University of Texas in Austin, which offered me a fellowship. Then at the urging of Abeyu Berlie, then Mezy's boyfriend who was attending Yale School of Management, I sent my application package to Yale just weeks before the deadline. To my surprise, I was admitted to Yale.

In May 1986, I received my Master's in Public and Private Management (MPPM). Burdened with a student loan close to $30,000 ($10,000 from my undergraduate education), I accepted the first job offer I got from Tennessee State University Foundation as business manager and started my professional career in the United States. Since then I had worked at Paine College, College of Southern Maryland, and now at American Public University System.

*   *   *

The year I came to the United States, I wrote a letter to United Nations High Commission for Refugees office in the Sudan seeking assistance in locating Lt. Omar M. Shifaw. I knew Omar had left his position as police office in Gondar, but was not sure where he lived and was determined to get to him out. I was also not sure if he was alive or dead and suspected that he might have been involved with EPRP and I might have unwittingly contributed to that. Gerry said he would sponsor him to come to the United States.

My letter was posted at the Khartoum office of the UNHCR. After a few months, I received a reply from Tsedale Egigu who had read the letter. She wrote back saying that Omar was wounded in a fight between the forces of the Ethiopian Democratic Union and Ethiopian government near the Sudan border. He was treated in London and had finally settled in Germany. Then a few months later I heard from Mezy, who had also read my letter. Gerry sponsored both Mezy and Omar to come to Philadelphia. Mezy's boyfriend, Abeyu, was sponsored by the Nationalities Center in New York, but moved back to Philadelphia to live with her later.

I also managed to find a sponsor for many of my friends from Djibouti, including Adam Mohammed and Elisabeth Asfaha, and brought them to Philadelphia, forming one of the first groups of Ethiopian immigrants to settle in Philadelphia.

Mezy and I occasionally talked about the revolution and our past. She told me that she cried for days when she heard that I had died in Ethiopia.

A few times we raised the *anja* issue and the death of the prisoners who were killed in Asimba. I was raising very strong objections to the information and questioning the motives of the leaders who were responsible for that. She told me that because the action happened after she came to Asimba, people assumed that she contributed to the atmosphere of repression in the army. I knew Mezy had concluded in her mind that Birhanu's death was attributable to *anja*. It was more a visceral reaction than a cool-headed observation supported by facts. She composed a famous poem about Birhanu and recited it to the army in Asimba. I sensed that she was hurt by all the insinuation she may have wittingly or unwittingly contributed to the death of the *anja* suspects.

That was the extent of our conversation about *anja*. The only other thing I remember was a letter she received from Tsegaye Gebremedhin a few months or a few years after she settled. The gist of the letter was an expression of Tsegaye Gebremedhin's determination to fight it out to the end. He was not going to migrate to the United States like the rest of EPRA fighters. Mezy kept these letters and other documents from EPRA with her before she was tragically murdered in 1988.

Mezy's murder was as shocking as it was unexpected. By this time she had broken up with Abeyu and was dating a person who had earned a PhD from the University of Pennsylvania. He seemed nice and personable, but became dangerously obsessive with the relationship, monitoring every move and action. Around noon one day, when her sister returned from work, Mezy was found dead with multiple stab wounds and blunt trauma to the head. The suspicion centered on the boyfriend, who hired a well-known criminal lawyer. Since the suspect had been in the classroom the morning of the incident, his lawyer argued his client had an alibi and could not have had the opportunity to murder. This threw a monkey wrench in the investigation and the police could not find enough evidence to indict. Although there was enough circumstantial evidence with regard to motive, jealousy, and an abusive past, the investigation did not make any headway. Her case remains unresolved and the murderer is still at large.

Mezy's promising life was cut short in such a terrible way. Had she lived, I am sure Mezy would have written a book on EPRP that would have significantly contributed to the understanding of the organization. She had the insider information, the writing talent, and passion to make it happen. It is in reaction to her death that I decided to draft this book two years after she was murdered. I realized that our life is precarious, that we should tell our stories so future generations can learn from our experience.

I sometimes wonder if the brutal ending of Mezy's life was not in some way connected to the infighting within the organization. Could someone have killed her in revenge for her perceived role against the *anja*? Could anybody have the heart to drag what happened in Ethiopia to the United States? Could the suspect, her boyfriend, have played this role? Could the suspect, who seemed mentally capable of planning and executing such a devious scheme, been a vehicle for exacting some kind of revenge? This is far-fetched conjuncture, but it can't be ruled out.

Mezy was a student at University of Pennsylvania when she was murdered. One night, she came home completely distraught. It was in the midst of an exam, and while writing an essay she completely broke down and started crying. She said she could not stop crying. The professor told her to go home and calm herself, obviously distressed by what she saw. What triggered such a terrible memory that would break her down in the middle of an exam? Could it be her daughter who was still in Ethiopia, her deceased husband, her life as a revolutionary? We never discussed it further.

Weeks before she died, Mezy told me that she received a disturbing phone call from a person who said he had just arrived in Philadelphia by train. This was someone she knew, but did not tell me how and where. She was uneasy about the phone call, that I remember. I have never made sense of this information, although I can't push it out of my head either.

I wish Mezy had lived long enough for us to have discussed our history much more openly. We were all busy trying to make a new life for ourselves that the uncomfortable intrusion of our past was often deliberately shunned. Mezy was obsessed about bringing her daughter to the United States. She repeatedly told me that she would never marry a husband before she saw her daughter, Martha, and talked to her about Birhanu's life and her past. She wanted to be the person to tell her daughter about Birhanu, who was an unknown entity to his daughter. Martha may have seen him once or twice when she was a baby, but she probably had no recollection. It seemed to me Mezy felt enormously guilty for having "abandoned" her only child in favor of the cause of the revolution. She wanted to provide an explanation and maybe even ask for forgiveness and understanding from a child who would never make sense of the revolution.

Mezy's story is a double tragedy. Who would have thought this brave, caring, and sensible woman would escape the Red Terror and Asimba, only to meet her violent death in America? If only she had lived long enough to make sense of her past and reconcile herself to the future, how much she could have helped us to understand the phenomenon we call EPRP.

In 1993, I went back to Ethiopia to visit my mother. My father was deceased in 1988 after a prolonged struggle with asthma and liver disease.

Two weeks before I returned to America, I was introduced to my future wife, who worked as a nurse in Boru Hospital. This was love at first sight. Within four months, Lubaba came to the United States and we were married. Marriage and the raising my two daughters, Muna Yimam and Sarah Yimam, anchored my life and have given me a wonderful sense of purpose.

*   *   *

Over the past thirty years, I have visited and revisited in my mind the profound moral dilemma of my association with an organization that is equally loved and hated, ridiculed and respected, and generates intense passion, both pro and against. Just what is EPRP? This is not an attempt to define the party by what it stood for, commendable though it might have been. Who are its members? Were they bad people, as the prevailing narrative of the public that has understandably turned against it would have us believe? Were they good people, as most members of the organization are inclined to think? Were they good people who did bad things in an act of self-defense or were they bad actors who did what they did because it was in their nature to do so? Were they bad people masquerading as good people whose real character was unmasked by the difficulty of the struggle? Were they good people who descended into darkness in the barbarity of the environment they helped to create? Is it fair to accuse the party of having committed crimes against the Ethiopian people? Is the party guilty of serious violations of basic decency and humanity as alleged by Meison and other critics? Can we use current standards and views on human rights, tolerance, and democratic values against a revolutionary organization in the '70s? How about my own role in this?

These are very serious questions for which I don't believe anybody has the right answer. Then why raise them, especially if there are no satisfying answers anyway? Is it not better that they are left unquestioned? The easiest thing to do for EPRP critics is to enumerate the many failings of the party and simply declare it as a destructive force that should never have existed. That is very simplistic and can be neither enlightening nor informative. On the other hand, the easiest thing for its adherents, whose numbers though dwindling may still be significant, is to seek cover behind the sacrifices of its dedicated members, some of whom, needless to say, were among the most talented and brilliant Ethiopians, and deny the wrongs done by their organization. Their members lost their lives for a cause they believed was right. It does not mean, as Nuruddin Fararh, the prominent Somali novelist writes, quoting Mark Twain, if people die for a cause the cause is necessarily noble.

To treat this sacrifice as sacred and not deal with their past may seem righteous for EPRP members, but does not address the very serious nature of things that happened in the name of the party that may never be morally defensible. It is a fairly complicated issue that reasonable people may argue about for years to come without any closure.

What about my role? I have been unbelievably torn between my good feelings toward the individuals I knew and the organization's excusable misdeeds, which can be justifiably called crimes. I have defended EPRP when I felt it was attacked unjustifiably by its critics. I have also criticized the party using language as harsh as any used by its most implacable enemies. EPRP was a phenomenon; it was a contradiction; it was as bad as its enemies say it was and was as noble as its supporters fervently claim. Everyone can find something to love or hate about it.

Often, I have taken the absurd position that it is possible to separate the individuals from the organization as a whole. EPRP, I endlessly argue with myself, is less than or worse than the sum total of its members. Most of its members were good and noble, but the party was bad and dysfunctional. That is to say, its members, in certain occasions, acted in an abominable way within the party structure than they would otherwise have if they were not shackled by the party discipline. What EPRP did, I reasoned, did not reflect on the goodness and idealism of the individuals I knew and associated with. Deep down, I know my friends who died at such a tender age were good and decent human beings. Had they lived, they would have been wonderful husbands or wives, caring parents, and good citizens. I know they would have been as successful as I was in reconstituting their lives here in America or elsewhere, and many would have exceeded my achievements in academia or professional endeavors.

But EPRP is not just about those who were murdered by the government. EPRP also had a role in the murder of others, both within and outside the party. This is the story of EPRP that does not necessarily square very well with the narrative of those who hold it dear to their heart, partly out of loyalty to their fallen comrades. This is probably why these individuals might consider what I am attempting to do here, albeit in a tortured way, as nothing less than betrayal of their friends. I would only say here that because of the emotional investment in EPRP, it is not necessarily all right to shy away from criticism. It is admirable to stay true to an ideal, but the organization is not necessarily an embodiment of the ideal, not the way we know it. Loyalty to one's fallen brothers should not deter one from an honest and critical look at one's own and comrades' role in the tragedy of the of Ethiopian revolution. The easiest and the laziest thing to do is blame Meison and the Derg only for what happened and exonerate our own organization and comrades. That does not help us grow individually or understand the situation better.

We have had decades of life experience that our friends were deprived of to reflect on what our participation in EPRP meant to us individually and to the Ethiopian people as a whole. We were not innocent bystanders, nor were we just helpless victims. We were individual actors with a mind of our own, notwithstanding the fact that we were neither mature nor sophisticated enough to handle the issues we faced. But that does not make us innocent. Things have happened. Bad things have happened. Innocent people were killed. Innocent children were lost—some by our organization's direct effort, some in reaction to these efforts. We must face our past.

It is often said that time is a great healer. Those of us who survived this ordeal have had time to heal and time to reflect. One thing that time and distance from the past creates is an opportunity to see our former adversaries in a different light. We have had enough time to reintroduce ourselves to our former enemies, and we have no doubt found them to be not different from us. There are of course truly sadistic people in all the organizations that could be described as evil. Now, I think we should be able to appreciate what Meison members did was not in any way different from what we did. It should now be obvious that they were also motivated by high ideals. In fact, the vast majority of Ethiopian youth engaged in one or the other of the revolutionary organizations—EPRP, Meison, Malered, TPLF, EPLF, OLF and ELF—and were motivated by a commitment to an ideal, a dedication to the poor and the oppressed of Ethiopia. Many of these were selfless youth who were willing to pay "the last measure of sacrifice" for what they thought was the betterment of Ethiopian people. To the extent this experiment failed, we are collectively responsible for what happened. But the fact the achievements were less than desirable, or on the contrary, catastrophic, does not affect the quality of their ideals, nor can it take away from the humanity of these youth, whose contribution to the building of a nation was lost forever. As a result, the country was significantly diminished, morally, intellectually, and socially.

It is our responsibility to learn from our past and chart a more hopeful, democratic, and civil society for our country. We need to remember our lost generation and do everything we can so something similar does not happen again.

Now the country still struggles to find its footing. For whatever it is worth, a part of the Ethiopian left came to power and is attempting to shape its future. Needless to say, there is an enormous conflict simmering in and outside the country about the nature and the future of Ethiopia. The strife of the 1970s should offer some lesson in how we approach the next phase of the country's endless struggle.

Mohamed Yimam

INDEX

O

OAU, 63, 78, 91-93

P

pen names, 56, 77-78, 86, 101
Pennsylvania, 211, 213-14
Philadelphia, 211-12, 214
poems, 77-79, 122, 158-59, 182, 191, 195, 213
politburo, 42, 101-2, 126, 129, 131
proletariat, 62-63, 69-70, 78, 97-98, 100

R

Red Star over China, 53
Red Terror, 47, 117, 122, 142-43, 146-47, 152, 165-66, 176-77, 185
regime, 40, 49, 59, 61, 65, 86, 98, 100, 102, 107-8, 133, 147-49, 156, 205
revolutionaries, 22, 41, 43, 46, 50, 54-55, 64, 89, 100, 120, 134, 151, 214
revolutionary squads, 163, 166, 193

S

Sarah, 75-77, 80, 83, 93, 105, 128
Saudi Arabia, 27, 199, 209
Seleshi, 205-6
Seti, 184-85
Sidamo, 31, 74, 88, 112, 131, 139, 164
Silk Amba, 24, 26
Snow, Edgar, 53
Soviet Union, 77, 93, 98, 149
strife, factional, 126-27, 154

T

Tadesse, Kiflu, 66-67
Teferra, Sirak, 16, 187-88

Tekle, Afework, 78
Teodros, 16, 112
Tigray, 39, 48, 65, 107-9, 113, 127, 151, 163, 173, 185, 187, 194-95
Tikalegne, 164-65, 168-69
Time, 29, 71, 208
TPLF, 15, 48, 108, 113, 149-51, 217
Trotsky, Leon, 35, 111, 124
TTI (teacher training institute), 27, 29, 31-33, 56

U

United States of America, 4, 21, 29, 33, 36, 49, 71, 73, 92-93, 124, 150-51, 153-55, 160, 186, 207-16
University of Pennsylvania, 211, 213-14

W

Woizero Siheen, 22, 27-28, 40, 45, 206, 208
Wolde Abe, 78-79, 112-13, 143, 150, 166
Wollega, 52, 126, 164
Wollo, 21-22, 24, 39-40, 120, 180, 187, 200, 206
Wonji, 67-68, 70-71, 74, 99-100

Y

Yared Music School, 51, 82, 205
Yohannes, 16, 42, 56, 89-90, 92, 101-2, 104, 107-12, 114, 118, 129-30, 139, 158

Z

Zebiba, 205-7, 209
Zemecha, 45, 73-74
Zenebe, 31-33

CPSIA information can be obtained
at www.ICGtesting.com
Printed in the USA
LVHW020505130821
695223LV00010B/755

9 781483 698960